THE MEDIEVAL THEATRE

GLYNNE WICKHAM

Professor of Drama, University of Bristol

THE MEDIEVAL THEATRE

WEIDENFELD AND NICOLSON
London

Weidenfeld and Nicolson
11 St John's Hill London SW11

822

30561

ISBN 0 297 76778 X
Printed in Great Britain by
Willmer Brothers Limited, Birkenhead

To
S.G.W.

CONTENTS

ILLUSTRATIONS

A•

16. King David with musicians and dancers (*Psalterium Aureum*, St Gall, *c*.900)
17. The ascension of St Mary Magdalene (Sforza Book of Hours, British Museum, Add.Ms. 34294, f.211ᵛ, late fifteenth century)
18. Self-portrait of Nikolas Manuel (Cathedral Church, Berne, Switzerland, early sixteenth century)
19. The Dance of Death (Campo Santo, Pisa Cathedral, Italy, late thirteenth century)
20. The building of Noah's Ark (Scene from the 1969 production of the *Cornish Cycle* in St Piran's 'Round', Perranporth, Cornwall)
21. The Head of a pastoral staff representing the Adoration of the Magi (Victoria and Albert Museum, London, late fourteenth century)
22. Visit of the Magi and the Nativity (Detail from 'The Triumph of Isabella', by Denis van Alsloot, Brussels, 1615, Victoria and Albert Museum)
23. The martyrdom of St Appollonia (MS. illumination by Jean Fouquet to the Hours of Etienne Chevalier, Musée Condé, Chantilly, France, fifteenth century)
24. The Seven Virtues (Painting from the studio of Francesco Perellino, fifteenth century. Birmingham Museum of Art, Birmingham, Alabama, USA)
25. Hell-castle (MS. illumination from the Hours of Catherine of Cleeves, fifteenth century)
26. The owl as a symbol of Hell (Illumination in a fifteenth-century MS. of Ovid in the Bibliothèque Nationale, Paris)
27. Battle between the good and the bad angel for the soul of the deceased (MS. illumination in the Hours of Catherine of Cleeves, fifteenth century)
28. *Below,* Modesty challenges Lust, while *above* Faith crushes despair (? persecution) and offers the wreath of victory to four martyrs (MS. illumination in a copy of Prudentius's *Psychomachia*. Staatsbibliothek, Berne, Switzerland. Codex 264, p. 70)

29. Fortune and Wisdom (An early sixteenth-century wood-engraving: Theatre Collection, University of Bristol)
30. Antichrist, alias the Pope (An early sixteenth century wood-engraving. Theatre Collection, University of Bristol)
31. A wildman and a wildwoman (Swiss tapestry of the mid-fifteenth century: Victoria and Albert Museum)
32. A knight slaying a wildman (Enamelled silver-gilt perfume case of the mid-fifteenth century. Victoria and Albert Museum)
33. The Market Cross, Shepton Mallet, Somerset, early fifteenth century
34. Burlesque Tournament of Abstinence versus Gluttony (Bibliothèque Nationale, Paris, MS. Français 146, early fourteenth century)
35. The strife of Lent with Shrovetide (Painting by Peter Breughel the Elder, c.1550. Royal Museum of Fine Art, Copenhagen, Denmark)
36. Nigerian masquerade, photographed in Lagos, 1965
37. St George (Farleigh Hungerford Castle, Somerset, early fourteenth century, Department of the Environment)
38. Knights tilting before ladies (British Museum, MS. Harley, 4431, f.150, early fifteenth century)
39. Sir Geoffrey Luttrel with his wife and daughter (MS. illumination to the Luttrel Psalter, c.1340)
40. An 'entremet' representing the Conquest of Jerusalem performed before the King of France and the Holy Roman Emperor in Paris, 1378 (MS. illumination from *Chronique de Charles V*, Bibliothèque Nationale, Paris, MS. Français, 2813, f.473ᵛ)
41. The Court of Mirth (Bodleian Library, MS. Douce 195, late fifteenth century)
42. Bishop Beckington's Jester (Wells Cathedral, Somerset, fifteenth century)
43. The Mummers' Play at Marshfield, Gloucestershire (Photo, 1970)
44. Pageant-stage with mechanical rose and lily erected in

Paris for the marriage of Margaret Tudor, daughter of Henry VII, to Louis XII of France, 1514 (British Museum, MS. Cot.Vesp. BII.f10.)

II. Figures

ACKNOWLEDGEMENTS

My thanks are due in the preparation of this book to my col-
leagues in the University of Bristol for their help in checking the
translations of quotations from Latin, Old French, German,
Italian and Spanish sources: Mr Jim Tester (Department of
Classics), Dr T. Hemming (Department of French), Mr George
Brandt (Department of Drama), Mr Higgins (Italian) and
Professor Metford (Spanish).

I must also express my gratitude to the British Museum; the
Victoria and Albert Museum; the Bodleian Library, Oxford;
Corpus Christi College, Cambridge; the Theatre Collection and
the Arts Faculty Photographic Unit of Bristol University; the
Bibliothèque Nationale, Paris; the Musée Municipale,
Avranches; Staatsbibliothek, Munich; Staatsbibliothek, Berne; the
Royal Museum of Fine Arts, Copenhagen; Max Niemeyer
Verlag, Tübingen; the Birmingham Museum of Fine Art,
Birmingham, Alabama; and the Ministry of the Environment,
London, for permission to reproduce paintings, manuscript
illuminations, tapestries, and other materials in their possession
as illustrations to this book.

To John Northam, Professor of Modern and Comparative
Drama in the University of Bristol, my especial thanks are expressed for assistance with the reading of the proofs.

Glynne Wickham
Department of Drama
University of Bristol
20 November 1973

INTRODUCTION

This book attempts to give an account of how dramatic art developed in Europe between the tenth and the sixteenth centuries. This is a formidable undertaking within the covers of a single volume; but if the subject is viewed as a whole and not century by century or play by play, three features emerge with such clarity as to suggest that each was a guiding force within the period and thus a useful signpost towards a possible treatment of the subject today. These features are the predominant and pervasive influence of religion, recreation and commerce.

Throughout the six centuries in question the drama is informed by a concern for religious aspirations in general and doctrinal orthodoxy in particular. This is the salient factor. Next, there is evidence of a growing preoccupation with leisure and the possible uses of leisure time, in a word, with recreation. This is a social phenomenon, but one which in its several aspects embraces all strata of medieval society as effectively as religion. Third, there is the dawning realization that dramatic art, whether used as religious propaganda or for purposes of social recreation, becomes more costly as it becomes more elaborate : in other words, any serious development of the art is intimately related to questions of money, of finding capital with which to finance production on the one hand and of determining appropriate rewards for services rendered on the other.

These three aspects of dramatic activity in medieval Europe – religion, recreation and commerce – are never wholly distinct from one another; but they do denote marked differences of approach. It is this difference of approach which I shall attempt to preserve in dividing this book into three parts : theatres of worship, theatres of leisure and pleasure, and theatres and commerce.

Such a method of handling a large subject is bound to introduce artificial divisions of varying sorts which were never present
in the minds of the organizers, actors or audiences of the
time. It also makes some measure of repetition inevitable. Yet if
drama is to be respected for what it is, a living art, this is a price
that must be paid for rejecting the temptation to treat it as history
(and thus in strict chronological sequence), or as literature (and
thus text by text and author by author) without much care for
either its moral content or its political and social environment.

There is a fourth feature of the drama of the whole period that
seems, at first glance, to warrant dismissal within a few para-
graphs, but which, as one becomes more closely acquainted with
the subject, clamours repeatedly for more detailed comment : this
is the legacy which, notwithstanding the collapse of organized
play-production within the Roman Empire, the Middle Ages in
fact inherited from classical antiquity and Byzantium and from
the more primitive Celto-Teutonic cultures of Northern and
Western Europe. This legacy was of course more distinctly preserved and appreciated in countries colonized by the Romans
than in countries where the *pax romana* had not been experienced. Even so, we have to remember missionaries based on
Rome and using Latin as the language of their cause preserved
memories of Roman life and manners wherever they succeeded in
establishing themselves. It is thus not only the physical remains of
Roman theatres and amphitheatres which continued to stand in
the early Middle Ages as witnesses to Roman notions of entertainment, but also a large vocabulary of words and phrases which
could never be wholly divorced from their original meanings. Of
these words, *ludus* eclipses all others in importance since it can be
translated with equal justification as 'recreation', as 'game' or as
'play', and since the significance of these English words to medieval drama is obvious enough.

The Romans were themselves aware of the ambiguity residing
in the word *ludus* and took pains to couple with it qualifying
words to make the particular meaning to be attached to it in a
given context as precise as possible. Gladiatorial games, for
example, were qualitatively very different from mimetic games;
and just as the words *gladiatorum* and *proscenium* or *scenicus*
were used to distinguish the one form of *ludus* from the other, so
the words *venalis* and *circensis* served both to define games in-

volving animals and athletes respectively, and to distinguish these recreational activities from others. There is, nevertheless, a common factor linking all uses of the word *ludus*, however precisely qualified – an underlying sense of energy released in action. It is this imperative quality of something done, of doing, of activity that links the athlete to the actor. The quality they possess in common is bodily movement: where they part company is in the respective objectives to which their energies are applied. Yet even in this respect at least one important affinity between the two may be discerned: however different the characteristics of the *ludus* athletic or mimetic, the game or recreational element is paramount. The stage actor *imitates* people and their actions in real life: the athlete *regulates* the limits of his skill and prowess by the rules within which his competitive games are played. Thus a tournament, to take an extreme case, though it could result in injury or death for one or more of the contestants was conceived of as a violent game to test individual skill and endurance, never as war. However nearly it approaches the reality of battle, rules exist to prevent the imitation extending to the actual, just as the tragic heroes of mimetic games, however realistically their deaths may be portrayed, arise to repeat their performances on other occasions. Both are imitations 'in game' and not 'in earnest'. No account of medieval drama and theatre therefore which ignores the survival of the word *ludus* and all it represented in the Roman Empire is likely to do much justice to the subject.

Another word requiring scarcely less attention is *jocus*. Here the English word 'joke' retains the original Latin meaning of a purely verbal game. Paradoxically it was in the Latin countries bordering the Mediterranean – Italy, France and Spain – that the word *jocus* came to absorb into itself, as vernacular languages developed, the meanings formerly associated with *ludus*. Thus the ambiguity of the latter comes first to encroach upon and then to survive in the Italian *giuoco*, the French *jeu* and the Spanish *juego*. In French it becomes permissible to use the noun *jeu* or the verb *jouer* to cover jokes (*jeu de mots*), a game of cards or tennis (*jeu de cartes, jeu de paume*), or the acting of a play (*jouer une comédie*). In Northern Europe no such equation between *ludus* and *jocus* was effected: writers or orators had accordingly to make a conscious choice between continued use of the Latin originals and the vernacular alternative which, in German, was

Spiel and, in Anglo-Saxon, *pleg* or *gomen*.* In this way the vernacular words, which were at first restricted to describe very primitive forms of recreation, had expanded and developed by the end of the Middle Ages to embrace and contain most of the more sophisticated nuances associated with *ludus* and *jocus*.

The essential point at issue here is that throughout the Middle Ages and throughout Europe the concept of a game in which words might or might not play an important part dominated both courtly and popular attitudes to drama. Development of such games thus owed much more to experimental and pragmatic considerations than to any theoretical concepts of a literary and architectural character of the sort that have governed European drama and theatre from the seventeenth century to the present day. If we are to approach the drama of the Middle Ages intelligently therefore we must first dismiss all our own contemporary notions of what a theatre should be and of how a play should be written, and then go on to substitute the idea of community games in which the actors are the contestants (mimetic or athletic or both) and the theatre is any place appropriate and convenient both to them as performers and to the rest of the community as spectators. If the contemporary catch-phrase 'total theatre' has any meaning it finds a truer expression in medieval than in modern terms of reference; for song, dance, wrestling, sword-play, contests between animals, disguise, spectacle, jokes, disputation and ritual all figure, separately or compounded, in the drama of the Middle Ages which was devised in celebration of leisure and for a local community. It was a preponderantly social art which could be given a religious, political or sexual dynamic as need and occasion demanded, but which was only rarely concerned with questions of literary theory and genre such as inform our own concepts of comedy, farce, tragedy, melodrama, opera, ballet and so on. Clerics could involve themselves in dramatic parodies of sacred rituals like the Feast of the Ass or the Boy Bishop just as easily as artisans of city guilds could devote themselves to the re-enactment of the Crucifixion or the Last Judgement : knights who by day could risk death jousting in the lists, disguised in armour and heraldic blazon, could as readily display

---

* Other important words which, from a philological standpoint, illuminate this discussion are the Anglo-Saxon *lac* and *waffen*, and the Old French *battre* and *behorder*.

themselves before their ladies as dancers in a disguising in the course of the banquet-hall revels the same evening.

If it requires an effort of imagination to rid our minds of the image of the normal modern theatre built deliberately to exclude daylight, and illuminated artificially by electricity, it takes an even stronger imaginative effort to come to grips with the society and its environment in which the dramatic *ludus*, or game, of the Middle Ages developed. Somehow we must imitate our cosmonauts of today and tomorrow in erasing preconceptions from our minds when we launch ourselves on a scholarly journey that propels us backwards a thousand years in time and lands us in the Europe of the tenth century.

The Europe that awaits us, if we make this journey, is one much more closely in touch with nature than that familiar to us. The climate may not have been very different, but human kind, being far less cushioned against its rigours, was far more conscious of its dangers. Winter and hunger were virtually synonyms: starvation and cold far fiercer enemies than they are to us. Spring and summer brought not only a physical release from these perils but a psychological release from the fear of them. Summer was a time to be enjoyed, but also a time in which to protect oneself against the inevitable advent of another winter. When that winter came, nights were long and dark, and time lay heavy on one's hands. Travel was difficult, often impossible. Coal was not unknown, but its commercial uses were; in consequence, landscapes were clean and not fouled with soot and smog. Concentrations of people were small and buildings could be viewed individually, each in terms of its shape and decoration. Noise was abnormal and human ears proportionately were responsive to delicate sounds, more easily satisfied with melodic line. Fabrics were the product of individual labour and thus more readily compared, contrasted and valued for the merit and elaborateness of the craftsmanship. Ornament was recognizably the fruit of labour and skill, and not the product of some mould in an impersonal, mechanical process in a distant and unknown factory.

Johan Huizinga in *The Waning of the Middle Ages* drew attention in a forceful yet sensitive manner to another contrast between life then and now, the prevalence of illiteracy and the corresponding declaration in visual signs and symbols of everyman's place in society. While we pride ourselves on having banished illiteracy and on sending all children to school until they are at least fifteen, we still struggle to conceal our own individuality in anonymity. In housing, furnishings and personal attire we strive to prevent anybody else from recognizing who we are, what we do and, above all, what we think or believe. Men and women of the Middle Ages behaved very differently. As Huizinga put it :

> All things in life were of a proud or cruel publicity. Lepers sounded their rattles and went about in processions, beggars exhibited their deformity and their misery in churches. Every order and estate, every rank and profession, was distinguished by its costume. The great lords never moved about without a glorious display of arms and liveries, exciting fear and envy. Executions and other public acts of justice, hawking, marriages and funerals, were all announced by cries and processions, songs and music. The lover wore the colours of his lady; companions the emblem of their confraternity; parties and servants the badges or blazon of their lords (Penguin ed., pp. 9–10).

The emphasis which Huizinga laid on costume, emblems, ceremonies and processions serves to direct our attention towards the dramatic tenor of daily life in the Middle Ages which, on account of rather than despite its relative simplicity, was coloured by the violence of its contrasts and by the slow but varied rhythm of the recurring seasons. Violent contrast is best figured both verbally and visually as contest, rhythms in ritual. It was from these sources in real life that the imitative dance-drama of peasant communities throughout Europe had arisen, and it was in them again that the mimetic drama of Christ's triumph over sin and death on Easter morning was to find a more sophisticated reflection in the early Middle Ages. Still more sophisticated, if less sharply defined, ripples are to be seen in the revels of the medieval banquet hall celebrating the recurring cycle of courtship, marriages and christenings securing for human kind a victory over death at one remove.

A sense of occasion is never absent from medieval drama : ceremonies of a joyous kind reflect, in activity, thankfulness for life and energy, while those of a more solemn kind recall the constant threat of a loss of both. The significance of the occasion was an important factor in determining the particular structure of all three types of dramatic game – folk play, Christian religious drama and court revels. The Boy Bishop thus has affinities with the Lord of Misrule although the former was no more likely to order festivities in the banquet hall than the latter those in a Church : the link is provided by the season of the year (the winter solstice, the Christmas holiday), the Lord of Misrule presiding over the twelve days of Christmas (25 December – 6 January) and the Boy Bishop usurping the authority of his mentors in Christmas week (25 December – 1 January)*. Similarly the Feast of Corpus Christi gives its name to the type of drama associated with it, the cyclic Mystery Plays; while Disguisings and Masques can be said to have existed as opportunities to comment on the occasion celebrated.

Masques and Disguisings which in the fifteenth and sixteenth centuries were so closely associated with Twelfth Night festivities as to be almost obligatory, normally culminated in the presentation of gifts from the masquers to the master of the house, a feature reflecting both the libations to the Goddess *Fortuna* at the Roman Kalends or New Year in pre-Christian times and the offerings of the Magi at Epiphany in Christian Europe. Twelfth Night, the final festival of the Christmas holiday in the Middle Ages, thus serves as yet another bridge between the old world and the new.

This brings us very close to the heart of the matter, the *raison d'être* of the medieval *ludus* of all descriptions : this can fairly be claimed to have been a formal externalization, by recourse to the playing of games, of moments of abnormal significance in the recurrent patterns of daily life. The origins and earliest steps in the development of athletic and mimetic games for this purpose are shrouded in the mists of an oral and not a written tradition of transmission from one generation to the next. Roman society, however, formalized these games and recorded them with sufficient precision to outlast the assaults of both barbarian invasion and Christian evangelism over five centuries of political and social turmoil, and thus to serve as the basis for new games of both kinds reshaped to conform with the changed conditions of medieval life. In this process of reshaping the old forms, by far the most

---

* The wider term 'Feast of Fools' covers three groups of individuals – priests, deacons and choristers – and three separate Festivals – The Nativity, Circumcision and Holy Innocents – all appropriately associated with children.

important new factors were Christian philosophy and the vernacular languages of the new Europe.

It is these two factors which provide the principal justification
for discussing medieval drama first under the general heading of
'Theatres of Worship' (Part I of this book) and then under the
general heading of 'Theatres of Social Recreation' (Part II).
Neither type of dramatic activity was seriously dependent on or
concerned with money in the first instance; but success, in the
form of ever-growing popularity, carried within itself a need for
elaboration and variety, and this could not be met without regard
to cost. The increasing attention paid first to production costs and
then to rewards for services rendered came, with the passing of
time, to involve the patrons and promoters of medieval drama in
a growing traffic with artisans and proportionately deeper en-
tanglements in questions of profit and loss. No discussion therefore
of the theatres of worship and theatres of social recreation in the
Middle Ages would be complete without a third general heading,
'Theatres and Commerce', conducted here in the third and final
part of this book.

Part I:
Theatres of Worship

I

DRAMA OF PRAISE
AND THANKSGIVING

A. LEGACIES FROM PALESTINE AND ROME

The earliest Christian drama is that which arose spontaneously as part of a much wider process of elaborating and ornamenting the services appropriate to the principal commemorative festivals of the Christian year. The liturgies in question were conducted in Latin, were sung by priests alternating with the choir, and were constructed to contain some subject-matter of an ordinary and invariable kind and some that was appropriate and unique to the particular occasion – Christmas, Epiphany, Good Friday, or Easter as the case might be. Thus, just as the festivals were commemorations of events in Palestine between the years AD 1–33, sandwiched into the confines of a single year and repeated annually, so the drama which arose out of the liturgies proper to these festivals was commemorative in essence and ritualistic in character.

There is no short cut to any genuine understanding of the evolution of a process that was at once historical and doctrinal, musical and artistic, evangelical and monastic. Christianity could not establish itself in Europe without combating the cults and rites of primitive religions which commanded the allegiance of the peoples whom the missionaries wished to convert: E. K. Chambers devoted an entire volume of *The Mediaeval Stage* to discussion of the religious and dramatic antecedents of Christian drama in Europe. Nor is the shaping of the Christian liturgy itself any less complex since different rites established themselves in Egypt, North Africa, Spain, France and Ireland as well as in the Eastern and Western Empires centered on Byzantium and Rome :

the triumph of the Roman rite over its Syrian, Coptic, Mozarabic and Gallican competitors took the better part of seven centuries and is the subject of Dom Gregory Dix's *The Shape of the Liturgy*. With it the supremacy of the Books of the Old Testament in Hebrew and the New Testament in Greek gave way in Western and Northern Europe to St Jerome's Latin Bible, the Vulgate. Thereafter, throughout Europe, works of commentary on both the Bible and the liturgy, frequently in the form of sermons, began to multiply rapidly following the examples set in the fourth and fifth centuries by St Ambrose, Pope Gregory the Great and St Augustine. The need to expound and explain grew proportionately with the spread of Christianity into Ireland, Scotland, England and the lands to the north of the Rhine and the Danube in the course of the sixth and seventh centuries : and with it grew the methods of explanation and analysis adopted by the Church. Outstanding among these was interpretation through allegory, and the prime exponent of this technique by the end of the eighth century was Amalarius of Metz. Whether or not he was the first person to perceive the essentially dramatic structure of the Latin Mass is an open question; but, as O. B. Hardison demonstrated in his book *Christian Rite and Christian Drama in the Middle Ages*, Amalarius thought it necessary to stress the fact that celebration of Mass had an immediate and recurring significance for all who partook of it as well as an historical significance in commemorating past events. With the allegorical interpretation of the Mass, set out by Amalarius in his *Liber Officialis* and copied by others, the way was at least open to regard the Church as a theatre for the re-enactment of Christ's triumph over sin and death and his redemption of mankind : and with an invitation to make such a mental equation the distance between the concept and practical fulfilment was not large. It was in fact made around the middle of the tenth century.

It will be noticed that I have been skipping through ten centuries as if they were mere months in a single year. In what I have said, however, it is obvious enough that no one can hope to come to terms with the origins of Christian drama without first familiarizing himself with the structure of the Mass and the history of its development. No less evident is the fact that any theatrical representation of the sacred drama latent within the Mass must involve visual and aural aspects of the service in action : thus any comprehension of it now must correspondingly involve some acquaintanceship with ecclesiastical iconography in architecture and the fine arts, together with some knowledge of the Church's attitude to music.

Of the two, the musical situation is much the more difficult to approach with any degree of certainty since the musical notation of the period that has survived is so sparsely documented that scholars cannot agree on how to interpret it.

The early Christian fathers in the days of persecution disapproved of music in the context of worship on the grounds that noise was incompatible with secrecy and that music distracted attention from the words of the service and the true spirit of devotion. Nevertheless it had to be admitted that musical instruments featured prominently in the Old Testament and that the Psalms were unquestionably intended to be sung. Following the conversion of the Emperor Constantine to Christianity, worship could become public. This proved a great stimulus to artistic embellishment of the liturgy of all kinds, since it served both to attract publicity for the faith and to assist in converting others to it. Where music was concerned the first-fruits of liberty appeared in the adaptation of Jewish psalmody, borrowed from the synagogue, to specifically Christian liturgies. An original contribution soon followed in the invention of the hymn, a lyric poem of a devotional kind, together with melodies drawn from Greek as well as Jewish sources.

By the start of the sixth century the Church was ready to standardize its attitudes to music both in theory and practice. This was achieved in two works destined to exercise a controlling influence over music throughout the Middle Ages and beyond – Boethius's *De Institutione Musica* and Pope Gregory's *Antiphonarium*. It must not be thought, however, that the production of these two works introduced a new era admitting instrumental music, harmony and polyphony to Church services. Alec Harman in *Man and His Music* demonstrated that the Church still justified the use of music as being an enhancement to audibility and to the meaning of the words used. When speaking of liturgical music in the sixth century therefore, we are talking strictly about vocal music and simple melody or plain-chant. It is this that Pope Gregory regulated in his *Antiphonarium*. Boethius's work was much more comprehensive, but it took another three

centuries for his theoretical precepts in respect of harmony, polyphony and instrumentation to become applicable to Church
services in any general way.

Historically, therefore, we possess a fair knowledge of what
music existed and how it was performed when the equation
between the sacred drama in the Mass and the enactment of it as
an integral part of the liturgy was made in the tenth century; but
this does not resolve the problems of pitch, tempo, instrumentation, if any, and other questions relating to the techniques of
performance actually employed. Extreme caution must still be
employed when approaching the antiphons and tropes which
formed the musical basis of the earliest liturgical dramas, notwithstanding the somewhat imaginative reconstructions which
have recently been recorded by fine singers and venturesome
musicians* (see Plate I and p. 33).

No less taxing to the theatre historian are the visual aspects of
liturgical practice, although documentation in respect of both
architecture and the fine arts is much fuller. That the new religion brought with it a new art can be stated with the utmost
confidence since so many buildings, mosaics, frescoes, ivories and
statues survive to convince us. How this new art was formulated,
what the sources of its inspiration were and what controls were
imposed on its development are questions, however, which are
open to widely diverging answers since tracing the cross-currents
between Byzantine, Roman, Celtic and even Islamic influences is
no easy task.[1]

At first the new art was practical and functional, since there
was neither time nor money for it to be anything else : nor, in the
days of persecution, could Christian communities afford to allow
their meeting places and the furnishings of them to be so con-
spicuous as to attract attention. For the historian it is always
important to try to relate art to the society that creates – or fails to
create it. Within the context of the particular society with which
he is dealing he must ask two questions. What is art for? What
does art do? We, in our time, are still heirs to the heresy
bequeathed us by the aesthetic movement in the nineteenth
century that art exists for its own sake. Art is *not* for art's sake :

* The two most noteworthy recordings are: *Ludus Paschalis*, Valois (Ensemble
Polyphonique de Paris) MB.444. Mono, and *The Play of Daniel*, Brunswick (New
York Pro Musica) SXA.4001. Stereo.

once it is (as with us it is often assumed to be) it quickly becomes art for the artist's sake (which, with us, many artists have convinced themselves it is). The artist then comes to believe that society owes him a living, which it does not.

Because these self-indulgent attitudes have become so commonplace in our society it is necessary to stir our imaginations once again before approaching architecture and the fine arts in the Middle Ages, and to try to understand that buildings and their ornaments were commissioned to meet specific needs.

Early Christian communities, when at last they were free to abandon secrecy of worship and declare their existence publicly by building shrines, churches and tombs, could choose between adapting existing buildings, notably temples, to their own requirements and inventing new buildings designed to meet their own needs: the former course of action recommended itself by virtue of being cheaper and of purging such places of their pagan associations, while the latter, if much more costly and time-consuming, served to proclaim the advent of the new faith both more vigorously and more ostentatiously. Either way, however, the architects were bound to derive a major part of their engineering and aesthetic ideas from existing buildings. This meant that Christian communities within the Byzantine Empire of the fourth and fifth centuries AD enjoyed a wide range of prototypes to copy or improve upon. Syrian, Egyptian and even Persian example came to play as large a part in determining the architectural character of early churches as Greek or Roman precedent. Materials too played their part – stone, brick, wood – according to availability and climatic conditions. Nor was it easy for these communities to divorce their thinking about the shape and style of God's house from what had formerly been thought appropriate as an environment for the God-Emperor. The one requirement of the new churches however that was uniquely Christian was the provision of a meeting place large enough to accommodate the whole community in any one locality for the specific purpose of celebrating the rites that were particular to the new religion. Two spaces were thus needed, one for assembly of the community of believers (the nave) the other for the celebration of the rites (the chancel). The two were linked together within a building described as a basilica. The chancel frequently ended in a semi-circular apse. Larger communities and extended rituals made additional space desirable; yet strict limits were imposed upon the size of nave, chancel and apse respectively by practical considerations about the roof. To meet the problems associated with spanning the distance between the walls with a roof and at the same time preventing the walls that supported it from collapsing, side aisles, transepts, supplementary apses and a central dome were added to the simplest form of basilica.

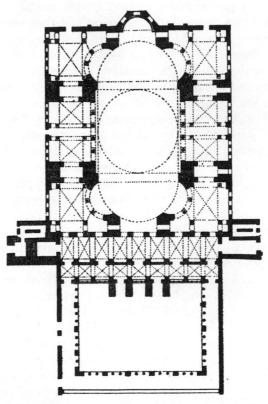

1   Ground-plan of Santa Sophia, Constantinople, consecrated in 537 AD

No less important to early Christian communities than a place of common assembly were suitable buildings in which to baptize converts to the faith and shrines or mausoleums as memorials to those heroes who had given their lives for the faith and who had died as martyrs at the hands of their persecutors. The basilica thus

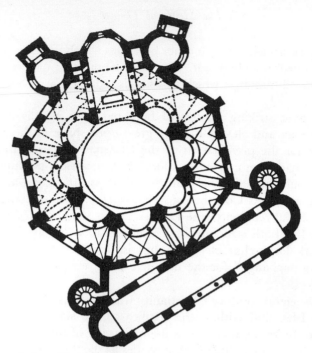

2 Ground-plan of San Vitale, Ravenna, consecrated 547 AD

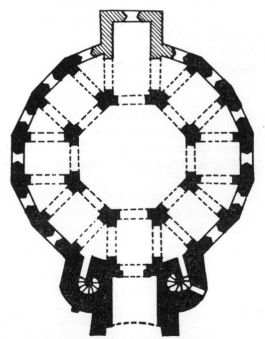

3 Ground-plan of the chapel of Charlemagne's Palace, Aachen, c.800 AD

came to be associated with other buildings which were frequently incorporated in or beside it. The most magnificent of these more complicated buildings which still stands today is Santa Sophia in Istanbul.

The most striking feature of buildings such as this both in ground plan and elevation is the great open space in the centre, an area for the presentation of the Christian mysteries that the building had been erected to contain: in theatrical parlance this space would unhesitatingly be described as 'an acting-area for performances'. As Christianity spread north, south, east and west as the official religion of the Empire so this style of building was modified in both structure and ornamentation for local reasons and with local characteristics; but its basic pattern remained virtually unchanged for the next five centuries (see Figures 1, 2 and 3.)

By the eighth century Christianity was firmly established in the British Isles, and with it the basilica as the standard place of worship. In Western countries the basic plan of the building had been modified to include such novelties as the three parallel apses at the eastern end of the chancel, a crypt beneath it to serve as a mausoleum, an elaborate porch at the western end and an ambulatory. Roofs however continued to be made of timber. It was not until the eleventh century, and then in France, that it became possible to span the nave and chancel with stone barrel-vaulting instead of timber beams (see Figure 4). This became possible because of the relative lightness of the limestone available in North-Western France; but the stresses which this stone vaulting imposed on the outer walls were such as to force architects to make fundamental changes in the structure and ground-plan of the whole building in succeeding centuries as churches grew in size.

The possession of buildings dedicated to the worship of Christ presented the elders of Christian communities from the fourth century AD onwards with both a problem and an opportunity in respect of the treatment to be accorded to the interior surfaces of the new churches. Should they be decorated, or should they not? If they were not to remain starkly un-ornamented, what kind of decoration was permissible and appropriate to the furnishing of God's House?

4 Diagrammatic sketch of barrel-vaulting at St Sernin, Toulouse, eleventh century

As might be expected, these questions were answered as much in terms of existing traditions of interior decoration known to the artists and craftsmen available as in terms of specifically Christian attitudes to the fine arts themselves. The matter was further complicated, however, by the dichotomy between the austere simplicity of the Christian philosophy of life on the one hand, and a natural desire to celebrate the end of persecution in a display of power and creative vitality on the other. A compromise was reached in a form of decorative art that deliberately abandoned the sensuous realism of Roman painting and sculpture in favour of more abstract and spiritual forms borrowed from Eastern art. This compromise was not reached without bitter controversy. As Christian communities began to establish themselves in Syria, Israel and countries further to the east and south, they encountered a total ban on all figurative art among the Islamic peoples by whom they found themselves surrounded and whom they were hoping to convert. A no less forceful disinclination to encourage the realistic as opposed to the spiritual in art emerged among Christian communities themselves in Ireland and was carried eastwards to England and France by Irish missionaries.

While it was easy enough for the elders of the Church in Byzantium and in Rome to accept the argument that detachment from physical reality helped to enhance the growth of the inner life of the spirit, it was far less easy to abandon all figurative art as a teaching aid, more especially as missionaries sought to propagate the gospel among peoples who spoke neither Greek, Hebrew nor Latin, the majority of whom were totally illiterate. Controversy was bound to arise therefore over the balance to be struck between decoration and ornament desired for reasons of prestige on the one hand, and the rival claims of spiritual detachment from the physical world and pictorial art as an explanatory device in missionary work within the actual decoration and ornament permitted.

The compromise that evolved admitted figurative art, but within very strict limits : chief among these was the emphasis to be placed upon the symbolic or emblematic significance of the figure or figures represented and their relationship to the divinity of Christ and the salvation of the human soul. The figure of Christ as Emperor thus came to assume far greater importance than that of Christ as man.[2] Figures of the Virgin Mary or of the disciples were allowed to be depicted in fresco, mosaic or in bas-relief as signposts to personal redemption from original sin : as such they were formalized the better to project their message – Mary enthroned and presenting Emanuel, St Peter holding a Church in one hand and the keys to Heaven's gate in the other, Moses displaying the commandments engraved on stone tablets, and so on. Never were these figures allowed to appear against a pictorially realistic background. A formalized treatment of the river Jordan could be permitted as an essential identification device in the portrayal of St John the Baptist, as could a tree to represent Paradise; but these and other concessions to pictorial realism were never organized pictorially as representations of place or scenic background for its own sake, only to assist speedy recognition of the figure and of that figure's contribution to the Christian way of life (see Plates 4 and 16).

The Romanesque style in Christian art and architecture is thus formal, austere, and derived as much from Eastern as from

Western precedents. It aspired to depict Christ in Majesty and to assist the faithful to find their own way to salvation through the example of the prophets, the apostles and the saints and martyrs. Its development between the fifth and the eleventh centuries was subject to frequent jolts and reversals occasioned as much by internal disputes about the rival claims of one code of liturgical practice over another and the never-ending effort to establish orthodoxy of belief in the face of heresy, as by sporadic waves of invaders from the north and east who destroyed and plundered what they found before accommodating themselves to a new way of life and becoming absorbed into Christian society.[3]

If the attitude of the early Christian Churches towards music, architecture and the fine arts was both pragmatic and cautious, their approach to dramatic art was no less ambiguous. Like the other arts drama possessed a distinguished past in Greek and Roman plays, theatres and works of criticism. The Greeks had carried this heritage east and south into Asia Minor, the Middle East, Alexandria and North Africa : the Romans had extended its influence northwards and westwards into Germany, France and Britain. In the fourth century AD, however, when Christianity claimed its first Emperor as a convert, Christian communities had no cause to admire the *ludi scenici* and the *spectacula* presented in theatres and amphitheatres throughout the Empire. It was not the tragedies of Aeschylus, Sophocles and Euripides or even the comedies of Aristophanes, Menander, Plautus and Terence which figured on the playbills known to them; for dramatic entertainment had by then degenerated into sequences of amusements that were both crude and rude. Mimes, pantomimes, dancers, musicians and keepers of performing animals mingled with tumblers, wrestlers, charioteers and gladiators to provide that strange mixture of mimetic and athletic *ludi* which I have already discussed. Designed to kill time and to deflect attention from the more serious aspects of political and social life within the boundaries of the Empire, these pastimes could scarcely be expected to appeal to the Christian priesthood, more especially in the light of the ridicule and physical suffering meted out to fellow Christians by these entertainers in the days of persecution. Worse still, all of these recreations were formally organized and presented within the frame of festivals dedicated to pagan deities and frequently financed by members of the secular government, metropolitan or provincial, Roman or Byzantine : the performers by contrast, who in Republican Rome had been permitted to exist on sufferance only (denied voting rights, debarred from holding political office and regarded socially as little better than slaves and harlots) came, under the Empire, to enjoy wealth, position and a degree of license in their conduct both on and off the stage that became a byword for luxurious living and sexual promiscuity. Under Constantine and Julian (despite the latter's apostasy) a reaction set in. The Emperors however found themselves in a difficult position. As E. K. Chambers remarked, 'They stood between bishops pleading for decency and humanity and populaces now traditionally entitled to their *panem et spectacula*' (*The Mediaeval Stage*, I,13).

In the Eastern Empire the Emperors' embarrassment on this score was brought to an abrupt end by the Saracen invasions in the seventh century. In the West the problem was solved by similar means although from a different quarter. The invading Goths, Ostogoths, Vandals, Lombards and other barbarian tribes that swept over the Alps into Italy and North Africa during the sixth century despised the showmen and their shows, mimetic and athletic, and eventually suppressed them, thus doing for the Church what its most distinguished leaders from St Chrysostom to St Augustine and St Jerome had for so long argued should be done, but had so signally failed to achieve.

With the election of Gregory the Great to the Papacy in 590 the old theatrical world of Greece and Rome had come to its end as an organized institution in Western civilization : paradoxically, before his tenure of the Papal office ended with his death in 604, Gregory had effected reforms within the Church which were of their very nature destined in the fullness of time to prepare the way for the advent of a new drama and a new theatre, Christian in inspiration and Romanesque in style.

It is a mistake, however, to suppose as many historians of the drama have done that the collapse of the theatre as an organized institution meant that all knowledge and recollection of dramatic art and theatre practice perished without trace for the next four hundred years; for neither Christian clerics nor barbarian magistrates could altogether banish or ignore the mimetic instinct in human kind or the Hellenistic heritage to which they were the direct heirs. Just as Christian society, in coming to terms with

music, architecture and the fine arts at an earlier point in its
history, had found itself obliged to compromise with Greek,
Roman, Hebrew and even Islamic traditions in these arts, so it
did with drama.

First, and most important, the mimetic instinct renewed itself
with each generation, like the annual return of spring after
winter, and expressed itself throughout Europe in the festive
games and dances associated with the sowing and harvesting of
crops and with the progress of the seasons as remarked in the sun's
passage through the heavens, notably at the solstices (December/
June) and the equinoxes (March/September). For the peasant
communities of Northern and Western Europe, whom the
hierarchy of the Roman Church sought to convert and to control,
these festivals of the agricultural year held an economic as well as
a religious significance. The Church therefore could not ignore
them, nor could it suppress them : it had to come to terms with
them and attempt to endow them with a Christian significance.
With that achieved through the equation of the major Commemorative Feasts in the Christian Calendar (Christmas, Shrovetide, Easter, Pentecost, All Saints, etc.) with those of the agricultural year, an accommodation with the *ludi* of social recreation in these holiday seasons could be reached.

Scarcely less important to the survival of earlier dramatic
traditions was the triumph of Latin as the universal language of
the new Church and the new Europe. No one could hope to
acquire fluency in this language without studying its literature;
and, since it was necessary to speak it as well as to write it, an
acquaintance with the works of the classical orators and playwrights was at least as desirable as knowledge of epic poetry,
philosophy and history. Ecclesiastical libraries, more especially
those in the monasteries that concerned themselves with teaching,
thus continued to contain some writings of Aristotle and some
Greek dramatists (albeit in Latin translation), and those of
Seneca, Terence and Horace.[4] A series of grammarians preserved
some notion in their writings about the nature of tragic and comic
form in literary narrative, while in Germany, at Gandersheim,
the nun Hrostwitha as late as the tenth century knew her Terence
well enough to imitate him in Latin prose plays glorifying
Christian martyrs.

Not all theatres and amphitheatres of the Roman Empire were

destroyed by the barbarians : many survived as buildings to be devoted to communal recreations that were still permitted, such as bull-fighting, wrestling and other sports (see Plate 6). Stripped of their former luxurious ornamentation and frequently used as quarries, they nevertheless continued to provide an open space for these activities, and convenient, if rudimentary, seating for spectators.

Thus, when Christian society felt ready in the course of the eleventh and twelfth centuries to approach dramatic art as a teaching instrument in the service of the faith, it found models and precedents both for composition and performance much closer to hand than has often been imagined. That this approach, when eventually it came, should have been transformed into something recognizably new and strange by those same influences which had modified and changed Christian attitudes to all the other arts should not surprise us : rather should it reveal to us the sort of mould in which it was likely to be cast. The starting point could only have been the liturgy and its purpose to enhance the worship of Christus Rex.

B. LITURGY AND RITUAL

Having learned by experience that university students can no longer be expected to know the meaning of either of these words, it will perhaps be as well to start by referring to dictionary definitions of them.

In the Christian Church the term 'liturgy' was originally limited to the commemoration of the Last Supper in the celebration of the Eucharist; but in the course of time the term was extended in its meaning to describe any or all of the Offices or services devised for public worship. Thus the term 'The Mass' as used in the Roman Catholic Church today still resembles the term 'liturgy' as used in its original restricted sense among the earliest Christian communities : by contrast the word liturgy as used in the Anglican Church today extends to embrace the entire contents of the Book of Common Prayer. It is the physical conduct of the services covered by the term 'liturgy' that is described by the word ritual in a Christian context : it thus embraces both the order of the service and the ceremonies carried out in association with it.

Our concern is the Mass; and, later on, some other liturgies, the significance of which was expressed visually in the rituals which accompanied them : for it was within the visual external-ization of the inner meaning of the rites which priests and con-gregations had met together to celebrate that the mimetic instinct in man came to be harnessed to the service of the Church.

Once it is realized that the Church we are talking about was entrenching itself from the fourth century onwards around the entire circumference of the Mediterranean, it becomes obvious that several liturgies would develop simultaneously, each coloured by variants of language, artistic traditions and other local factors particular to the country in question. The student of Christian worship thus finds himself obliged to take notice of the differences distinguishing the conduct of the same service in Asia Minor, Syria, Ethiopia, Spain, Gaul and Italy. Sooner or later a struggle for the supremacy of one corpus of liturgical practice over another was bound to develop. This struggle has been studied, and its progress carefully documented, by Dom Gregory Dix in *The Shape of the Liturgy*. For our purposes however it suffices to take note of two facts : the first is that in Europe two liturgies triumphed at the expense of all others, one in Greek in Eastern countries, the other in Latin in the West, and the second is that in the West the Latin or Roman liturgy had displaced its rivals by the end of the seventh century. What is thus of immediate con-cern to the historian of the drama is the conduct of the Roman liturgy between the accession of Charlemagne at the end of the eighth century and the compilation by St Ethelwold, Bishop of Winchester, of the *Regularis Concordia* in the last quarter of the tenth century when we first read of liturgical practices that are recognizably dramatic.[5]

With that said, it is still necessary to recognize that all the liturgies that came to be incorporated within the Roman – the Ambrosian of Northern Italy and Central Europe, the Gallican in Ireland, Britain and France, and the Mozarabic in Spain – had grown out of common roots in the Byzantine Empire under Constantine and his immediate successors in the fourth and fifth centuries. This is obvious enough in the Romanesque style of architecture, painting and sculpture : it is less obvious (because so much less familiar) in most aspects of liturgical ceremonial. This included the vestments of the clergy and the actual movements of

priests and congregations in the conduct of their collective
worship.

As I have already remarked, it proved difficult in the fourth
century for peoples accustomed for centuries to acknowledge
Emperors accepted as Gods to imagine how better to conduct
themselves in the house of the Christian God than had been their
wont in Imperial palaces. Much of the ritual therefore in the
Church legitimatized by the Emperor Constantine was simply
transferred from the palace to the basilica. As the Emperor was
omnipotent on earth, so Christ, as Pantocrator, commanded
heaven, earth and hell. This image found its way into the domes
and vaulted apses of Christian basilicas (see Plate 3). In its wake
came both a sense of hierarchy and of opulence derived from
Eastern rather than from Western models. The impact and
endurance of these images is instantly recognizable in the mosaic
ornamentation of interior walls of the Romanesque Churches of
Northern Italy and in the sculptured western elevations of
Romanesque Churches in France, Spain and Britain (see Plates
7, 8 and 9). An appropriate austerity of artistic treatment
matches the severely simplified contrasts between the good and
the bad, heaven and hell, saints and sinners. The dualism implicit
from the outset in these contrasts was consistently reinforced by
the steady development of the idea of an everlasting tug-of-war
between God and Lucifer, with men's souls as the prize, that
would not end until the day of final judgement. One of the most
important steps towards formalizing these abstract concepts into
an iconography which, as a result of constant repetition, came to
possess the realism of actual characters in actual situations, was
taken by St Augustine early in the fifth century. Between 413 and
426 he wrote *The City of God* in which he sought first to prove
that Christianity was not responsible for the fall of Rome at the
hands of Alaric the Goth, and then to contrast the corruption and
decay of all human achievement with the immortal and incor-
ruptible city-state of God's creation, which embraces the former,
but transiently for a particular purpose and a mere moment. The
vision proclaimed by Augustine was of a new empire of the future
centred upon a Christian Rome. Deeply indebted both to Plato
and to Virgil, this quasi-historical, quasi-philosophical work laid
the foundation-stones, as it were, of the Holy Roman Empire of

the Middle Ages in the Christian imagination. The link between God in heaven and the Emperor on earth was to be the Bishop of Eternal Rome. With a chain of being – God, the Saints as intercessors, Pope, Emperor – thus formulated, corresponding hierarchies of ministers, servants and subjects were bound to develop in its wake. The link between God and the entire hierarchy of mankind, between mortal and immortal, visible and invisible was the Mass.

It was only a short step from this contrast between heaven and earth to that between earth and hell. The Roman 'Avernus', with its smoking cave at the entrance, its many-headed guard-dog and its Stygian gloom, became a legitimate starting point for an iconography that drew its realistic detail from whatever was bestial in human conduct and whatever occasioned fear or pain or grief in the human mind and heart (see Plates 10, 11, 25 and 26).

If the City of God could be depicted visually as a castellated town, so could Satan's city : if the former could be defended by an army of angels and archangels led by St Michael with his flaming sword, Lucifer could muster a no less formidable force of professional executioners, torturers and licentious, brutalized soldiery under the leadership of Beelzebub and the other Princes of Darkness. If in heaven all was light and harmony, in hell cacophony reigned along with noisome fumes and intolerable extremes of heat and cold. It soon became legitimate, therefore, to visualize heaven in terms of the Garden of Eden as a pastoral idyll, or as a never-ending succession of state rooms in a royal palace or baronial fortress. Hell, in appropriate contrast, resembled in its furnishings the privies, cess-pits, dungeons and torture chambers of these same palaces and castles, or a wild country of hostile forests, barren deserts and volcanic eruptions.

The same pattern of thinking came to be applied to the respective populations of these contrasted city-states beyond the frontiers of the known world. That of heaven was idealized and that of hell appropriately distorted : both were hierarchically structured, each rank of society taking its orders from its superior and its dress from its rank : status was thus outwardly advertised in costume. In time these contrasted ranks of angels and devils came to be augmented by their agents on earth in the battle for men's souls, the Virtues and Vices.

B*

5   Angels at War with Devils: early sixteenth-century woodcut illustration
of St Augustine's *Civitatis Dei*

Undoubtedly such realistically grounded concepts of the physical characteristics of the life of the soul after death formulated by Augustine and his followers in Christian literature encouraged artists to attempt to depict such scenes in mural decoration. By the eighth century the drift in this direction was gaining such momentum that it provoked a sharp reaction. In AD 730 the Emperor Leo III, who was himself a Syrian, forbade the use of images in rituals accompanying Christian services: this edict was ratified by the assembled bishops of the Church twenty-four years later, and there followed three decades of systematic destruction of representational images in Churches. It was directed with especial energy against icons and thus became known as iconoclasm. A brief reprieve arrived under the Empress Irene during the closing years of the century; but it was not until the middle of the ninth century that artists could again regard themselves as free in the Eastern Church to depict Christian life and thought in figurative terms.

It was in the West however, rather than in the East, that the traditions of Roman representational art found their most enthusiastic supporters in the ninth century, under the Emperor

Charlemagne. With his coronation on Christmas Day 800, a new era had begun for art in the service of Christianity in which the painter, the sculptor, the illuminator of manuscripts and workers in ivory, stained glass and metal could begin tentatively to explore once again the possibilities of depicting heaven, earth, hell and scriptural history in terms both of the daily life that was familiar to them and of the Roman works of art that survived in their midst as models to be copied and adapted to new needs.

If, in the early centuries AD, artists had experienced difficulty in depicting Christ, the prophets, and the apostles, and had solved their problem by idealizing these figures in recognizably imperial terms of reference, no less difficulty was experienced by the elders of the Church in determining how to behave when communicating with God in the new basilicas. Again the solution was found in imitating the ceremonial of the imperial Court at Byzantium. On greeting the Emperor one prostrated oneself: in his presence subjects removed their headgear: when he passed they fell on their knees and bowed their heads. Slowly, the movements, dress and gesture necessary to the *execution* of the liturgy – indeed the whole aura of worship under the gaze of the Pantocrator in the dome or apse – came to assimilate the traditional rituals of Court life. Whether private audience or public ceremonial was the order of the day, no one in the imperial household was at a loss how to behave: models therefore existed to be directly copied or appropriately adapted for every Christian occasion by the priest-servants and officials of Christ the King.

The closeness of this imitative practice may be recognized most clearly in the vestments worn by priests in the early Church (see Plates 12 and 13). Here again we must banish our modern notions of costume as a weapon in the sex-war or as dress prescribed by the exigencies of work and occupation: instead we must try to recreate in our imaginations a costume ethic that flatly contradicts both of these modern assumptions. Costume was intended then to *conceal* the shape (and thus the sex) of the person wearing it: yet it was also required to be as opulent and sensual in appearance as the proximity of Byzantium to the silks and jewels of the Orient permitted. Garments which we recognize as the cloaks, surplices, albs, dalmatics and stoles of the clergy today on ceremonial occasions were thus the normal attire of Emperor, Empress and Court Officials in Constantinople. Ankles, legs, waists and chests were concealed from view making the male form indistinguishable from the female. Variety was provided in the fabrics from which these enveloping garments were made, and in the embroidery and jewelry applied upon them. As these luxuries were not denied to men, their use was naturally transferred from Court vestments to those adopted by clergy.

A no less obvious reflection of the influence of imperial ceremonial on Christian worship is to be perceived in the division of the Mass into two principal parts, the Ordinary and the Proper. The Ordinary, as the title implies, covers that part of the service that is appropriate to daily celebration of the Office, and its texts are thus invariable : the Proper, again as the title implies, covers that part of the service which is uniquely appropriate to a particular festival in the Church's Calendar of commemorative feats and its texts thus vary from festival to festival. A similar distinction applies to High and Low Mass, the former describing the conduct of the liturgy on a major public occasion and the latter its conduct on routine and relatively private occasions. The Greek word 'Eucharist' meant thanksgiving, and the original ceremony was a simple one : by the tenth century, however, it had been heavily elaborated, ornamented, and expanded into a sequence of ceremonies known as the Mass. The Roman Mass, out of which a new dramatic art was destined to emerge in the tenth century, was thus compounded of several distinct components, each of which took its appointed place within the full liturgy. For convenience and for subsequent reference the component parts of the Ordinary and the Proper are here set out side by side.

The Proper	*The Ordinary*
Introit (Introduction)	
	Kyrie
	Gloria*
Gradual	
Tract or Alleluia	
	Credo
Offertory	
	Sanctus
	Agnus Dei
Communion Prayer	
* This was dropped during Lent.	Dismissal

In the earliest Christian communities the Eucharist was preceded by a vigil or period of meditation. This vigil was also
elaborated and expanded into what, by the tenth century, had
become known in the West as the Canonical Hours or Offices. Of
these there were eight : Matins (at midnight), Lauds (at day-
break), Prime (at 6.00 am), Terce (at 9.00 am), Sext (at noon),
None (around 2 or 3.00 pm), Vespers (at 6.00 pm) and Compline
(at 9.00 pm). The shape and content of all these liturgies were
developed within monastic communities whose principal concern
was with the form and order of worship. Each Office came to be
varied and decorated with suitable psalms, hymns, readings from
scripture and even commentaries upon these readings. These
additions and variations were further reinforced by the musical
treatment accorded to them, the emblematic use made of the
architecture of the basilica, darkness and light, vestments, movement and gesture.

By the tenth century melodies adapted from Greek and Jewish
originals and standardized within Pope Gregory the Great's *Antiphonarium* were in use throughout the West, and attached to
liturgical texts in forms inherited from Jewish synagogues known
collectively as psalmody. There were three principal types —
direct, responsorial and antiphonal. These types are still indicative of the relative importance attached to the words and to the
melodies. Chanting of texts, as opposed to the speaking of them,
made for better audibility in echoing basilicas; and since the
object of chant was to ensure that the words were heard, direct
psalmody, or plain-chant, allocated one note of the melody to one
syllable of the text. This came to be known as syllabic chant.
Hymns were handled in this way and usually allocated to the
congregation to be sung in unison. Psalms however admitted
more complicated treatment. One form resembled that of question and answer, a text divided between a single singer (*cantor*)
and the rest of the community (*decani responsores*). This could
be done in two ways. Either all the verses could be allocated to
the cantor with only the briefest of repeated answers left to the
others (responsorial plain-chant) or the text could be more
equally divided between two or more groups of singers (antiphonal plain-chant). It will be noticed that any move away from
direct syllabic chant towards antiphonal singing implied a shift
in the balance of interest between words and music : the presence

of elaborate antiphons in the liturgies of the tenth century therefore indicates a steadily developing interest in music for its own
sake.

In the course of the ninth and tenth centuries elaboration of
the liturgy developed in several directions. Instruments were
introduced to accompany the singers. Voices were divided into
groups to sing the same melody, but at two different pitches,
making for simple harmony as opposed to strict unison. With that
achieved (and enjoyed) the next step was to vary the tempo of
one melodic line while retaining that of the other. In these ways
liturgical music moved inescapably towards what we know as
descant and counterpoint, and thus imperceptibly towards full
polyphony.

This progression towards this end starts with the addition of
'group-chant' to syllabic chant. By 'group' was meant simply the
admission of several notes as opposed to one note to some syllables : thus the word *Benedicamus*, for example, containing five
syllables, could span perhaps ten notes by spinning out the original '*Ben* . . .' with a group of three notes and the penultimate '. . .
cam . . .' with a group of four. Acceptance of this principle
opened the way to a still more elaborate variation which took the
form of introducing a group so large as to be virtually a new
melody in itself, and then attaching this to the final syllable of the
word. In the case of 'Benedicamus' therefore, while four notes
sufficed to cover the first four syllables, the final '. . .us' could be
decorated with a tune of its own of forty notes or more. This
practice was known as melismatic chant, the word 'melisma'
describing the musical ornamentation of the final syllable. It is
important to grasp the originality of this creative process which
resulted in a supply of new texts on the one hand and of new
melodies on the other. Once this is understood, it will be seen that
a temptation existed to supply a further text to take up the spare
notes of the melisma, thus bridling melodic fantasy and harnes-
sing it once again to the truly devotional purpose of the liturgy.
Widespread acceptance of this practice called for a new word to
describe it : the answer was supplied in the Latin word *tropus*
meaning 'added melody', the anglicized version of which is trope.
The added words were also known as tropes, but the term trope
came to cover new texts, new melismas and new texts wedded to
the new melismas, while the actual tasks of matching additional

words and notes and linking them appropriately to text and melody on either side came to be described as troping. The monastic centres in which this initiative was pursued most vigorously were those of St Gall in Switzerland and St Martial at Limoges in France.[6]

Among the more famous of these troped sequences to find a permanent place in the liturgy are the *Dies Irae*, the *Stabat Mater* and the *Victimae Paschali* : the last of these was destined to play an important part in the growth of the new drama. Among other troped sequences designed to be chanted antiphonally was one item of the Proper in the Mass, the Introit particular to Easter Sunday. The text was taken from scripture and was then treated musically as an antiphon to be sung responsorially, i.e. with a single cantor supported by a small group of responders.

Int[errogatio]
Quem que - ri - tis in se - pul - chro,   O   Chri - sti - co-le

R[esponsio]
Je - sum Na-za-re - num cru-ci-fi - xum,   O   cae - li - co-lae

Non est hic, sur-re-xit   si-cut pre-di-xe-rat, I-te, nun-ti-a-te quia sur - re - xit de sepulchro

(See plate 1)

The full text, with its further questions and answers but lacking rubrics prescribing anything other than responsorial plain-chant, lasts a little more than a minute. Much argument has surrounded the question of whether this Introit in its original form when it lacked rubrics specifying direct impersonation of the angel and the three Maries was or was not dramatic. In the closing years of the last century Marius Septet alerted scholarly opinion in *Les Prophètes du Christ* and *Origines Catholiques du Théâtre Moderne* to the intimate connections between theatrical representation and the musical representation and the *musical* elaboration of the Mass, isolating the superimposition of responsorial chant upon texts in dialogue form as the *fons et origo* of Christian drama : yet Karl Young in *The Drama of the Mediaeval Church*, possibly because he was more concerned with texts than with music, insisted that only after the Introit had been displaced from Mass to Matins and rubrics added prescribing impersonation can it be said to have become a drama. His is a precise view; in my opinion too precise. The truth, as I see it, lies somewhere between Septet's view and Young's in that mysterious realm of the human imagination when the emotional response to the Introit of certain celebrants and witnesses was strong enough to equate singers and dialogue on the one hand with the angel and the Maries of the Gospels on the other. Such an equation of the musical treatment accorded to this troped Introit – soloist and liturgical chorus – and commemorative re-enactment of the original event was only made the easier by the habit of submitting the whole of the Mass to allegorical interpretation which had been popularized a century earlier by one of Charlemagne's most influential Churchmen, Amalrius, Bishop of Metz.

In this way the basilica itself had come to be regarded as a kind of theatre in which the actions and gestures of the ritual accompanying the liturgy linked the events of the historical past commemorated by the office with the immediate present for celebrants and congregations alike. What is beyond doubt is that many recipients of Holy Communion on Easter Sunday in the the tenth century in those monastic communities where the use of this troped Introit was adopted made just that equation and found that it enhanced the joyous quality of their worship at this climax of the Christian year : for shortly afterwards another troped Introit, again built upon an appropriate text from scripture in dialogue form and again chanted responsorially, was added to the Proper for Christmas Day. This time it is the shepherds who ask the angel where they may find their saviour.

Thus although in neither case was there any deliberate attempt initially to impersonate the angel, the Maries or the shepherds, dialogue plain-chant and emotional response to both served to create a mystical re-enactment of historical event, simultaneously within the liturgy of the Eucharist on two of the Church's principal commemorative Feasts and in the imaginations of the worshippers, as a natural extension of normal worship. Once this had occurred it was bound to be recognized, sooner rather than later, that the art of drama had come to take its place among the other arts in the Church triumphant in the service of Christ its King.

C. THE DRAMA OF CHRIST THE KING

If I have succeeded in my purpose in the two preceding sections of this chapter, the reader will have noticed that the earliest form of drama to appear within the Christian Church was artificial, mystical and lyrical – in a word, operatic – rather than realistic and didactic. It was chanted, not spoken; it was sung in Latin, not in vernacular languages; it formed an integral part of the liturgy proper to particular Calendar Feasts and was not in any sense either a scripture lesson or an entertainment. In short, the most striking feature about the Introits for Easter Sunday and Christmas Day as presented at St Gall, Limoges or Winchester in the late tenth century was the naturalness of their evolution. Like mosaic, fresco, and every form of musical addition to the Church's liturgies between the eighth and the tenth centuries, it was initially no more than an ornamental and explanatory elaboration, the purpose of which was to mark the special nature and the outstanding importance of particular festivals for Christians.

To understand the inevitability of this development it is necessary to relate the Feasts of Easter and Christmas to the aesthetic contrast between the Feasts themselves and the long periods of carefully controlled preparation – Lent and Advent – which preceded them. These contrasts of course were not entirely manmade since they took their origin from natural phenomena : the steadily diminishing hours of daylight culminating in the winter solstice in the latter half of December, and the weeks of near-famine conditions in February and March before the melting of the winter snow. To this extent then Christmas continued to reflect the fact that the balance between darkness and light had shifted in favour of lengthening daylight, and Easter, linked as it was to the equinoctial moon continued to reflect the annual rebirth of nature in spring: but for the Christian there was the new spiritual significance which Christ's birth and resurrection from the dead had added to these natural phenomena to be thankful for as well. Both festivals were thus charged with optimism, romantic in spirit, and joyous in character : as such they invited imaginative ornament and artistic exposition inside Christian basilicas.

Pitfalls await the student who seeks to reconstruct these ceremonies in terms of the modern Roman Catholic Mass or the

Anglican Communion Service. The liturgy of the tenth century was different and so were the buildings : so too were the religious and social attitudes of the men and women who participated. Nevertheless, it is still possible to descry, however dimly, something of the nature and quality of the earliest liturgical music-drama from surviving records if these are properly used. Texts, taken on their own, will not help us : they must be coupled with the musical notation that accompanies them in the surviving manuscripts if they are to inform us accurately of what actually happened. Stage directions, in the form of rubrics, cannot assist us taken on their own because they are so brief and scanty : they too must be coupled to what we know of the architecture and decoration of early churches. Nor can the actors and audiences help since they are dead and have left no memorial : and here the only clue we have to guide us is the knowledge that their actions and reactions formed an integral part of their worship.

On these slender foundations it is possible to make a tentative appraisal of how the Introit for Easter Sunday, and other liturgical sequences of a dramatic character developed from it, were executed.

When we talk about 'the performance of a play' we are automatically, if uncritically, speaking about five things at once. We cannot think of a performance without assuming the existence of a theatre, that is a stage and auditorium to contain it. We assume imitation of actions in sequence, that is, a story line. We take for granted some means of identifying person and place, costumes and setting : and we assume the existence of both actors and an audience. If we now apply these concepts to certain liturgical ceremonies of the tenth century which are recognizably dramatic in character what do we find?

If we start with the word 'theatre' we will find nothing to help us; for neither in the liturgical rubrics nor in descriptive accounts of the ritual do such Latin words as *teatrum, amphiteatrum* or *arena* occur. Instead we find *platea*, another Latin word that is surprisingly accurate in its very vagueness. It means simply 'the place', no more, no less. The only qualifications, deducible from the context but not specified, are that this place should be flat and open enough for the clerics who are impersonating characters described in the Gospels to move about and be seen. Our own word 'acting-area' is a remarkably close equivalent. If we now

relate that concept to the ground-plans and elevations of Byzantine and Romanesque architecture it will be quickly seen how
appropriate it is (see Plates 2 and 7, and Figures 2 and 3 p.17).

The fact, however, that the *platea* is contained within a basilica
at once endows it with a special quality; for it forms an integral
part of a place of worship. What is done on or in the *platea* will
thus reflect some of this quality : if it does not, it will appear
discordant, even offensive. It will absorb this quality of worship
not only from the architectural environment, the basilica, but also
from the people assembled in the basilica, priests and congregation. Our stage is thus an open space containing an altar, and our
auditorium those areas of the basilica surrounding this open space
reserved to accommodate the worshippers.

Turning next to the action of the drama presented, we notice
that the worship of which it forms a component part is itself a
response to instinct, something that we both feel and perceive to
be desirable : it is neither an exclusively emotional response nor an
exclusively intellectual one. It is shaped, ordered and controlled
by the intellect while it provokes, stimulates and ultimately
releases emotional energy. The double-barrelled quality of this
response is apparent in the Latin words chosen to describe the
function of the *platea* in respect of the stage action. These are
Officium, *Ordo* and, at a later date, *Representatio*.

Officium, or Office, simply means a ceremony or rite. *Ordo*, in
this liturgical context, means the Order or sequence in which a
particular ceremony is to be conducted. Thus use of these two
words in the rubrics of early service books to cover those
ceremonies we recognize as dramatic tells us quite plainly that
whatever else this drama was for its pioneers it was never conceived or regarded as some sort of visual-aid to Bible reading for
the education of illiterate peasants – why, in heaven's name,
should it have been conducted in plain-chant and in Latin if it
were? – but as a new dimension to the depth of emotional
response to the event commemorated and thus as an enhancement of its abiding significance. Viewed in this light, Easter can
at once be seen as the most important Feast of the entire Church
year and thus as the occasion that demanded both ceremonies
and an order of service to contain them commensurate with
Christian joy and thanksgiving for the miracle of Christ's
resurrection. That *these* ceremonies on *this* occasion should thus

come ultimately to stretch beyond painting and beyond music into commemoration of the event itself by annual re-enactment of it was well-nigh inevitable.

We can therefore establish with certainty that the *platea* of tenth-century basilicas contained on major festive occasions special rituals that involved brief and simple re-enactment of historical events of critical importance to the Christian faith. Scarcely less important to our understanding of the nature of this drama is the fact that repetition of this re-enactment on any occasion other than that which it had come into existence to celebrate would be intellectually meaningless and emotionally inappropriate. So far, therefore, *platea*, occasion and dramatic ceremony can be seen to have been as tightly linked to each other artistically as they were doctrinally; and only when a discordant element of some kind creeps in to disturb this balance is any reason for change likely to declare itself.

Nothing inappropriate, and thus discordant, reveals itself in the directions governing the performance of these early liturgical music-dramas dedicated to Christ the King. Commemoration of an historical event, by mimetic imitation, whether it be the first Easter, the first Christmas or the first Epiphany, covers two aspects of the original occasion; the facts and the emotions associated with or arising from the facts. It also involves the provision of suitable techniques to meet these two objectives. In other words the imitation must both narrate the facts and demonstrate their emotional quality.

The facts of the Easter story could scarcely be simpler. Three women are looking for a tomb intending to dress the corpse of a friend : they meet an angel who tells them that the corpse has risen from the tomb* (see Plates 14 and 15).

The accompanying emotions are equally simple. The women are overcome with grief as they approach the tomb. The angel's news translates this grief into joy.

Notwithstanding this, however, and the dialogue form in which the Easter Introit was cast, the troped Introit itself was likely to develop in the direction of liturgical exhortation rather

---

* Quem quaeritis in sepulchro, Christicole?
  Jesum Nazarenum crucifixum, o coelicolae.
  Non est hic, surrexit.
  Alleluia. (See p. 33 above.)

than dramatic narrative for so long as it served to introduce the Mass. Once it was shifted to the first of the Canonical Offices – Matins (midnight) – sufficient time was allowable for the reverse to happen. There, in its new position at the close of Matins between final response and the *Te Deum*, dramatic narrative could expand.[7] The means adopted to meet these needs only involved the application of existing rituals to the new forms. Processions, song, symbolic gesture and vestments, as we have seen, had long since been appropriately geared to the emotion and significance of the occasion in Christian worship : thus, in the case of dramatic representation, nothing more was needed than to apply existing audible and visible symbols which were already codified to each new sequence of actions. This becomes readily apparent in a document originating from the Benedictine reform of the tenth century in the diocese of Winchester – *Regularis Concordia*.

With the accession of Edgar as King in 959 reform in England began in earnest with the translation of three outstanding clerics to bishoprics : St Dunstan to Canterbury, St Oswald to Worcester and St Ethelwold to Winchester between 960 and 963. These three men met in Winchester, which was then King Edgar's capital city, and the capital of a recently reunited country, *c*.970, and called a Synod or Council of Churchmen the purpose of which was to settle earlier disputes (*concordia*) relating to the new reforms, both in monastic life and liturgical practice which, as Benedictine monks, they had introduced when still employed as Abbots. This Synod links England with Benedictine reform on the Continent in those monastic houses where the troped *Quem quaeritis* Introit had first made its appearance : through the decisions reached and promulgated in the *Regularis Concordia* this Synod also links Winchester with the rest of the Church in England since its recommendations were swiftly to be copied elsewhere.

It is in the wide context of this truly momentous ecclesiastical Council that St Ethelwold's instructions for the correct conduct of the *Quem quaeritis* trope at Matins must be viewed.

While the third lesson is being chanted, let four brethren vest themselves. Let one of these, vested in an alb (see Plate 13), enter as though to take part in the service, and let him approach the sepulchre without attracting attention and sit there quietly with a palm in his hand. While the third respond is chanted, let the remaining three follow, and let them all, vested in copes (Plates 14, 15) bearing in their hands thuribles with incense, and stepping delicately as those who seek something, approach the sepulchre. These things are done in imitation of the angel sitting in the monument, and the women with spices coming to anoint the body of Jesus. When therefore he who sits there beholds the three approach him like folk lost and seeking something, let him begin in a dulcet voice of medium pitch to sing *Quem quaeritis . . .* ? And when he has sung it to the end, let the three reply in unison, *Ieshu Nazarenum.* So he *Non est hic, surrexit sicut praedixerat Ite, nuntiate quia surrexit a mortuis.* At the word of his bidding let those three turn to the choir and say *Alleluia! resurrexit Dominus!* This said, let the one, still sitting there and as if recalling them, say the anthem *Venite et videte locum.* And saying this, let him rise, and lift the veil, and show them the place bare of the cross [i.e. the altar-cross which had been placed in the sepulchre below the altar on Good Friday]* but only the cloths laid there in which the cross was wrapped. And when they have seen this, let them set down the thuribles which they bore in that same sepulchre, and take the cloth, and hold it up in the face of the clergy, and as if to demonstrate that the Lord has risen and is no longer wrapped therein, let them sing the anthem *Surrexit Dominus de sepulchro,* and lay the cloth upon the altar. When the anthem is done, let the prior, sharing in their gladness at the triumph of our King, in that, having vanquished death, He rose again, begin the hymn *Te Deum laudamus.* And this begun, all the bells shall chime out together.[8]

The importance of these instructions can scarcely be exaggerated: not only do they inform us that the Easter Introit was conceived of in the tenth century as *officium,* not *ludus,* liturgical office *not* play or game, but they give us a vivid picture of the style of acting and the means adopted to identify character and locality in this 'imitation of the angel sitting in the monument,

---

* This was done within the liturgical office known as the *Ordo Deposito Crucis* which is also described in the *Regularis Concordia.* For a full account of the form and conduct of this Office see Karl Young, *The Drama of the Mediaeval Church,* vol. II, pp. 112–48.

and the women with spices coming to anoint the body of Jesus'. It was clearly intended that the congregation should be confronted with a double image. The Maries are men, not women. They wear copes, not fashionable female attire or historical 'period' dress. The dialogue is in Latin, not English; chanted, not spoken; and punctuated with hymns and anthems. The climax is the *Te Deum*, the most famous and familiar Christian hymn of praise and thanksgiving in which actors and audience participate together. Thus the event of Christ's resurrection is commemorated by re-enactment in the most artificial and formal manner imaginable : yet what is patently a highly ornate ritual from one standpoint is just as patently a dramatic representation of a turning point in Christian history when viewed from another. This dichotomy of visual image exactly parallels the dichotomy that was present in the fusion of historical time with actual time to form ritual time, and resulted in a form of dramatic representation that existed simultaneously as liturgical ritual and mimetic re-enactment. The result is liturgical music-drama, for which the theatre is the basilica itself, the occasion a festival of rejoicing. The style is recognizably Romanesque.

Once a ceremony of this kind has been standardized in the manner prescribed by St Ethelwold, and once it has come to be widely adopted, three developments are likely to follow : the original ceremony may be embellished and expanded, similar ceremonies modelled on it may legitimately figure in the liturgies for other festivals, and the individuals responsible for creating them may develop a technical awareness of what they are actually doing. The imitative aspect of the ceremony may thus come to possess an importance of its own, artistic rather than strictly religious. Proof exists that all three of these developments overtook liturgical music drama in the course of the eleventh century. Not only does the practice spread south to Italy, north-east to Germany and west to Ireland, but we find the Christmas crib being substituted for the Easter sepulchre at Matins on Christmas Day and an *Officium Stellae* to celebrate the coming of the Magi to Bethlehem at the Epiphany or *Festum Trium Regum*. The latter attached itself as naturally to the Offertory in the Mass as the other two had originally done to the Introit : this too was later displaced to precede the Mass (see Figure 6). Texts, moreover, become longer and, at least in some cases, the accompanying

6 *Trium Regum*: manuscript illumination from the eleventh century
   Wolfenbütteler Evangeliar, Codex Guelf, 16.1. Aug. 2.

rubrics become fuller. In these extended forms where narrative
has come to assert its own claims we also encounter a recognition
of the dramatic qualities present in the ceremonies in a gradual
change of title. *Ordo Visitatio Sepulchri, Officium Pastorum* and
Officium Regum Trium indicate plainly an emphasis upon
action and upon character within these commemorative ceremonies that has come to rival their liturgical quality implicit in
the words *Ordo* and *Officium*. Not surprisingly therefore a new
word *Representatio*, or representation, comes into use as an
alternative to *Ordo* and *Officium*. Once this has happened, as is
the case with *Ordo representacionis Adae*, an Anglo-Norman text
of the twelfth century, the drama of the Church is approaching
perilously close to what the Romans had known as a *ludus* and to
what we describe as a play.

The inescapable inference to be drawn from this is that repetition, expansion and variety combined to endow these ceremonies
with a special attraction of their own both for their begetters and

for those who participated in them. I think this may be described as joy mixed with pleasure : if this is the case, what we then have to recognize is that actors and audiences and the relationships between them must loom as large as priests and congregations in any discussion of the subject. In short, entertainment has become a factor of consequence alongside worship. The Church itself acknowledged this in the twelfth century when it came to encourage the use of the word *ludus* as a title for biblical narrative presented in dramatic form.

D. DRAMA OF THE PROPHETS, SAINTS AND MARTYRS

Central to the genesis of the drama of Christ the King, historically, physically and symbolically, was the place occupied by the altar in Christian basilicas. In the development of the troped Easter Introit into the *Visitatio Sepulchri*, the altar was not only the centre of the *platea*, or acting-area, but served also to symbolize the sepulchre. Historically, association of the altar in the tenth century with the sepulchre of Christ took its origin from the much earlier practice of constructing the altar immediately above the tomb of a local saint or martyr. With time, it became as normal to construct altars with a cavity below the altar-table and to place a casket containing the bones or other physical remains of a saint or martyr in this cavity.

The fact that the first liturgical music-dramas developed in close proximity to the *Te Deum* within the liturgy only reinforced this association of the dramatic Offices with the saints and martyrs, and added the apostles and prophets as well, in a context of praise and thanksgiving.

Holy, Holy, Holy : Lord God of Sabaoth;
Heaven and earth are full of the Majesty : of thy glory.
The glorious company of the Apostles: praise thee.
The goodly fellowship of the Prophets : praise thee.
The noble army of Martyrs: praise thee.
The holy Church throughout the world: doth acknowledge thee;
    The Father: of an infinite Majesty;
    Thine honourable, true : and only Son;
    Also the Holy Ghost : the Comforter.
    Thou art the King of glory : O Christ.

Moreover, as liturgical exhortation was the base on which the earliest dramatic Offices were grounded, nothing could be more natural than to recall prophetic prefigurations of Christ and subsequent saintly imitations at appropriate Calendar festivals. The season of Advent was ideal for the former and that of Whitsun no less suitable for the latter. Yet for reasons which are not known, neither season in fact supplied additional plays: instead it was the twelve-day feast of Christmas that served to widen the dramatic repertoire of liturgical music dramas. Three reasons for this come to mind, but they can only be regarded as speculations. The first is that late December and early January was the season of the year when work could stop for nearly two weeks together: the second is that the Church had grouped several important festivals into this holiday period – the Nativity, St Stephen, St John the Evangelist, Holy Innocents, the Circumcision, and Epiphany – all of which were preceded by St Nicholas's Day on 6 December: the third is that young scholar-clerks and deacons were encouraged to turn their leisure time to profitable ends in the service of God and thus had ample incentive to deploy their literary and musical gifts to the embellishment of this succession of Feasts in the holiday season.

A combination of all three reasons at least corresponds with the sudden expansion in both the number and type of play associated with the liturgy that developed around this particular season in the Church's Calendar during the eleventh and twelfth centuries. Two other facts have to be taken into account in this context, both of which point to the same conclusion. The first is the subject matter of the dramas that have survived to us: this is almost wholly concerned with the slaughter of the Innocents, St Nicholas, the exhortations of the prophets and the life of the Virgin Mary. There can be no doubt that the source of the many plays related to the prophets is the *lectiones*, or readings, taken during the Advent season from the fifth-century homily *Contra Judaeos, Paganos, et Arianos Sermo de Symbolo*. This commentary arraigns the Jews, and by implication pagans and heretics of the Christian era, for their refusal to accept Christ as the promised Messiah, and summons the major prophets to testify to the contrary. Because this testimony took the form of direct speech, like the dialogue form of the Easter and Christmas Introits it invited dramatic treatment. This it received in the liturgical music drama known as the *Ordo Prophetarum*, or Procession of the Prophets. Advent liturgies provided a no less obvious cue to develop dramatic rituals in honour of the Virgin Mary.

The other fact to be reckoned with in the Christmas season is the genesis of dramatic parody within a liturgical context in the guise of the Boy Bishop, the Feast of the Ass and the Feast of Fools. The root of all these ceremonies derives in large measure from the play of Balaam and his Ass within the *Ordo Prophetarum* and plays relating to St Nicholas. The inversion of normal hierarchical order and of social status that is a common factor in these festivals reflects customs formerly associated with the Roman Saturnalia but given a Christian significance appropriate to the Christmas holiday: the dominant part played by students and children in all these liturgies suggests just as powerfully a deliberate policy on the part of their elders to keep idle hands and minds profitably employed by preparing festivities that were at once enjoyable and appropriate to the season.

Whatever the reasons for these extensions of dramatic art in the service of worship, the results were a self-evident stretching of the original *officium* towards *representatio* and a gradual transformation of *representatio* into *ludus*. The truth of this claim is obvious enough in the changing character of the rubrics ordering the presentation of these liturgies. Here are some examples.

Ysaias:	barbatus, dalmatica indutus, stola rubea
Isaiah:	*bearded, dressed in a dalmatic, with a red stole*
	per medium uerticis ante et retro dependens.
	hanging from the neck down the middle in front and behind.
Iheremias:	similiter, absque stola.
Jeremiah:	*similarly clothed, but without the stole.*
Daniel:	adolescens, ueste splendida indutus.
Daniel:	*a young man, dressed in a gorgeous robe.*
Moyses:	cum dalmatica, barbatus, tabulas legis ferens.
Moses:	*with a dalmatic, bearded and carrying the tablets of the Law.*
David:	regio habitu.
David:	*dressed as a king.*

Abacuc: barbatus, curuus, gibosus.
Habbakuk: bearded, stooping and hunch-backed.
Elizabeth: femineo habitu, pregnans.
Elizabeth: dressed as a woman, pregnant.

... etc.[9]

This rubric comes from Laon Cathedral in North-East France and is of the thirteenth century. The costume is appropriate to and identifies each character, but it goes well beyond strict liturgical vestment and towards realism. If a beard is the only concession towards realism where Isaiah and Jeremiah are concerned, David and Elizabeth are wholly free of ecclesiastical vestments. The same ambivalence is observable in the rubrics relating to the action. The most realistic applies to Balaam :

Hic veniat Angelus cum gladio. Balaam tangit Asinam,
Here let there come an Angel with a sword. Balaam prods the Ass,
et illa non procedente, dicit iratus.
but since it will not move he speaks angrily.

Compiègne, in North-East France, provides a similar example from the eleventh century of an *Officium Stellae* expanded to contain King Herod, a Court Officer, a Soldier and Women and Magi with individual names; but no rubrics relating either to costume or stage-action are supplied. Our knowledge of both, however, is amplified by the *Visitatio Sepulchri* from Dublin.* It starts as follows :

Finito iij R(esposori)o cum suo V(ersu)et Gl(o)ria p(at)ri
At the close of the 3rd Response with its verse and the Gloria
uenient tres p(er)sone in s(uper)pell(iceis)
three people will advance [clothed] in surplices
et in capis s(er)icis capitib(us) uelatis quasi
and with their heads covered with silk caps as if they were
tres Marie querentes Ih(esu)m, si(n)gule
the three Maries seeking Jesus, each one of them
portantes pixidem in manib(us) q(uas)i
carrying a box in her hands as though it were

---

* This probably originally belonged to Salisbury and is thus related in its rubrics to those prescribed in the *Regularis Concordia*.

aromatib(us), qua(rum) prima ad ingressu(m)
a casket of spices, of whom the first at the entrance
chori usque sepulcru(m) procedat p(er) se
to the choir is to proceed as far as the entrance to the sepulchre
quasi lamentando dicat: ... etc.
on his own, and let him say, as if weeping: ... *etc.*
(see Plates 14 and 15).

The repeated *quasi* ('as if', or, 'in the manner of') emphasizes the double image of deacon and character, vestment and costume, altar and tomb. Further vivid stage-directions accompany the arrival of the apostles Peter and John:

Int(er)im ueniant ad ingressu(m) cho(ri)
Meanwhile let there come to the entrance of the choir
due p(er)sone nude pedes sub personis ap(osto)lo(rum)
two people with bare feet as if representing the apostles
Iohannis (et) Pet(ri) indute albis sine paruris cu(m) tunicis,
John and Peter clothed in white albs without ornamentation
with surcoats,
quo(rum) Ioh(ann)es amictus tunica alba palma(m) in manu
gestans
of whom John wears his white surcoat wrapped round him and
carries
Petrus uero rubea tunica indutus claues in manu ferens ...
a palm in his hand, but Peter wears a red surcoat and carries
keys in his hands ...

A St Nicholas play in the Fleury group supplies information about the conventions adopted to assist recognition of place when more than one locality had to be depicted. It starts as follows:

Ad representandum quomodo Sanctus Nich(o)laus Get-
ron(is)
To represent how St Nicholas freed the son of Getron
Filium de manu Marmorini, Regis Agarenorum, liberauit,
paretur
from the hands of Marmorinus, King of the Agareni, let there
be prepared
in competenti loco cum Ministris suis armatis Rex Marmorinus
in alta

*in a suitable place King Marmorinus with his armed Knights
on a high*
sede, quasi in regno suo sedens. Paretur et in alio loco
Excoranda,
*throne as if seated in Majesty. Let there also be prepared in
another*
Getronis civitas, et in ea Getron, et cum Consolatricibus suis,
uxor
*place, Excoranda, Getron's city, and in it Getron himself
and, together*
eius, Eufrosina, et Filius eorum Adeodatus. Sitque ab orientali
parte
*with his Consolers, his wife Eufrosina and their son Adeodatus.
And*
ciutatis Excorande ecclesia Sancti Nicholai, in qua puer
rapietur.
*on the eastern side of the city of Excoranda let there be the
Church of St Nicholas, in which the boy will be abducted.*

This elaborate and relatively spectacular piece has progressed
far beyond simple *officium* and is demonstrably a *representatio*.
Three separate locations are required to identify the locality of
the action. The problem is solved by placing three physical
objects on the perimeter of the *platea*. These objects are not
described in detail; but one of them is placed in the eastern
quarter and represents the Church of St Nicholas. This is flanked
on one side by a seat, more specifically a throne, for King
Marmorinus, and on the other side a device – possibly a pavillion
– representing the city of Excoranda.

Once the *platea* comes to be used for action as complex as that
postulated by the text of this play, problems of a strictly theatrical
kind arise in respect of the handling of entrances, exits and
characterization. The former appear to have been met by liturgical means, that is to say by adapting processional ritual to cover
the arrival and departure of the principal characters in the
drama. Each thus arrives escorted by his or her entourage. The
method is clearly illustrated in the twelfth-century *Ludus Danielis*
from Beauvais.
The opening rubric reads:

Dum venerit Rex Balthasar, Principes sui cantabunt
When King Belshazzar shall come, his Princes will sing
ante eum hanc prosam.
before him this text.

Thirty lines later Belshazzar arrives at his throne (*solium*) and
sits down while his courtiers prostrate themselves. This processional entrance is concluded with the chorus line

Rex, in eternum vive!
King, live for ever!

After the sinister appearance of the writing on the wall a similar
processional entry is employed to bring the Queen into the *platea.*
This occupies twenty-five lines and again concludes with the
salutation,

Rex, in eternum vive!

A third processional entry is prescribed for King Darius :

Statim apparebit Darius rex cum Principibus suis,
Immediately King Darius shall appear with his Princes;
venientque ante eum Cythariste et Principes sui psallentes hec.
and they will come before him, the musicians and his Princes
singing as follows.

This entry again occupies some thirty lines and concludes with
a graphic description of the musical escort followed by a lengthy
stage-direction.

Simul omnes gratulemur; resonent et tympana;
Let us all rejoice together; let the drums sound;
Cythariste tangant cordas; musicorum organa
Let the harpists pluck the strings; let the musicians' instruments
resonent ad eius preconia.
sound to herald his approach.
Antequam perveniat Rex ad solium suum, duo precurrentes
Before the King reaches his throne, two men running ahead
expellent Balthasar quasi interficientes eum. Tunc sedente
shall drive Belshazzar out as if killing him. Then as King
Dario Rege in maiestate sua, Curia exclamabit
Dario sits in his majesty, the Court shall exclaim
Rex, in eternum vive!
King, live for ever!

The final exit of all the performers from the *platea* is covered by the singing of the *Te Deum* (see Plate 16).

Besides providing clear evidence of how entrances and exits were stage-managed, *Ludus Danielis* offers us useful information about the origin and authorship of such plays.

The opening lines tell us that it was devised by the '*iuventus*' [lit. youth, *i.e.* deacons] in honour of Christ. The subject-matter is an elaborate extension of a single episode from the *Ordo Prophetarum*. The closing lines are given to an angel who announces the birth of Christ in Bethlehem and the fulfilment of prophecy. It is thus clearly a play prepared as an appropriate prelude to the Feast of the Nativity; but although liturgical in all its forms it is recognizably a *ludus*, not an *officium*.

Much the same can be said of the very few extant liturgical music-dramas based on New Testament subjects and again associated with the twelve-day Feast of Christmas, though none of them is described as a *ludus*. One of these, *The Conversion of St Paul*, from Fleury is a *representatio*; another, this time from Limoges, is simply called *Sponsus* (lit. Spouse) and deals with the Wise and Foolish Virgins; another, also from Fleury and relating to the raising of Lazarus, has the title *Versus*.

The most striking feature of all these plays is their greatly extended narrative scope with action in or between several localities. The *platea* has become self-consciously an acting area: rubrics are needed to specify the existence, and sometimes the placement and appearance of these localities in relation to each other and to the acting-area. The texts remain versified and in Latin, but occasional vernacular words and phrases make a surprising appearance: secular melodies and instrumentation obtrude forcefully within the strictly clerical musical frame. Non-Christian characters appear with increasing frequency, and the Fleury *Sponsus* closes with the rubric

Modo accipient eos Demones, et precipitentur in infernum.
Now let the Devils receive them, and let them be cast forth into hell
(see Plate 10.)

Transition however from the world of *officium* to that of *ludus* is at its most obvious in the text and rubrics of a music drama on the subject of the False Messiah, Antichrist, surviving from

Tegernsee in Bavaria and dating from the twelfth century. Here, no less than eight *sedes* (localities, lit., seats) are demanded in the rubrics and much stage action of a violent nature is carefully described : at times this occupies much more space in the manuscript than the dialogue.

No less violent and antithetical to the true meditative spirit of devotion were the quasi-dramatic liturgies associated with the Feasts of the Holy Innocents (28 December) and the Circumcision (1 January) – *De Episcopo Puerum* (The Boy Bishop), *Officium Follarum* (*Festum Fatuorum,* the Feast of Fools), *Prosa De Asino* (Prose of the Ass). In one sense it was quite natural that after the long preparatory meditations of Advent and the serious, if joyous, devotions of Christmas Day itself, a reaction should set in, and that provision should be made for a much more relaxed and informal celebration of the two other festivals devoted to children which followed swiftly after : nor is it surprising that the liturgies actually devised to meet these circumstances should have been derived in some measure from the *Ordo Prophetarum* and from liturgies dedicated to St Nicholas. Human nature being what it is, however, any relaxation of order and precedence whether in respect of hierarchy or ceremonial, is likely to turn quickly to inversion of normal social status and to parody; and once this has occurred it is very difficult to draw firm dividing lines between the permissible and the outrageous, decency and obscenity, jocularity and blasphemy. What did become apparent to serious churchmen was a sharply discordant clash between the intention and the fulfilment of it, responsibility for which rested squarely with the histrionically-minded minor clergy.

By the end of the twelfth century, therefore, dramatic art had both established itself firmly throughout Christendom, but had also begun to lose its way. No longer a simple *officium* enhancing the significance of a particular liturgy, but not yet a *ludus* in the sense of an entertainment; still firmly harnessed to the rituals appropriate to particular Calendar Feasts, yet in danger of occupying a disproportionate amount of time and of disrupting the devotional quality of the liturgy in question; severely distanced from everyday life by plain-chant and the Latin tongue, yet straining towards realistic representation as expanding narrative content placed an increasing strain on the conventions

c

adopted to identify person and place; and here and there inviting question, if not outright condemnation, for local failures to distinguish between liberty and abuse.

The root cause of this dilemma which was overtaking the drama of the Christian Church and which reformers of the thirteenth century would have to tackle, is to be discerned in the consequences of admitting non-Christian characters to liturgical music-dramas: for this provoked a need to contrast the *behaviour*, both in word and deed, of Christians and their opposites – Daniel with Belshazzar, Paul with Saul, a Wise Virgin with a Foolish one. Initially it was not hard to solve this problem. Christians were, *a priori*, serious and therefore good; granted that they were subject to original sin, they nevertheless strove, in imitating Christ's example, to purify their hearts and minds and to conduct themselves in a manner befitting their King and Saviour. As he himself had said, 'Those that are not for me are against me.' All non-believers, worshippers of other gods and persecutors who could be classed as enemies of Christ and his Church were bad and therefore ridiculous. Impersonators of Christian heroes and heroines had thus only to handle emotions ranging between joy and grief, in a manner that befitted the circumstances and was worthy of imitation. With the possible exception of joy, which could be expressed in ways that were regarded as unseemly (dancing is an example), the imitation of Christian conduct and emotion presented few problems.

The special relationship between the frame of *officium* and the imitation of emotion in liturgical music-drama ensured that motivation played no part in the actors' thinking: the characters they represented were stereotyped in advance by their faith and works. Their emotions were thus pre-set, as it were, even in matters of degree, together with appropriate actions indicative of them. Thus respect or reverence could be represented by a bowing of the head, genuflexion, kneeling accompanied by bowing of the head, or total prostration. With Christ the King at the centre of these early essays in theatrical representation, the code of conduct taken over wholesale from the Imperial Court in Byzantium and allegorized to possess a Christian significance sufficed to instruct the actors in how to behave in the *platea* of a Christian basilica.

Conduct unbecoming for Christians in such an environment

sufficed, by simple contrast, to indicate the character, actions and emotions of Christ's enemies. As the subjects of these liturgical music-dramas grew in number, however, and as the narrative component expanded, so non-Christian characters began to obtrude: and it was within the range of 'bad' or 'ridiculous' behaviour necessary to identify them that the germ of entertainment through laughter resided. Unlike the serene joy of Christians, their joy must be overstated in noisy shouting or fiendish convulsions that were so absurd as to be funny. No less important, the modesty and humility of the Christian Emperor's behaviour before his own master, God, must be contrasted in non-Christian rulers by the adjuncts of tyranny – uncontrolled anger, vain boasting and general ostentation – and once again, just as it is a relatively easy step to equate bad conduct with ridiculous or absurd conduct, so only a further small step is needed for absurd or ridiculous behaviour to become comic. In other words the impersonation of non-Christian characters carried with it an innate risk that the means adopted to represent them would come to possess an entertainment value : and any actor knows that if an audience responds warmly to the manner in which he executes an action on the stage this carries with it an automatic temptation to repeat or enlarge the same device.

In this way the entertainment value of non-Christian characters and non-Christian emotions became embarrassing to the begetters of liturgical music-drama, and doubly so when the impersonators were themselves clerics. It was this lack of seemliness, or appropriateness, and not drama *per se* which gave rise to ecclesiastical doubts and protests in the twelfth and thirteenth centuries, since this indecorum was clearly at odds with the place and occasion which the ritual existed to illuminate. Since, moreover, the best sources for the imitation of unseemly conduct were secular, pagan, or both, this development could be construed as doctrinally dangerous and thus to be condemned. Other aspects of the drama which struck its begetters as equally discordant with the liturgical character of *officium* may be seen both in the elaboration of polyphony in the music and in the number and quality of visual aids required to identify character and place. The expression of non-Christian emotions and the use of dialogue unworthy of Christians encouraged the adaptation of music drawn from secular sources, while the need to distinguish a multiplicity of Old and New Testament characters encouraged some degree of visual realism.

The awareness within the Church that these discordant elements presented a threat to the gravity of the original *officium* is apparent in the shift first to the word *representatio* and then to the word *ludus* and in the adoption of these words as alternatives to distinguish these more developed, commemorative impersonations where entertainment, however appropriate to the occasion, came near to destroying the original devotional purpose of the ritual : *Ordo Prophetarum* is one thing, *Ludus Danielis* quite another.

These changes obliged the Church to rethink its attitude to the representation of biblical history in drama. It thus became the major concern of what we may call the transitional style to deal with three problems. The first was to determine what further development, if any, could be permitted either within the framework of the Canonical Offices or on a *platea* inside the basilica itself. The second was to redefine the balance between music and language within an art form that had come to find Latin verse and antiphonal singing more of a hindrance than a help to its full expression. The third was to come to terms with the technical aspects of theatrical representation in respect of both human emotions and the visual identification of persons and places.

Of these three problems only the first was still strictly religious : the other two were aesthetic and technical. The solutions found inform the Gothic style.

Before embarking upon a study of the new style it is as well to be sure that we still recognize the boundaries of the earlier Romanesque style. The most important of these is the closeness of the liturgical ceremonial to the occasion celebrated, the one taking its life from the other. The starting point is always the significance then, now and hereafter of the event re-enacted : the event dictates the ritual and the ritual reflects the event. This relationship between the two militates absolutely against the fusion of one commemorative music-drama with another, and thus against any process of gradual coalescence which an expanding narrative component might otherwise suggest. The occasion (i.e. the particular Feast celebrated) effectively placed its own limits on the degree and quality of narrative expansion.*

The second major control upon the nature of permissible development was the relationship of these commemorative re-enactments of historical events within ritual time to the worship of Christ the King. Praise and thanksgiving provoked these exceptionally elaborate ceremonies and militated against similar treatment being accorded to sequences of events ending in seeming disaster. The Fall of Lucifer, Noah's Flood, and above all the Crucifixion therefore found no place in this kind of liturgical development. The studious avoidance of any serious treatment of Christ's Passion before the end of the twelfth century, and then only in Italy, is one of the most remarkable features of this early drama, and a clear signpost to both the artistic and liturgical quality of its origins : nor, without a serious dramatic treatment of the Crucifixion, would it ever be possible to link any of the Advent, Christmas or Epiphany sequences to those of the Easter season.

A third boundary of the old style is to be found in the limitations imposed upon development by Latin verse and plain-chant. Both factors served to confine its composition and execution to a professionally trained, intellectual élite closely associated with monastic seminaries. Furthermore, since this activity was occasional rather than regular and derived from a constant obligation to improve the quality of Christian liturgies, it was never touched by commerce. There is thus a strange dichotomy about the quality of liturgical music-drama : this is apparent in the professionalism required of the singers needed to perform it successfully on the one hand and in the absence on the other hand of any of those financial anxieties that usually accompany the use of professionally trained performers. There is an extraordinary, not to say unique, purity about this drama unsullied by any of the vulgar considerations that stem from human exhibitionism and ego-centricity or from doubts about its likely audience appeal and consequent box-office receipts. It existed as praise and thanksgiving, an offertory from man to his Maker, freely and gladly given in poetry, in song and in mime.

* There is one exception, the Christmas Play from the *Carmina Burana* which starts with the *Ordo Prophetarum* and concludes with *The Slaughter of the Innocents*; but this play, sometimes known as the Benediktbeuern Christmas Play, dates from the thirteenth century and is properly a play in the transitional rather than in the Romanesque style.

2

DRAMA OF REPENTANCE

A. LANGUAGE AND DRAMA

Most people amplify what they say with gesture. This assists them to emphasize, to define and to enliven a viewpoint in a highly personal manner. We speak of an expressive face, articulate movements, a demonstrative stance. In mime, dance and pantomime much can be communicated – actions, emotions, jokes. By these means skilful actors can transcend barriers of hearing, speech and language, and entertain collectively audiences of different nationality, creed and race. Granted familiarity with the story, such audiences can follow a narrative of considerable complexity presented by actors in movement and gesture alone without recourse to words : the most talented of mimes and dancers can even persuade spectators to follow and comprehend a story that is not familiar.

Nevertheless spectators and performers alike quickly discover that a point exists at which it becomes necessary to formulate an elaborate notation of hand movements and other visual conventions if any precision is to be imposed upon the information conveyed in a mime or ballet. When this point is reached the temptation to employ language, more especially to define the drift of an argument, becomes compelling. The addition of words at once restores an essentially realistic, human characteristic to a world of make-believe, since it is more natural for men and women to speak to each other than to pretend that they are dumb : even so the language actually used can itself be highly artificial and far removed from that of everyday speech. The Latin verse of liturgical music-drama is a case in point.

Transition from the Romanesque to the Gothic style in the religious drama in the Middle Ages, as we have already seen, is discernible as much in a noticeable change of attitude to the use of language as in any other aspect of surviving plays. A drift towards use of vernacular languages rather than Latin, and away from song towards speech is as observable in such texts as we possess as in the realistic details of costume and setting prescribed in some of the stage-directions. The change may be minimal, as is the case with an occasional line like '*Pauper et exulans envuois al Roi par vos*', which suddenly obtrudes upon the Latin text of *Ludus Danielis*; or it may be all-pervasive, as is the case with the Anglo-Norman *Ordo representacionis Adae*. This fact has frequently tempted scholars to equate use of the vernacular as indicative of steadily increasing 'secularization' of religious drama. Little or no thought is given, however, when this argument is advanced, to the possibility that the vernacular languages of medieval Europe might be acquiring a respectability of their own. In fact they were.

Provence in Southern France during the eleventh and twelfth centuries was the centre of pioneer experiments with language which, in their time, were as revolutionary in their effects upon European literature as the invention of printing was destined to be four centuries later, or as television is proving to be in our own. Provence was so situated geographically as to be the cross-roads of Western Christendom, and it was there that the writers and entertainers of the Latin South met the authors and reciters of saga and epic romance from the Gothic North. Slowly, these exchanges of mode and method of composition and of form and style of presentation resulted in the creation of a new literary language – Provençal – and of a new poetry – the *chanson de geste* – which convinced educated society that a modern language was as suitable for original composition as an ancient one.[10] The new verses conveyed old stories from classical antiquity in a familiar tongue that was as intelligible to the ladies as it was to the men : it also added an incentive to embellish contemporary exploits of an heroic character undertaken in the name of Christ and for the glory of the Church in the course of the Crusades against Islam.

Lying between classical epic with its tales of King Priam, Ulysses, Aeneas, Queen Dido, and tales of modern chivalry, were those of the Bible and the Christian saints and martyrs; and these too found their way into the new literature. Simultaneously they began to find their way into manuscript illumination, ivories, tapestry, fresco and stained glass. This heroic and chivalric approach corresponded with the new Christocentric attitude to Christian history developing at the time in Southern Italy. As a result therefore the Crucifixion and Christ's eternal struggle with Lucifer for the souls of men emerged as the two nuclei around which a new romantic and specifically Christian vernacular literature began to shape : something of this interest also focused itself upon the suffering figure of Mary at the foot of the Cross and her subsequent intercessions for sinful mankind[11] (see Plates 27 and 28).

As Grace Frank observed in *The Mediaeval French Drama* (1954), these poems came swiftly to rival the new secular epics. Discussing the so-called *Passion des Jongleurs* of the late twelfth or early thirteenth century, she remarks upon prologues 'scolding audiences that prefer to hear about Roland and Oliver rather than about our Lord's Passion' (p. 125) and then gives an example.

> *Plus volentiers oroit conter*
> More willingly would he hear tell,
> *coment Rolan(s) ala joster*
> how Roland went to joust with,
> *a Olivier, son compaignon,*
> [i.e. against] Oliver, his companion,
> *K'il ne feroit la passion*
> than he would [sc. hear tell of],
> *Ke Dex soufri o grant enhan*
> the passion that God suffered with great pain,
> *par le pechié ke fist Adan.*
> for the sin that Adam did.

Such poems were soon translated into English, and were joined by similar original compositions in English, German and Italian. In England the sorrowful figure of Mary met with an especially warm response and was sympathetically elaborated in the Northern and Southern Passions and in the Stanzaic Life of Christ of the fourteenth century. In this way the scene came to be set for the forging of a new Christian epic starting with the fall of Lucifer and Adam, concluding with the Judgement and centred upon Christ's triumph over death and the Devil in the Passion, Harrowing of Hell and Resurrection which was not only available to those able to read it for themselves but to everyone willing to hear it read aloud because of the authors' use of the vernacular.

Poetic versions of this epic were quickly supplemented by prose versions which in their time were projected still further afield in the sermons of the new Orders of mendicant friars, notably the Dominicans and the Franciscans, who set out in the thirteenth and fourteenth centuries to reconvert Europe to a way of life more nearly in keeping with Christ's example.

With the literary and iconographic foundations thus firmly laid, the way was open at any time in the late thirteenth century for the new epic to be transferred from narrative to dramatic art within a code of theatrical representation already formulated to accommodate liturgical music-drama. The double catalyst that effected this transference is to be found in the promulgation of the doctrine of transubstantiation in 1215, followed by the institution of the Feast of Corpus Christi in 1264 and its adoption in 1311.

B. THE FEAST OF CORPUS CHRISTI

In Vienna on the first Thursday after Trinity Sunday the city's residents (and the more alert of its tourists) rise early enough in the morning to find a place in St Stephen's Cathedral by seven o'clock to hear the Philharmonic Choir and Orchestra, and soloists of international reputation, sing a Mozart Mass celebrated by the Cardinal Archbishop. The celebrants and the cathedral choir then leave the Cathedral in procession, carrying the Communion bread and wine with them, and celebrate Mass again, this time in the open air in front of the West doors of the city's other churches. They may be seen doing this all morning.

In London (as elsewhere in Britain), the Thursday after Trinity Sunday passes unnoticed in the Anglican Calendar.

The reason for this sharp contrast of behaviour in two metropolitan cities that were once united within Christendom is to be found in the Reformation and the Protestant rejection of both the papal doctrine of transubstantiation and the Feast of Corpus Christi. In Roman Catholic communities this festival is still observed; in Protestant communities it is not. In England it was officially suppressed in 1548, briefly revived by Mary I in 1553, and suppressed again, this time forever, on the accession of Elizabeth I in 1558. Yet it was this festival, which was celebrated annually in

C*

most churches throughout the kingdom for rather more than two hundred years between 1311 and 1557, that laid the foundations for the development of a vernacular drama, epic in scale and cosmic in scope that won the enthusiastic support of the whole nation regardless of educational opportunity or achievement, and bequeathed to Marlowe, Shakespeare, Jonson, Middleton and Massinger the conventions of theatrical representations which were to project so many masterpieces of dramatic art to audiences of the late sixteenth and early seventeenth centuries. The same theatrical legacy served Hans Sachs, Pierre Corneille, Lope de Vega and Calderon no less profitably within the same era.

The Feast of Corpus Christi and the drama which grew out of it are so intimately linked that the drama came to take the name of the feast: this fact went virtually unnoticed until Professor V. A. Kolve restored to this connection its true significance by publishing his important book on the subject under the title of *The Play Called Corpus Christi.**

If we seek the reason for this phenomenon we have first to consider the doctrine of transubstantiation instituted by the papacy in 1215; for this gave to the Eucharist a new importance – the status of a miracle on a par with those of virgin birth and resurrection from the dead. Yet the liturgical Calendar, developed over twelve centuries, was not equipped to deal adequately with this new concept: and while some ecclesiastics were preoccupied with this problem, others were no less deeply engaged in that of finding ways and means of projecting the newly formulated intellectual and philosophical concepts of God as man in Christ to an unsophisticated and largely illiterate laity. This radical reappraisal of both forms of worship and preaching methods brought with it, amongst other changes, a new drama centred on the Eucharist, emphasizing the humanity rather than the divinity of Christ's ministry and avowedly didactic in intention rather than ritualistic and devotional. In consequence it was conceived from the outset as a *ludus*, 'game' or 'play', and never as an *ordo* or *officium*; it was scripted in the vernacular languages of the individual nations of Christendom and not in universal Latin; it

---

* 'The Play Called Corpus Christi' is in fact the sub-title of *Ludus Coventriae* (ed. K. S. Black for EETS, 1922: reprinted, 1952): other Cycles, however, were also frequently referred to as Corpus Christi plays.

was designed to be spoken rather than to be chanted, and to invite the participation of laymen rather than to be confined to literate clerics trained as singers.

The crucial link between this new drama and the miraculous status accorded to the Eucharist by the doctrine of transubstantiation was the institution of a new Calendar Festival created for the specific purpose of celebrating its new significance in Christian worship. It took the Church half a century to determine how this was to be done : then, in 1264, Pope Urban IV announced the new Feast Day of Corpus Christi.* In justifying its promulgation, Pope Urban referred believers to the Eucharist, saying :

> For on the day of the Supper of our Lord [i.e. Maundy Thursday, or the Eve of Good Friday] – the day on which Christ himself instituted this sacrament – the entire church, fully occupied as she is with the reconciliation of penitents, the ritual administration of the holy oil, the fulfilling of the commandment concerning the washing of feet, and other matters, does not have adequate time for the celebration of this greatest sacrament.[12]

Thus, since the mood is wrong and the time is inadequate on Maundy Thursday itself, Pope Urban recommends another Thursday, the first after Trinity Sunday, when the Church is less preoccupied, for the proper celebration of the redemptive power of the Eucharist itself.

Unlike Easter Sunday or Christmas Day, therefore, the prime purpose of this new festival was not to be commemoration of an historical event, but to give thanks for man's salvation through God's decision to become man and to pay the price, through Christ's crucifixion, of man's redemption from original sin. We are thus taken out of ritual time into universal time : for the Eucharist has no significance in this context of man's salvation without taking account of the Fall of Lucifer and Adam on the one hand and of Christ's Harrowing of Hell and Doomsday on the other, and thus of the judgement of man himself.

Here then, in the doctrinal purpose and the didactic nature of the new Feast we also possess the key to the dramatic structure of the new vernacular plays which were to be so closely associated

---

* In the event, Pope Urban died before effect could be given to his Bull, and it was left to his successor, Clement V, to institute the new Feast in 1311.

with the Feast as to bear its name. Once this has been grasped, it becomes obvious that the size and scope of medieval cyclic drama is in no way dependent on the translation out of Latin, the gradual coalescence and the so-called 'secularization' of liturgical music-drama : the plays are possessed of what we call cyclic form from their inception – a *doctrinal pattern* of Fall, Redemption and Judgement. This pattern happens to bear a marked resemblance to that prescribed by Aristotle for Greek dramatists with its sharply defined beginning, middle and end, and which the Greeks in their turn bequeathed to the Romans.

From the outset therefore Christ's Passion, covering the Entry into Jerusalem, the trials before Herod and Pilate, the Crucifixion, Deposition, Harrowing of Hell and Resurrection, formed the climax, or 'middle' in the Aristotelian sense, of this new vernacular and didactic drama of Corpus Christi. Experimental versions of the Passion had been attempted, first in Italy and then in France and Switzerland partly in Latin and partly in the vernacular in the course of the thirteenth century.[18] Full treatments of the *Visitatio Sepulchri* and the *Victimae Paschali* existed in liturgical Latin throughout Christendom. It was thus a relatively easy matter respectively to copy and translate these versions and splice them together, or alternatively to return to the Gospels and wholly rewrite both sequences as a single entity, within vernacular languages now ready to receive them. Similar treatment could be accorded to the substantial nuclei of plays that had already grown up around the prophets and Christ's Nativity. Nor was there any difficulty in adapting the conventions already established in liturgical music-drama for the identification of person and place to the new needs : both had only to be expanded to accommodate a wider range of character and locality. Acting was another matter, since Latin texts were to be replaced by vernacular ones and plain-chant by spoken dialogue. However those problems were largely resolved by the approach adopted to the two sections of the new epic narrative that flanked the central climax of the Passion and the Resurrection. Here the critical factor was the deliberate abandonment of the earlier association of drama with ritual time and the substitution of a drama in which historical time was brought into conjunction with universal time and in which both remained linked to ritual time in the new Feast of Corpus Chrsti.

For this reason Old Testament history was presented as prefigurement of New Testament history; Christ replaces Adam, Mary replaces Eve, and the Cross on Calvary replaces the Tree of Knowledge in the Garden of Eden: Noah's Flood prefigures the general Doom. In this new context of universal time where the past was reflected in the present and the future, the proper narrative environment for the depiction of all these events was fourteenth-century Europe. For the script-writers and the actors this meant translation of Pontius Pilate into Sir Pilate, J.P. or into a German Burgomeister, Annas and Caiaphas into Bishops of the Roman Catholic Church, the shepherds of Bethlehem into those of the Alps, the Jura or the Cotswolds; Herod behaves like any ducal tyrant and swears by Mahomet; Noah becomes a shipwright of the Adriatic or the North Sea ports. Of course these changes served to 'secularize' the drama in point of locality, character, costume and dialogue; but they did so consistently in externals. They did nothing to undermine the religious motivation of this dramatic activity : rather did they establish its instructional purpose and spiritual appeal upon the firmest of foundations, universal suffrage (see Plates 21 and 22).

Corpus Christi drama was no less faithful to this concept of time *sub specie aeternitatis* in the flexibility of the equation that it made between the physical universe, as understood at that time, and the theatrical representation of it for actors and audiences alike : for in a Christian ordered universe concepts of space were as carefully defined from a doctrinal standpoint as those of time. Concepts of spatial distance, therefore, and of the relative placement and proximity of the spiritual worlds of heaven and hell were savagely foreshortened and depicted emblematically, every concrete image having its universal analogue. For the playmaker this had been made easy by the readiness of theologians from St Augustine onwards to compare God's creation with a theatre, and by the familiarity with which audiences could be reckoned to approach allegorical representation of the invisible worlds of heaven, limbo and hell in sermons, art and literature. God and Lucifer viewed mankind's brief struggle in the theatre of mortal existence as audiences watched actors strut and gesticulate upon the stage. It was thus as natural (and as easy) for an angel to descend to earth or for a devil to materialize from hell as it was for an actor to pass from Jerusalem to Damascus, from Israel to

Italy or from Africa to Europe. This notion of *Teatrum Mundi*, of the macrocosm reflected in the microcosm, established itself firmly enough in the play called Corpus Christi to suggest first 'The Theatre' and then 'The Globe' to the Burbage Company as names for their playhouses in Elizabethan London, and *El Gran Teatro Del Mundo* to Calderon as a suitable title for an *auto* in 1645.

The scarcity of detailed factual records surviving from the fourteenth century, more especially from countries ravaged by the wars of religion in the sixteenth and seventeenth centuries, makes it difficult to say in what precise way and at what precise date the continental Passion Plays and the English Cycles came into being as part of the Corpus Christi festivities. What we do know is that the Feast began to be generally observed within a year or two of its institution by Pope Clement v in 1311; that apart from an obligation to carry the Host out of the principal church in any district and to process with it round the town visiting other churches within walking distance, bishops were allowed to determine what form the celebration of the Feast should take; we know that the trade guilds marched in the procession accompanying the Host in their distinctive ceremonial liveries and carrying banners displaying emblems of their crafts, and that the Black Death swept across Europe between 1340 and 1360 decimating the population and giving vernacular languages an ascendancy over Latin in city life. We know too that the newly founded universities served to centralize knowledge and to encourage philosophical speculation.

Partly on account of the liberty of action accorded to the bishops in devising forms of celebrating the new Feast in the manner most acceptable to the local community, and partly as a result of those violent shifts in religious, political and social philosophy that were serving to change not only art forms and folk customs but life itself in the fourteenth century, the new vernacular *ludi* found a ready welcome from churchmen and laymen alike. The appearance at this time of the heretical movements led by Wycliff and his Lollards in England, by Hus and his followers in Czechoslovakia, and the penitential movement that copied and elaborated upon the example of the Italian *Flagellanti* in the preceding century provides evidence of this spiritual turmoil; no less remarkable politically were the recurrent efforts of an exploited and rebellious peasantry to liberate themselves from the bonds of feudal tyranny which, at least in Switzerland, succeeded to the point of emanicipating the Cantons, and thus in opening the way to ultimate release from German imperialism in the following century. Economically, the growth of a merchant class whose collective wealth in the cities that they were busily creating outstripped that of many feudal lords (whose wealth had traditionally lain in the ownership of agricultural land) only served to accelerate change, especially in Germany and England where city life came to be distinguished by a boastful and competitive materialism.

It is against this background that the Feast of Corpus Christi took root in Europe and it is not surprising then that it should have been to cities and to the merchant princes who governed the trading life of these communities that the lords spiritual and the new orders of mendicant preachers of the fourteenth century addressed their redemptive message.[14] From the outset the drama associated with Corpus Christi was directed towards the frivolous rich and the covetous tradesman in an effort to re-dedicate society to Christ and Christ's service in the remembrance that Christ had died to save mankind. The Dance Macabre survives to us in innumerable graphic representations depicting this time and this message : the spectral figure of Death, sometimes on foot, sometimes on horseback, armed always with his scythe and summoning pope, emperor, king, queen, merchant, lawyer, artisan, artist and peasant to follow him to the grave grew out of the time and gave force to the message (see Plate 19).

In Italy the *Sacre Rappresentazioni*, in Spain the *Autos* and *Farsas*, in German-speaking countries and in France the Passion Play, and in England the Corpus Christi Cycles were as much a civic response to this message as an ecclesiastical initiative. Market-squares were thus as appropriate a *platea* or acting-area for these performances as convent courtyards, laymen more desirable as actors than clerics, and civic wealth as necessary to finance production of these *ludi* as clerical scribes to provide the texts. And nowhere did text, production or place of performance conform to a stereotyped pattern. On the basic common factors of the Feast-day itself, of vernacular speech, of condensed typological exegesis of the Old and New Testaments, and of a tradition of theatrical representation copied from the coexisting music dramas of the liturgical Calendar, each local community embroidered its own variants to suit its own climate, its own topography and its own managerial expertise.

For a variety of reasons, both the driving force and the sheet anchor of the new drama resided in those distinctively medieval social units known as the guild and the parish. These organizational structures were each of such complexity and importance in the life of the times as to warrant whole books devoted to them; here it must simply suffice to observe that where the parish was a topographical unit dominated by the church and the priest in charge, the guild was a social unit formed for a particular purpose which could be religious, charitable, artistic or commercial.[15] If parishes, moreover, were principally administrative units encompassing towns and country districts without discrimination, guilds were just as self-evidently fraternal organizations self-consciously established to advertise, promote and protect special interests. A guild could thus exist within a parish, but the membership of another guild could well include residents of several parishes. A guild dedicated to a patron saint within a parish, like that of St Thomas à Becket at Canterbury, is an example of the former; a guild representing a particular skill, like that of the shipwrights in Newcastle, exemplifies the latter. Acceptance of the Feast of Corpus Christi as a new festival in the Calendar served to activate both of these units, guild and parish, since each parish had to determine for itself how the Feast was to be observed and every guild had to decide what contribution it could and should make to the festivities. In many places a new guild was formed charged specifically with the task of organizing the festival annually and with responsibility for its finance and administration. Such a guild served to co-ordinate the efforts of several parishes.

Inevitably in such circumstances, towns, which themselves consisted of a multiplicity of parishes and supported a wide range of wealthy commercial guilds, swiftly eclipsed the more scattered and thinly populated parishes of country districts in the ostentatious display of costly ornament which they could contribute to the new festival; but in many places personal initiatives in country districts led to a feudal system of celebrating the Feast in which each village made a contribution proportionate to its size and resources (see pp. 103 and 195f).

In these ways guild liveries and banners came to be supplemented by three-dimensional emblems or tabernacles in the Corpus Christi procession : pride of place was reserved for the Host in its casket and statues of Christ and the Virgin, but craft pride asserted itself in the addition of Noah's Ark from the water-drawers, the Ark of the Covenant or the gifts of the Magi from the Goldsmiths and so on, as well as in increasingly lavish construction and ornamentation of these objects. In many places a similarly possessive and competitive attitude declared itself in respect of responsibility for particular sections of the dramatic narrative in the epic *ludi* that served to expound the *raison d'être* of the Feast to society at large.

Thus the centres of dramatic initiative in fourteenth- and fifteenth-century Europe shift from the large monastic communities of St Gall, Benedicktbeuern, Fleury, Limoges and Winchester which had dominated the drama of worship in the tenth, eleventh and twelfth centuries to the most prosperous centres of trade and industry, such as Coventry, London, Mons, Frankfurt, Lucerne, Florence and Valencia. Everywhere there is evidence of close collaboration between Church and city, laymen and clerics; but nowhere are the circumstances of textual composition, methods of production or conditions of performance ever quite the same. The differences are directly attributable to this implicit reliance upon self-help and self-determination.

The production of Corpus Christi drama therefore varies between fairly closely defined limits. At one end of the spectrum lies the type of play and production dominated by the clergy but receiving the assistance and co-operation of the civic authorities, and at the other the type of play and production in which the Church supplied the script and then encouraged the civic authorities to accept responsibility for almost every aspect of its theatrical representation. If the *Confrèries de la Passion* in France serve to represent the one extreme, the Miracle Cycles of the large cities of the North of England may be said just as fairly to reflect the other.

C. THE DRAMA OF CHRIST CRUCIFIED

I will that my son manhood take
For reason will that there be three,

A man, a maiden, and a tree :
Man for man, tree for tree
Maiden for maiden; thus shall it be.

In these words God introduces the sequence of New Testament plays in the Wakefield Cycle : Christ is to match Adam, Mary is to replace Eve, and Christ's Cross on Calvary is to possess in these plays the importance accorded to the tree of knowledge in the Paradise Garden in the plays already performed.

The manner in which this governing idea was to be given theatrical expression in Wakefield was left largely to the trade guilds. The same assumption governed rehearsals and performances in Chester, Coventry, and York, and in several other large towns from which no texts have survived. In Lincoln, in London and in Cornwall different assumptions pertained. In London responsibility for production, at least during the reigns of Richard II and Henry IV was assigned to the Guild of Parish Clerks; in Lincoln it rested with a special Guild of the patron saint of the Cathedral, St Anne; in Cornwall text and performance both appear to have rested with the monastic community of the collegiate church of Glasney, near Penryn. In Chester, at least up till the Reformation, a Corpus Christi Guild existed which possessed a play of its own that has been lost or destroyed. In York, Beverley and Lincoln, other plays – notably a Paternoster Play and a Creed Play – existed which could be substituted on occasion for the play called Corpus Christi, but no example survived the destruction of prompt books and actors' parts which accompanied the Reformation. In London Corpus Christi plays were revived under Mary I between 1553 and 1557, but no copies of the texts and no records relating to the methods of production have reached us. Records, but no texts, of similar revivals at New Romney in Kent have survived. In Shrewsbury Corpus Christi plays were performed in a natural amphitheatre formed by an old quarry and bounded by the River Severn. In Worcester and Chelmsford substantial hire-wardrobes for religious plays existed in the sixteenth century and were finally sold, presumably to professional actors, during the reign of Elizabeth I.

All this information, and much more, tells us that the drama of Christ Crucified was as popular as it was widespread in England, but it does not help the historian to provide a short and concise account of how it was organized, financed and stage-managed; the very diversity of the evidence prohibits simplification and generalization. Students must accept the fact that while it may be possible to define in some detail and with some claim to accuracy what occurred in one city or in a particular group of smaller townships and country parishes, the information supplied by the one may very well appear to contradict that supplied by the other. Even so, a few common factors are discernible; and with the caution that instances may exist which fail to conform, it is worth drawing attention to these.

Starting with the *platea* or 'acting-area', it is evident that local convenience governed the choice of a flat open space, a large raised stage or a sequence of mobile platforms assembled singly or collectively within an open space. A similarly observable lack of doctrinaire thinking governed the choice of auditorium and the arrangements made for accommodating spectators within it. Considered simply as a shape, the circle had a flying start over all other forms: for behind it lay not only the physical precedent set by the arenas of classical antiquity, but that of the *platea* of liturgical music-drama wholly surrounded by worshippers. It is also to be noted that spectators, if left to their own devices, will quickly define the circumference of an acting-area for any spectacle, whether it be a drunken brawl, a street accident, a group of morris-dancers, by simply surrounding it (see Plate 40). In certain circumstances, however, as in a town or in a palace, architectural and social pressures can easily give precedence to the square or the rectangle as the basic shape that must be adapted to contain both spectacle and spectators.

A third factor, no less important in as sophisticated an entertainment as the medieval *ludus*, is a changing-room for the actors, where they may effect changes of costume and store their stage properties and personal belongings out of sight and earshot of the audience. In the open air a tent will serve this purpose; in a house, an adjacent room; in a church, the vestry. The vestry of Christian basilicas had long recognized this need and was simply projected and adapted together with the drama as the drama's environment and purpose changed.

The possible combinations and permutations in type and relationship of stage, dressing-room and auditorium were thus theoretically innumerable. In practice however some order and

control were exercised over them by the dominant doctrinal concepts of a Christian ordered universe which defined a theatre as a
microscopic image of God's creation. Hierarchy and social precedence thus come to play a part in determining the allocation
of places in the auditorium: so do economic factors in determining whether spectators shall sit or stand and how production
costs are to be met. Nor can such physical factors of a performance as audibility, visibility and privacy be divorced from those of
social hierarchy; and in the self-consciously materialistic world of
medieval guild life all these factors played some part in determining the sort of stage, dressing-room and auditorium that was
most convenient and acceptable to the local community.

Being both epic and festive in character, the drama of Christ
Crucified had to cater for large crowds in holiday mood who were
nevertheless required to give their attention to the actors for
several consecutive days. This too created special problems, and
the varied responses to them actually adopted must be our next
concern.

i. THE SCRIPT

So often has it been stated in the course of the past hundred years
that anonymity governed the writing of the religious plays of the
Middle Ages, that we have come to forget or ignore the many
instances where a play can be directly associated with the name of
its author or authors. In fact a succession of individual names,
from the troper, Notker, in the tenth century and Hilarius, the
composer of plays devoted to Daniel, Lazarus and St Nicholas in
the eleventh century, accompanies both liturgical music-drama
and vernacular religious drama into the fifteenth and sixteenth
centuries. From France come the names of Jean Bodel, Rutbeuf,
and Arnoul Greban between the thirteenth and the fifteenth
centuries: from the Tirol and German-speaking countries to the
north the names of Benedikt Debs, Reneward Cysat, Canon
Mathias Gundefinger of Zurzach and Hans Baldung survive
among others in the context of Corpus Christi plays: nor are
Italian and Spanish records silent on this point, since Feo Belcari
and Gómez Manrique are remembered for their religious plays in
the fifteenth century, while in England Sir Henry Francis of St
Werburgh's Abbey at Chester in the fourteenth century, and

Dominus Hadton of Cornwall and Miles Blomfield of Chelmsford in the sixteenth century warn us against too ready an acceptance of the idea that all such plays were necessarily and invariably anonymous compositions. It is true that we would like to know who the so-called Wakefield Master was, and the names, for that matter, of his earlier associates and of their predecessors in York. It is true that more plays have reached us from all over Europe with no identifiable author associated with them than plays with an author's signature attached; but this must not lead us to suppose that such plays were in consequence the work of barely literate peasants who contributed playlets (the brevity of which matched their limited capacity) to a loosely linked whole that amounted in its entirety to nothing more than a consecution of scenes. This idea has established itself as much because publishers have preferred to print representative single plays or excerpts, and because school and university teachers have found it more convenient when drawing up a syllabus to prescribe these texts as set books, as for any other reason. Yet no student, told to read Noah's Deluge from the Chester Cycle, the Second Shepherd's Play from the Wakefield Cycle and *Everyman* as 'representative examples' of medieval drama has the faintest hope of understanding the structural principles and stage-conventions of Elizabethan drama, let alone those of its medieval antecedents.

By contrast, anyone who has seen a modern revival of an entire Cycle – and a far greater debt on this account is owed in recent years to the actors, designers and directors whose enterprise and labour have brought them to life for modern audiences than to generations of specialists in English literature – has some knowledge of their true dimensions and proportions, and can thus begin to appreciate their true quality as works of dramatic art.*

The first notion then that must be jettisoned in respect of these scripts is that of nameless authors of small intellectual capacity and smaller understanding of theatrical expertise. The second piece of critical nonsense that must follow it is the idea that each episode in the vernacular drama of Christ Crucified was scripted at Sunday-school level from biblical narrative and then strung together in the manner of Lamb's *Tales from Shakespeare*. The

* A check-list of modern revivals forms the Appendix pp. 221–6 below. Films and video-tapes of some of these performances are also available.

third is those mental pictures of quaint carts carrying groups of
straw-chewing yokels naïvely attired and ornamented in the garments of their social superiors playing some game resembling
charades. With that done, we can begin to recast our thoughts,
taking a cathedral such as that at Canterbury, Chartres, Rheims
or Cologne as our starting point; that, in architectural terms of
reference, will at least help us to recognize the epic scale of the
dramatic concept of *The Play Called Corpus Christi*; and that, in
its turn, may assist us to an understanding of the structural complexity of this epic drama and of the subtlety of the inter-relation-
ships between the many sections that compose the whole as
revealed in the prefigurative and typological techniques already
discussed. What we have to learn to recognize is that these plays
were the work of highly educated clerks, deeply versed in the
doctrines of the universal Church, highly skilled in the rhetorical
arts of preaching, and frequently capable of writing verse that
could rise above the merely pedestrian and touch the hearts of
those that heard it. To say that they were clerks does not imply
that they were all regular clergy. Some, in fact, were lawyers and
others notaries. In France, at least, some were Gentlemen Ushers
in royal households with quasi-professional literary pretensions.
In England we possess less information, but we should recall that
Geoffrey Chaucer was a Clerk of the Exchequer (i.e. a civil
servant) and not a priest, while John Lydgate as principal poet to
the Court of Henry vi was also a monk of the Benedictine Order.

All these men were artists in the service of the Church. Those
who wrote plays supplied one copy of the full-text. Scribes were
then employed to copy out individual parts and cue-sheets for
each actor : anything up to a hundred or more actors could be
involved, many of whom were expected to take two or more roles.
Provision of two hundred or more actors' parts was thus a normal
requirement.

The manuscript was known in England as the 'original' or
'register' and was used as the prompt-book. This was subject to
revision, variety being supplied year by year through the addition
of new material and the deletion or destruction of old. In this
way, with the passage of time, several authors came to be associated in succession with each prompt-copy. In some instances the
surviving manuscript is self-evidently the work of a single hand :
such is the case with Mathias Gundelfinger's Easter play from

Zurzach near Lucerne, with Greban's *Mystère de la Passion,* and also, in all probability, with the Cornish *Ordinalia.* In other instances the manuscript that we possess is just as obviously a compilation attributable to two or more authors widely separated in point of date. Such is the case with the Wakefield Cycle and with the Lucerne Passion Play. Shrewsbury offers us one of the rare surviving examples of a group of actors' parts and cues; these are for the Shepherd's play : another survives from Frankfurt where our knowledge of the local Passion Play is confined to the stage directions and actors' cues in the *Dirigierrolle.* Chester, by contrast, offers us five manuscripts of the full Cycle; but as all of them can be dated between 1591 and 1607, the earliest of these copies was made seventeen years after the last recorded medieval production of the Cycle in Chester.

Certain recurring features of these scripts derive directly from the conditions of performance which the authors recognized and allowed for. Such are the methods adapted from those practised by open-air preachers and other orators to obtain silence from a noisy crowd in holiday mood. So is the almost invariable use of verse which, apart from being appropriate to biblical subject-matter, is much easier for unlettered actors to memorize than prose : frequent alliteration within the verse is an additional aid to the same end, especially when the actor has to learn his part by repeating the lines read aloud to him by his instructor. Since machinery and music played an important role in these perform-ances, the playmakers had to take account of both, and thus to provide sufficient lines to cover particular stage effects and to incorporate appropriate hymns and psalms. In the French Passion Plays audiences are always exhorted at the end to recall the *raison d'être* of the performance they have just witnessed and to give thanks to God by singing the *Te Deum.* In cases where simultaneous action on a multi-locational acting-area was en-visaged, the playmaker could turn this convention to his own use for ironic effect : fine examples of this technique may be observed in *Ludus Coventriae* where Judas can be *seen* trafficking between the house of Caiaphas and the Upper room of the Last Supper, or in the Cornish Passion when Peter denies Christ while the trials before Herod and Pilate are proceeding. The constant use of deliberate anachronism has already been discussed (see p. 63 above). Yet another device to render the remote and unfamiliar swiftly understandable, was the use of analogue. The dramatist who sought to explain chaotic disorder in the world sufficient to provoke God into drowning his whole creation bar Noah and those who escape with him, employs the shrewish wife as his analogue who indulges herself by disobeying and contradicting her husband. Only when order is restored between husband and wife does the dove return and the rainbow appear.

Every script therefore was a sustained work of art, conforming to its own rules. These rules closely resemble those used in Shakespearean play making : but they are utterly different from those adopted in the theatre of pictorial realism of succeeding centuries. The script of an English Corpus Christi Cycle was dramatically structured on a doctrinal basis with as clearly defined a beginning, middle and end as any Greek tragedy : the epic dimensions and episodic character of the narrative were buttressed against disintegration and collapse by constant typological cross-referencing : and the needs of actors who were not scholars and of audiences who had to congregate in the open-air were met by means of familiar analogues and alliterative verse with strong rhythms which imbued past history with immediate relevance to the daily lives of all concerned. By any standards this is a not inconsiderable achievement and rarely even attempted by modern playwrights.

ii. MANAGEMENT

Considering the enormous number of local variants that accompanied production both of the scripts that have survived to us and of those that have not, it is impossible to give a brief and concise account of production methods that can claim to be accurate. Again, however, it is possible to single out certain features of the procedures employed that permit us to grasp imaginatively the major problems involved and the principal methods adopted to meet them.

The Church, having provided the script, had the choice of committing production of it to laymen, of retaining this responsibility in its own hands or of sharing it with others. In most cases the nature of the Feast of Corpus Christi itself suggested that responsibility for the enactment of the accompanying drama of Christ crucified should be shared with the laity; an added incentive to enlist lay help derived from and grew proportionately with increasing production costs. In Italy and Spain this was largely accomplished through the agency of the charitable organizations known respectively as *compagnie* and *confradiás*. In France it was normal for special guilds known as *confréries* to be formed, while in German-speaking countries and in England it was more usual to engage the active interest of the wealthy merchant princes and the trade guilds over which they ruled. Yet even these distinctions are dangerous if applied too literally or exclusively; for in France the mayor and officials of the town-hall frequently play as important a role in the mounting of a *mystère* as do their English counterparts, while in England the wards and parishes figure on occasion as prominently in the organization and finance of Corpus Christi drama as any Italian *contrada*. In Italy, moreover, at least during the fifteenth century, the *sacre rappresentazioni* came to be intimately associated with special guilds called *Compagnie* in which even the aristocracy deigned to participate, notably in Florence and Urbino. What I think one may state categorically is that the sheer size of each undertaking dictated committee government of some sort. How else is a play that stretches over three full days as in Chester, a week as in London or twenty-five days as in Valenciennes in 1547, to be handled? How else is a play requiring one hundred or more actors to be cast? How else is it to be rehearsed and its costs met? How else are order and discipline to be imposed upon crowds of spectators jostling for a good view of the proceedings and to get near enough to the actors to hear the dialogue.

Granted committee government of some sort, I think we may assume with equal certainty the existence in every case of a council of management: its composition varied from place to place, but it did not carry passengers. The cathedral chapter, or its ecclesiastical equivalent in smaller towns, contributed the book-men, substantial musical and costume resources and sometimes an auditorium and some money: it also handled the delicate task of checking the actual script against the authorized sources – Bible, Apocrypha, Golden Legend, etc. The town hall, through its contacts with artisans of every description and its paid agents for keeping law and order, provided most of the money and materials for the stage, scaffolds, scenic devices and machinery, as well as the food, lodgings and other necessary regulations and amenities for actors and spectators alike. Among the principal tasks of these management committees was the appointment of a producer and a stage-manager and the delegation of wide powers of selection, remuneration and punishment to these chosen officers. Contracts were normally drawn up establishing these duties, defining these powers and imposing penalties for failure to produce the required results.

Given this authority, producer and stage-manager (together with the author or the redactor and the town clerk) then solicited the co-operation of choristers, artisans, nobles, priests and casual labourers according to need : the choristers to sing or play the parts of boys and women, the artisans to make machines, stage-traps, smoke-bombs for hell-castle, trees, temples, ships and other scenic devices, the nobles to lend costumes, donate properties and money, the priests to copy actors' parts and keep accounts, the labourers to fetch and carry, prepare meals and build an auditorium. All of these groups might be called upon to supply actors according to social rank, talent and experience. The whole community came to be involved, not only in the performance itself but for months beforehand in the preparations for it. If therefore the question is asked – as it ought to be – how these epic dramas retained their popularity over the better part of three centuries and then had to be forcibly suppressed, the answer becomes self-evident : no other occasion in the life of that community could compare with them in promoting unity of purpose, self-fulfilment, and egalitarianism in the sight of the Almighty, notwithstanding the obvious distinctions of birth, wealth, education and skill dividing each member of that community from his fellows. If ever the romantic concept of a united Christendom was realized in practice, these annual theatrical representations of the drama of Christ Crucified could claim to have brought individual human beings as close to an experience of it as they were likely to come.

It would be foolish to suppose that these councils of management worked invariably in harmony and without discord; yet the popularity and longevity of the productions supply convincing evidence of their general suitability to the purpose in hand, and of their efficiency in discharging their multiple responsibilities. On occasion there was friction between the clerical and civic representatives, between one guild and another and between individuals who sensed themselves to have been slighted, underrated or overtaxed. Glimpses of such bickerings emerge from the Coventry Leet Book, from French and German accounting ledgers and in the records of an Italian *Compagnia* here or a Spanish *Confradiá* there; but the nature of the complaints and the remedies adopted themselves provide evidence of the strength of the managerial system and the self-confidence with which it was administered.

iii. REHEARSAL AND PUBLICITY

One of the hazards of open-air productions, now as in the Middle ages, is rain. The drama of Christ Crucified was subject to this hazard, as we know from records in France and England which tell of performances being postponed. Yet its intimate association with the Feast of Corpus Christi which fell between 23 May at the earliest and 24 June at the latest (depending on the date of Easter in any year) gave as firm a guarantee of fine warm weather as the European climate permits. Open-air production was a virtual necessity as much because of the epic scale of the script as because of the wish of the clergy to involve the laity in all

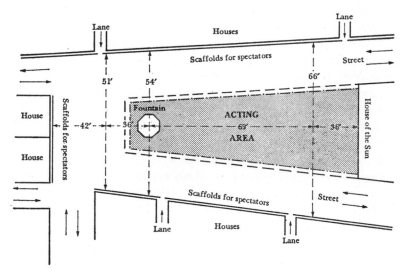

7 Lucerne wine-market: ground-plan of the square as it is today with dimensions and the lay-out of the acting area and auditorium for a performance of the Easter Play in the sixteenth century superimposed upon it.

aspects of the Feast. It then fell to the committee of management
to secure an appropriate *platea*. This could be a single site, such
as the wine-market square in Lucerne – (it stands for inspection
virtually unaltered today : see Figure 7) – the courtyard of a large
friary or convent or several smaller open spaces like the areas in
front of the abbey gates and the town hall in Chester. The stage
could be the flat ground itself as in the Cornish 'Rounds', or a
large raised platform as at Valenciennes, or several mobile platforms placed in conjunction with one another as in Madrid : it
could incorporate all these variables, making possible a stage
direction like the famous 'Herod rages in the pageant and in the
street also' from Coventry (see Plates 22 and 23). Hand in hand
with work on the stage went the preparation of the auditorium.
This had to fulfil two requirements : to control admission and to
give spectators as clear a view as possible of the play in performance following their admission. Attention had also to be paid to
social hierarchy and an appropriate price structure : this however
is a matter to be considered when we come to discuss the commercial aspects of the medieval theatre, including the construction and labour costs involved in providing costumes and scenic
equipment as well as the auditorium itself.

All these physical preparations proceeded alongside the
rehearsals. These were protracted and could cover a period of
several months depending upon the availability of the script, the
length of the play and the manner in which responsibility for
rehearsal had been subdivided by the management committee. As
always with amateur drama, a major problem confronting the
producers was the availability of actors who had to put in a full
day's work at some other occupation, and were only free to
rehearse a play in their spare time. Today this means that
rehearsals normally take place of an evening and at weekends :
then, it was more usual for rehearsals to be called very early in the
morning between first light and the start of the day's work. Thus
it is breakfasts and not teas or suppers that have to be organized,
paid for and recorded faithfully in the account books. The
Coopers' Company in Chester record in 1574 :

Item spent at the fyrste rehearse vj[d]
Item spend at the secunde rehearse xij[d]
Item spend at the thred rehearse xij[d]

It^e spend at our generall rehearse ij^s x^d

Twenty years earlier in 1554 the Chester Smiths' bill for food included 'flesh at the breckfast and bacon. ij^s 8^d, 'botord beere 4^{d}, 'bred ij^{d}, '6 chekens x^d, '2 cheeses xvj^{d}, and so on.[16] A banquet for the actors and technicians and for important guests in the evenings following performances was also a fairly regular occurrence. Details of such banquets survive in records from Lucerne and Valenciennes.[17]

In Romans, France, in 1509 rehearsals were held weekly over a period of seven weeks. They took place in the town hall and refreshments were provided.[18] In Spain we learn of rehearsals in the chapter house of the cathedral in Seville, and in the private apartments of members of the councils of management.[19] In England an example of a rehearsal in a private house comes from Lincoln, c.1479. In short, it would appear that then as now rehearsals were arranged in the largest room or rooms available at the smallest cost that suited local convenience. Nor does it appear from the fragmentary records which survive that amateur actors were any more reliable in point of punctuality and regularity of attendance then than now : at least the management committees found it necessary to draw up stringent regulations which I fancy would decimate many a dramatic society if implemented today.

At Beverley in Yorkshire as early as 1392 the Smiths were fined 40s for failing to present their play, and in 1520 the Painters were fined 2s 'because their play of The Three Kings of Colleyn was badly and confusedly played, in contempt of the whole community, before many strangers'.

To prevent such disgraces to Church and civic pride the management committee at Valenciennes presented all the actors with a contract (*l'obligation*) which they had to sign before a public notary. This document has survived and is highly informative. It consisted of fifteen articles, the first of which bound the actor to perform on the prescribed days, illness alone being admitted as an excuse for failing to do so. Next the actor had to bind himself to accept the part or parts allocated to him without argument. Third,

Les joueurs seront tenus d'arriver en temps
The actors will be required to present themselves
voulu aux répétitions, aux heures et

on time at rehearsals, on the days and at
jours indiqués, sous peine d'une
the times prescribed, under penalty of a
amende de trois patarts.
fine of three patarts.

Among the other stipulations, the actors are bound never to
indulge in recriminations with the producer and not to get drunk.
Every actor was required to hand over a deposit of one gold coin
(*un écu d'or*). This served two purposes: the first was to ensure
that the threat of fines for breaches of contract should be
meaningful, and the second was to secure the management committee against a possible deficit. At Lucerne, at least in the
sixteenth century, similar regulations governed rehearsals and
performances of the Easter Play. There, the council of management (*Verordneten*) assisted by the Director (*Regent*) drew up a
code of 'rules and penalties' ('*Leges*') which covered absence
from rehearsals, exchanging parts without permission, arguments
with the producer or the Council and, as at Valenciennes,
drunkeness. Anyone guilty of such misdemeanours became liable
to a fine.

Zuo den Tagen, da man das Spil probiert,
on the days when the play is being
sol keiner, der im spil ist, in kein zäch
rehearsed no one who is in the play is to go to the tavern
sitzen oder gan zächen gan, bis das er mitt
or to go drinking until he has completed his
synem stand fertig ist, by XB buoss der
part in the script on penalty of paying the Council X–
gesellschafft an iren umbkosten. Doch in
towards their expenses. However due exception
allweg das gebbot der kirchen und
and reservation being made for the rulings of the
der Oberkeit, wann es die Fasten bereicht
ecclesiastical and civic authorities concerning Lent if
ussgnommen und vorbehallten, dess fasten
an infringement of Lenten rules takes place.
bruchs halb.[20]

Despite the irritating shortage of detailed evidence, what has survived suggests a common, basic pattern of rehearsal procedure with the usual local variants. Broadly speaking, we shall not be far from the truth therefore if we assume that rehearsals normally started shortly after Easter and were contained within a period of at most two months. One of the advantages of the English method of dividing up the script into separate plays and apportioning each, as was the case in the Midlands and the North, to individual guilds, was to cut down the number of rehearsals to three or four, and thus to shorten the period of time in which the rehearsals were held. It is hardly likely however that this period could be cut to less than a month if the actors were to have adequate time to memorize their parts.

With this achieved the several 'pageant-masters', 'superintendents', alias 'producers' could meet together with their actors and, in the course of one or two dress-rehearsals, assemble all the component parts of the epic drama into a single performance with adequate continuity. This objective, however, was carefully coupled with publicity and public relations.

Once a committee of management had decided to authorize the production of a Corpus Christi Cycle or a Passion Play, news of the decision was carried abroad by means of a Proclamation. The principal objective was to advertise the title of the play and the dates of performance; but it also served as a recruiting device to arouse the interest of actors and craftsmen in the surrounding district. The Proclamation, being a simple document, could easily be handled by the town crier and his opposite number in neighbouring towns and villages: the church of course had its own means of purveying the same news throughout the diocese. It also served to publicize any necessary information about public holidays associated with the forthcoming performances and about public order and law enforcement. Thereafter, word of mouth could be reckoned to generate interest and mounting excitement as rehearsals and the preparation of costumes, scenic equipment and mechanical 'secrets' progressed, involving an ever increasing number of individuals and their families and friends. The climax of this advance publicity was reached with the dress rehearsals; for they were preceded by a grand procession which included members of the committee of management, actors in costume, some of the scenic devices and images, together with flag-bearers and musicians. This procession was called in Chester 'the riding of the Banns', in France *le Monstre,* in German speaking cities *Ordnungen* and in Spain *Muestra.* Ideally calculated to arouse enthusiasm, and to provoke the lazy-minded into deciding to attend, these processions provoked curiosity, kindled the spirit of devotion and served a strictly practical function in uniting the whole community in expectation of the celebrations to come : they concluded with a private view of the final 'general rehearse' or dress rehearsal for the benefit of the committee of management and individual benefactors, who had contributed money or who had loaned costumes and stage-properties for the play.[21]

In the course of this 'general rehearse' not only could a note be made of the many technical matters that needed to be completed or rearranged, and the continuity of action rehearsed, but anything that was considered offensive in the script or in individual performances could be suppressed. Finally the management committee could assure itself that everything in the auditorium was in order to permit the orderly reception of the spectators.[22]

With every aspect of this vast organizational undertaking attended to and ready to begin, the whole community could devote its undivided attention to the devotional purpose for which script, rehearsals, design and construction work, benefactions, labour, publicity and administration were simply means to an end, the Festival of Corpus Christi.

By modern standards the time allocated to the actual rehearsal of the text seems short. If the records we possess are representative and truthful, it would appear that the pageant-masters aimed to devote one rehearsal – the first – to what we would describe as 'blocking' – i.e. entrances, actions and exits. Two or three more sufficed to ensure that the actors were word-perfect and had memorized their moves successfully. The dress rehearsals brought the actors into contact with their costumes, stage-properties, music and machinery. If this seems a desperately short allowance of time to achieve anything but the most pedestrian standards of performance, it must be remembered that annual repetition of the plays meant that many of the actors would already be fully familiar with their roles. Thus, with the exception of a wholly new play, rehearsals could largely be devoted to *additions* to existing scripts, to the newcomers among the actors, to actors who had mislaid their scripts and failed to learn their lines, and to any *changes* in the running order of the performance occasioned by modifications to the script. Another factor of no less importance was the presence of the pageant-master on the stage during the actual performance. Here his function extended beyond that of the modern prompter to that of the repetiteur in opera who cues in all the singers by repeating the entire text loudly enough to be audible to them, but not to the audience. Graphic evidence of this practice is provided in the Fouquet miniature of the torture scene in a play of St Apollonia, and this is confirmed in Richard Carew's account of the Cornish plays.

> The players conne not their parts
> without booke, but are prompted by one
> called the Ordinary, who followeth at
> their back with the book in his hand,
> and telleth them softly what they must
> pronounce aloud.*

This is depicted precisely by Jean Fouquet in his miniature where the Ordinary may be seen in ecclesiastical costume with the prompt-book in his left hand and a conductor's baton in his right (see Plate 23).

As the music was provided by the local choirs and as the music itself consisted of familiar anthems, hymns and psalms, this aspect of the production needed little rehearsal. Unlike music in the drama of Christ the King, it was largely incidental in character and needed only to be fitted into place at the 'general rehearse'. However it played a vital part in these performances and involved choirs and instrumentalists. Standards of performance were also high since it was usual to employ professionals recruited from local choirs and the city 'waights'. In Lucerne the play (and prospects of remuneration for services rendered) attracted professional musicians from great distances. Some of the music for that play has survived (see Plate 2).

iv. PERFORMANCE

Performance was a celebration. It was prefaced by a High Mass

---

* This double negative must not be construed to mean that the actors were not required to learn their parts: had this been the case it would have been unnecessary to pay scribes to copy out actor's parts or to fine actors who did not know them.

D

of thanksgiving equal in its joyous character with those of Easter Sunday and Christmas Day. It marked the end of months of preparation and anticipation in which it was difficult for any individual not to have become personally involved. It was high summer and a public holiday. It ended with a service of general thanksgiving and a banquet.

Seats or standings could be reserved in advance and privacy obtained at a price : for others who were less circumspect or less affluent admission could be obtained on the day itself in close proximity to the acting-area. As an incentive to attend and for good behaviour in the auditorium the Church offered substantial remissions of time in Purgatory : threats of excommunication served as a similar deterrent to those disposed to make the holiday an excuse for drunkenness and punch-ups.

Silence was obtained at the start of each performance by the Prologue or Expositor by recourse to a prayer, an anthem or, on occasion, a brief sermon. At Angers, in 1486, the Committee of Management took care to ordain :

> *Item, et pour mieux commancer et avoir*
> Item, both to make a better start and to obtain
> *sillence, si l'on voit qu'il soit expediant,*
> silence, if he should see that it should be expedient,
> *sera dicte une messe ou jeu sur ung*
> he will say a mass from an altar properly
> *autel honnestement droissé.*
> furnished on the stage.

On the third day the comittee prescribes,

> *Et sus l'entree du parc, y aura enfans*
> And at the entrance to the enclosure let
> *chantans melodieusement jusques ad ce*
> there be children singing melodiously until
> *que bonne silence soit faite, en lieu de*
> complete silence is obtained, instead of a
> *prologue.*
> prologue.

The Mons Passion Play of 1501 starts as follows :
PROLOGUE : *In nomine Patris et filii et Spiritus Sancti, amen.* In the name of the Father, Son and Holy Spirit, amen.[23]

Ironically, the silence so assiduously courted at the start of these plays has also descended on descriptions of performances. The historian is thus left with a random selection of generalized comments jotted down by individuals with no pretensions to being professional critics, and which in some cases were received at second-hand and recorded by persons who were not themselves eye-witnesses of a performance. In the latter category, unfortunately, fall the familiar descriptions of the pageant-carts in Chester and Coventry recorded by Archdeacon Robert Rogers and Sir William Dugdale respectively in the first half of the seventeenth century. Richard Carew's *Survey of Cornwall* was written in 1602, so even his testimony concerning performances in the Cornish 'Rounds' has to be received with some caution. Such too is the case with Henri d'Outreman and Simon Le Boucq who described the Passion Play at Valenciennes in 1547. Simon was the son of one of the participants, Noel Le Bucq: d'Outreman, likewise, was only born in 1546.* Renward Cystatus of Lucerne is a different case. He was Town Clerk, was responsible for at least one complete revision of the text, directed the play on two occasions and left behind him copious prompt-book production notes. His usefulness as a witness, however, is marred by the fact that the productions for which he was responsible took place so late in the sixteenth century as to make it questionable how far his evidence can safely be applied to conditions of performance in the fifteenth century. The same is true of the recognizances which the players of New Romney in Kent had to subscribe to in the Marian revivals of their play.

Students of the subject are thus forced to read the play for themselves – their epic nature makes this a daunting task – and evaluate the characteristics of performance by imaginative readings of dialogue and stage-directions. The speculative quality of such evaluation can be controlled to some extent by reference to the factual details provided in the accompanying account books or in lists of bills which have survived without the accompanying texts. Visual aids also survive in paintings, stained-glass, roof bosses, alabaster shrines, frescoes and statuary; but all of

---

* Rogers', d'Outreman's and Carew's accounts are printed by A. M. Nagler in *Sources of Theatrical History* (New York 1952), pp. 47–53. The New Romney recognizances are printed in Malone Society *Collections VII*, ed. G. E. Dawson (1965), pp. 202–11.

these must be approached with extreme caution since it is seldom possible to separate a scene from a play (in a photographic sense) from the iconographic conventions to which the artists were bound and the licence which, as artists, they allowed themselves.[24]

With these warnings in the foreground some generalizations can be made about performances which extend beyond the claims for silence made at the outset. For example, extant texts supply ample evidence of the presence of an Expositor who, in manner of Chorus or compère, kept the audience informed not only of the action to be witnessed, but also of its relationship with earlier and later parts of the story and of its abiding significance for the spectator. However much the narrative might entertain therefore, its devotional and moral character was constantly expounded and reiterated. The Chester play of Abraham and Isaac provides a typical example : this concludes with an epilogue which, in modern translation, starts as follows :

> Lordings, the signification
> Of this deed of devotion,
> An you will, it is shewn
> May turn you to much good.
> This deed you see done in the place,
> In example of Jesus done it was
> That for to win mankind grace
> Was sacrificed on the rood.

Nor was the miraculous quality of much of the action underrated. Henri d'Outreman dwells on the technical 'secrets' at Valenciennes in his account of the 1547 performance.

Les secrets du Paradis et de l'Enfer estoient
The machines of Paradise and of Hell were
tout a faict prodigieux et capables d'estre
absolutely prodigious and capable of being
pris par la populace pour enchantemens. Car l'on
taken by the populace for magic. For there one
y voyait la Vérité et les Anges et divers autres personnages
saw Truth, the Angels and other characters
descendre de bien haut, tantost visiblement,
descend from on high, sometimes visibly
autrefois comme invisibles, puis paroistre tout à coup;

and sometimes invisibly and then without warning.
de l'Enfer Lucifer s'eslevait, sans qu'on vist comment,
Lucifer arose out of Hell, riding on a dragon, without
porté sur un dragon. La Verge de Moyse de seche et stérile
anyone being able to see how it was achieved. Moses's dry
ietoit tout à coup des fleurs et des fruits; les ames de
and sterile rod suddenly sprouted flowers and fruit; the souls of
Herode et de Judas estoient emportés en l'air par les diables . . .
Herod and Judas were carried up into the air by devils . . .

Such scenic marvels are not far removed in spirit from those
which still attract and delight audiences in British pantomimes or
at the *Folies Bergères:* it therefore behoves us to accord the
respect due to the technical sophistication of theatrical presentation in the late Middle Ages even if the differences between the
objectives informing their productions and our own are very
large. Nor should we ignore the spectacular quality of the
costumes and stage properties. These were as sumptuous in their
fabrics as they were expensive, and as ostentatious in the care
lavished upon the design and construction as if commissioned for
princes of Church and State.

Account books everywhere confirm these impressions. The
Smiths at Coventry between 1450 and 1550 record the purchase
of white leather for God, gold and silver foil for mitres and scarlet
cloth for a bishop's tabard. When Worcester Cathedral, in 1576,
sold its 'players gere', this included 'A K(ing)s cloke of Tysshew.
A Jerkyn and a payer of breches. A lytill cloke of tysshew. A
gowne of silk. A Jerkyn of greene, 2 cappes, and the devils
apparel'. Wigs, furs, armour, wings for angels, gloves, copes and
jewelry figure repeatedly in lists of expenditure with Italian
examples eclipsing all others in splendour and extravagance.

No less thought, time, labour and cost went into the scenic
arbours, cities, fountains, gardens, hills, pavilions and temples
into which the simple *loca* and *sedes* of the ancient drama of
Christ the King had been transformed in this more realistic and
humane world of Christ Crucified. Scenic devices remained true
to their origin both in their emblematic character and in the
simultaneous use of as many as were required to identify every
locality that figured in the script: technically, numerically and
artistically however they were greatly amplified. The scale and

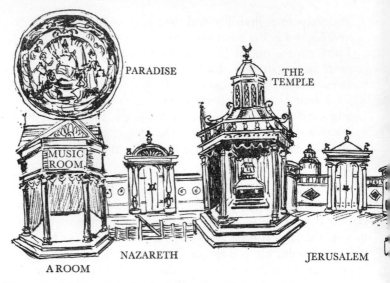

8 The stage and scenic units for the Passion Play, Valenciennes, 1547

9 Diagrammatic outline of the stage-setting for the play of St Lawrence, Cologne, 1581

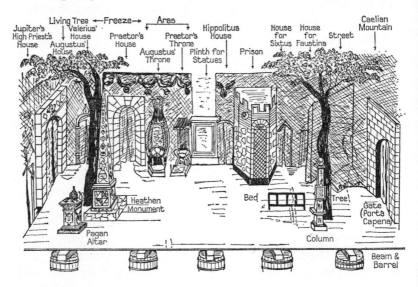

THE
PALACE

THE
GOLDEN GATE

LIMBO

HELL

THE HOUSE
OF THE
BISHOPS

THE SEA

nature of this amplification can be swiftly appreciated by a glance at Hubert Cailleau's drawings of the settings for the Valenciennes Passion Play of 1547 and an anonymous draftsman's sketch of those for Broelmann's play of St Lawrence at Cologne in 1581. Jean Fouquet's miniature of a play of St Apollonia, *c*.1460, depicts a much simpler stage setting; but it corresponds with the Cailleau drawings in two important respects. It depicts at least six separate *loca* as background to the stage action, and it places Heaven (or Paradise) on the actors' right and Hell on the actors' left; just as importantly, the central *loca* in both drawings is self-evidently a throne-room (see Plate 23 and Figures 8 and 9). This information, scanty though it is, fortunately suffices to indicate clearly that the concept of *teatrum mundi* which had informed the stage-conventions of liturgical music-drama in Christian basilicas of the tenth and eleventh centuries was carried forward in unbroken tradition into the vernacular religious drama of the fifteenth and sixteenth centuries (see pp. 40–51). Since the stage was still expected to represent the whole of God's creation, and not simply the mortal world, the invisible worlds of heaven and hell had to be accommodated not only in physical and tangible terms, but in their proper relationship to the visible world of daily experience. Heaven and hell are thus represented at the extremities of the stage's perimeter (in the Cornish 'rounds' heaven is set in the east and hell in the north): throne-room and judgement seat are set centre-stage and flanked by such other mortal *loca* as gardens, lakes and temples.

It was as easy for audiences to follow the symbolic meaning of the action from the evidence presented to their eyes as by the text itself. The *platea* with its adjacent *loca,* together with the costumes, continued to telescope the historical past and the future into the immediate present and space itself into the restricted view of the audience: thus the moral and doctrinal character of the performance continued to dominate it, notwithstanding those aspects of it that were specifically calculated to entertain.

The altar paintings of Corpus Domini in Urbino (now in the *Galleria Nazionale delle Marche* in the *Pallazzo Ducale*) – the altarpiece itself by Joos van Ghent and the predella by Paolo Uccello – illustrate this point graphically. For while Christ in the altarpiece administers the Eucharist to the apostles within a Romanesque basilica, the background figures depict Duke Frederico de Montefeltro and other individuals of importance to the guild at the time its members commissioned these paintings. The Uccello predella presents a pictorial narrative the significance of which is no less pertinent to both the Feast and the confraternity dedicated to its celebration.[25]

That the performance was a game and not in earnest was never in doubt. Games figure within the game: magician's games (the mechanical 'secrets'), games of chance (dicing for Christ's clothes), word-games. Thus the Townley crucifixion is skilfully turned into a parody of a tournament.

> 1st TORTURER :   In fayth, syr, sen ye callyd you a Kyng,
> You must prufe a worthy thyng
> That falles unto the were;
> Ye must J(o)ust in to(u)rnamente.

Setting Christ on the cross is then compared to putting him into the saddle on horseback.

> 4th TORTURER :   Stand thou yonder on yond syde,
> And we shall se how he can ryde,
> And how to w(i)eld a shaft.

The Townley cycle provides an even more spectacular example of this type of game in the three-dimensional parody of Christ's nativity that forms the sheep-stealing episode of *The Second Shepherds' Play*.

In performance I think it is fair to say that these techniques, so skilfully explored and exploited by the playmakers, serve a double purpose : they keep the audience alert and attentive on account of each individual spectator's familiarity with the game and interest in the use to which it is being turned; and, just as importantly, they assist the actors in their task of presenting scriptural characters to the audience *at a safe distance* from reality within the overall make-believe convention of the *ludus*. Thus blasphemy was avoided, and no actor was required to be anything other than himself fulfilling actions allotted to the character given to him to play.

A question that must remain open is the quality of the acting ability of the performers. All that we can say with certainty is that a difference was recognized between good performances and bad. There is factual evidence for this in the action taken by committees of management to reserve to the pageant-masters the right of auditioning and casting on their behalf, and to impose fines on lazy or forgetful performers themselves. There is the revealing entry in the Chester Coopers' accounts for 1574 : 'Item spend apon Thomas marler to get him to pleay ij[d]'.

Specific payments were made to actors in France and Germany as well as in England from time to time; but I think we must refrain from regarding this as evidence of professionalism in our sense of the word.[26] As in amateur dramatic societies today payments to individuals can simply represent reimbursement of wages lost, or of expenses incurred as a result of letting the play (rehearsal or performance) take precedence over normal work. On the other hand, it would not be odd in the case of performances in the late fifteenth century or the sixteenth to find management committees or pageant-masters recruiting one or more members of a small company of professional interluders in the service of a local dignitary and paying a modest fee. This might be the case with the actor in Coventry who was paid 3s. 4d. for playing the part of God. At Mons in 1501 at least five of the actors were professional rhetoricians.

In Spain a curious and seemingly unique feature of Corpus

D*

Christi drama was dancing (*bayles*). Dancing is a natural accompaniment to festivity as an expression of thanks or joy; but many of these dances appear to have lacked the gravity and seriousness that we might suppose to be appropriate to a religious festival. As late as 1593, the licentious *Zarabanda* was danced in the Corpus Christi *autos* in Seville.[27] Perhaps this only serves to prove that no matter how carefully the text of a play is scrutinized by a censor, the actors always have the last word when it comes to informing an audience how that text is to be interpreted.

Children were frequently recruited, especially choristers. Many of the Italian *sacre rappresentazioni* were played exclusively by boys. Thus the *Annunziazione* (Prologue) to the Florentine play of *Cleofas and Luca* begins:

E se anche vi molesta,	And although the speech
Di chi recita il dire	of the performers may
Col rozzo proferire	irritate you with their
Le parole e gli accenti,	uncouth delivery of word and
Deh! siate pazienti	accent, alack, be patient,
Perchè siam giovanetti,	since we're young.

In Germany, France and England it was habitual to cast boys as angels and to swell the ranks of the attendants upon such dignitaries as Pharaoh or the Magi with pages.

It is widely believed that women never performed in plays in the Middle Ages. As a rule they did not, but there are exceptions. The Chester play of the Assumption of the Virgin was allocated, according to the pre-Reformation Banns, to 'The wives of the town'. In France the role of St Catherine was played by a woman at Metz in 1468 and in *Le Mystère des Trois Doms* at Romans in 1509 all the female parts were performed by women. On that occasion their presence can be attributed in part at least to simple expediency since the play was written and performed as a form of thanksgiving for release from two years of plague. Women also took part in many of the dances which accompanied the Spanish *autos* of the sixteenth century. The trade guilds (*gremios*) met the costs of these dances and the performers received a fee.[28]

If women appeared rarely in the medieval theatre this was not because it was thought shameful: rather was this so because of factors that were particular to the theatre of the Middle Ages. In the first place responsibility for the organization of Corpus Christi drama rested with bishops, canons and city fathers : this exclusively male hierarchy then delegated executive responsibility to guilds, religious and commercial, that were only open to men. Moreover, liturgical music drama having relied for generations on choir-boys and junior clergy for treble roles, this provided an example to be imitated in the Corpus Christi drama. The quality of these voices suggests another and more practical reason for continuing to employ them rather than to recruit women – audibility in an open-air auditorium. Given the choice between trained and untrained voices, there can be little doubt that the producers would have given parts to individuals who could be trusted to project dialogue to the back of the auditorium and whose articulation was precise. In these circumstances few women in medieval society had much hope of securing a part in open competition : by the same token choristers and trained orators were always likely to be in keen demand.

Speculative, therefore, as conclusions must continue to be in the light of the scattered and fragmentary nature of the evidence that survives from a period spanning two whole centuries, the sum of that evidence points consistently at least to high standards of organization, production and performance. The committees of management were democratically constituted and comprised the best educated and most experienced leaders of the local community. They took care in their turn to delegate responsibility for the recruitment of actors and technicians to men whose reputations had been acquired from lengthy apprenticeships. These producers, whose continuance in office in subsequent years rested on the successful fulfilment of the commissions entrusted to them, sought out actors with trained voices and previous experience, and the finest master-craftsmen and their journeymen obtainable in the district for the provision of scenic emblems, stage properties and machinery. Scripts of epic dimensions were broken down into manageable units each of which was rehearsed separately and then brought together in one or more general rehearsals. Many participants were already familiar with what was expected of them from previous years : much of the scenic spectacle and many of the costumes, having been carefully stored away, had only to be brought out and refurbished with fresh paint or new ornaments to be fit for use again. A new section of text substituted for an old one here, a new pageant and new costumes there, with new faces here and there among the actors brought a breath of variety to the familiar and much loved spectacles. Little was left to chance. As Lucifer fell and Eve was born from Adam's ribs each year the spectators knew that the Tree of Knowledge in the Garden of Eden would later be translated into the true Cross on Calvary: as Christ died and Mary wept the audience knew that Anima Christi would harrow hell, redeem Adam, Eve, Patriarchs and Prophets and ascend to heaven in a mandorla surrounded with singing angels; but as the defeated Lucifer retreated into the smoking dungeons behind the shattered gates of hell-castle the audience also knew that Christ would appear again in majesty to occupy the throne in the audience chamber centre-stage to judge mankind – pope, cardinal, king, queen, merchant, lawyer, craftsman and peasant – separating those who had earned salvation through repentance and grace from those who had ignored their opportunity, and dispatching the latter to the flames of hell, stage-left, while guiding the former towards paradise, stage-right. The fitting conclusion was the time-honoured song of thanksgiving inherited from the liturgical plays, *Te Deum Laudamus*. The game was over. Its costs were counted. Scripts, costumes, properties and scaffolds were put back into store. Comparisons were made in taverns and private houses with earlier performances; and already the seeds were being sown of new ideas and improved techniques to form the subjects of experiment in a year's time within *The Play Called Corpus Christi*.

D. PATRON SAINTS

To provide a full account of the production of plays devoted to the lives of saints and martyrs would be as tedious as it was repetitious: for the fact is that such plays were frequently very similar both in structure and in performance to the drama of Christ Crucified. In one sense at least many of them were the logical extension, via the apostles, of New Testament history into more modern times. Plays like the East Anglian *St Mary Magdalene*, preserved in the Digby manuscript, the Cornish *St Meriasek*, the *Mystère des Apôtres* from Bourges or the *Mystère des Trois Doms* from Romans are virtually indistinguishable in their length and complexity of scenic requirements from Passion Plays or Corpus Christi Cycles.[29] Many Saint Plays, however, are much shorter, were clearly not associated with any of the major Feasts of Christendom but with strictly local festivals instead, and much more parochial in their administrative and production requirements. Some of these, indeed, are of so questionable an order as to raise doubts whether a fully scripted text ever existed or whether a tableau with images, processed around the streets following a service and as a prelude to a banquet, was all that was attempted : such was the case with many a festivity described as 'a Church ale' in English villages : nor was the case much different when certain tableaux devoted to particular saints appeared in Royal Entries into the larger towns. On the other hand a number of Saint Plays figure in the account rolls of academic foundations, performed indoors and at night, which more nearly resemble Interludes than Corpus Christi drama, and which were probably modelled on the shorter Morality Plays, of which *Everyman* may be taken as a typical example.

Within this exceptionally wide spectrum, therefore, generalizations are likely to be even more misleading than is the case with liturgical music-drama or the vernacular drama of Christ Crucified.

One such generalization which has gained credence in the past is that Saint Plays were a relatively late development in point of historical chronology and that they can accordingly be categorized as 'extensions' or 'offshoots' of the Mystery Cycles and Morality Plays. This hypothesis is one which fits in conveniently enough with a Protestant ethic and the wishful thinking of scientific humanists, since it suggests that such plays were the product of weariness with annual repetitions of the Cycles and Passion Plays : the obvious association that can thus be drawn between plays devoted to the miracles of obscure saints and the worst excesses of Roman Catholic superstition and idolatry can then be made to explain the collapse of the religious stage in the early decades of the sixteenth century. Unfortunately, the facts flatly contradict this argument.

To start with, liturgical music-drama itself produced the first Saint Play, that of St Nicholas (see pp. 47-8 above). Four episodes from this saint's life were treated dramatically in the course of the twelfth century: 'the dowry of the three daughters', 'the three clerks', 'the Image of St. Nicholas' and 'the son of Getron'. Plays on these subjects survive from Hildesheim, Ein-

siedeln, Fleury and from the pen of the scholar Hilarius. All
of them are short, in Latin verse and designed to be chanted in
a liturgical context. Records of such plays (but no texts) survive
from several other places in North-Western Europe, including
England.[30]

Records of plays particular to other saints reach us from the
latter half of the fourteenth century and are more or less contemporary with the earliest records of Corpus Christi plays.
Italian records abound with *Compagnie* charged with performing *sacre rappresentazioni* dedicated to saints – St Agnese
(Florence), St Antonio (Padua), St Leonardo (Aquila), St
Pietro (Modena) and many more. In England references survive
to a play of St Katherine in London in 1393 and to a play of St
Thomas the Martyr at King's Lynn in Norfolk in 1385 : these
take us back to Wycliff's strictures on miracle plays and to
Chaucer's Wife of Bath with her visits 'to pleyes of myracles and
to mariages'. As Chaucer states specifically that his Wife of Bath
made these visits 'in Lent', the plays in question can neither have
been liturgical music dramas nor Corpus Christi Cycles. That
such plays had become common in London at least by the end of
the twelfth century is vouched for in Fitzstephen's reference to
plays at Skinner's Well. 'London has a more holy type of
performance: representations of the miracles which holy saints
performed or of the sufferings by which the steadfastness of the
martyrs became renowned.'[31]

Plays of a similar kind were also being presented in Paris before
the end of the fourteenth century; and in 1402 a monopoly was
granted to the *Confrérie de la Passion* by Charles VI

> *jouer quelque Misterre que ce soit, soit de*
> To perform whatever Mystery it maybe, whether
> *la dicte Passion, et Résurreccion, ou autre*
> of the said Passion, and Resurrection, or any
> *quelconque tant de saincts comme de*
> other concerning the saints male or
> *sainctes*
> female.

A collection of plays devoted to the lives of saints and martyrs
from the Abbey of Saint Geneviève in Paris survives and may
well be a part of the repertoire of the *Confrérie de la Passion*. St

Fiacre, St Denis and St Geneviève herself figure in this group. In the fifteenth century other *Confréries* dedicated to particular saints possessed plays about their patrons, notably that of St Didier at Langres, St Remy at Rheims and St Crespinen in Paris. A play on the life of St Barbara survives which makes provision for one hundred roles and took five days to perform. Longer still was Gringore's *Life of St Louis*, which has two hundred and eighty characters. Both are comparable with the *Mystère des Trois Doms* (the Martyrs Séverin, Exupère and Félicien) which was performed at Romans in Provence in 1509, and for which we possess not only the complete text but also the account book. Grace Frank in *The Mediaeval French Drama* describes Gringore's *Life of St Louis* as 'potentially a historical and realistic play'. Much the same can be said of other French Saints Plays of the later period: this dictum applies with equal force to the Cornish *Life of St Meriasek*.[32]

In point of structure and incident these plays have much in common with the chronicle plays of the Elizabethan era, especially in respect of battles and scenes of torture and bawdy humour. Were any of them more often read and better known than they are, much of the writing which passes for criticism in editions of Marlowe's *Dr Faustus,* Shakespeare's *Titus Andronicus* or even Kyd's *The Spanish Tragedy* could be quietly dismissed: authors, actors and audiences who were accustomed to coping with the cures and cripples and other miracles performed by St Meriasek, the tearing off of St Barbara's breasts or the burning of St Lawrence on the stage would not have found the magic of Faustus, Lavinia's loss of hands and tongue, or old Jeronimo's revenge on his enemies as so shocking or so difficult to envisage in performance as we do. Jean Fouquet in his miniature of the play of St Apollonia obliges us with a picture of just such an incident (see Plate 23).

Records of Saint Plays in German-speaking countries are scanty; but if it is remembered that at one end of the chronological line St Nicholas's plays survive to us from Hildesheim and Einsiedeln, and that at the other the Cologne play of St Lawrence is of a much later date (1581) than anything like it in either France or England, it is much more probable that this dramatic genre found as much favour between the twelfth and the sixteenth centuries in German-speaking States as in other parts of

Europe than that it did not. Lucerne, for example, at least in the
sixteenth century, had its *Heiligenspiele,* its *Jüngstgerichtspiele*
and its *Fastnachtspiele* (Saints, Last Judgement and Carnival),
all of which were performed in the winemarket square in years
when the Easter Play was not performed, like the alternating
Creed and Paternoster plays in York.[33] The Reformation and
the Thirty Years War between them, it must be recalled,
worked as much havoc in the Protestant States on all expressions
of the Roman Catholic faith, including drama sponsored by
churches, as it did in Britain.

It was in Italy and Spain however that the cult of saints
achieved its apogee, and it should not be surprising therefore that
plays rehearsing the examples set by their faith and works should
have found elaborate expression in these countries. Unlike the
Corpus Christi drama in North-Western Europe, the Italian *sacre
rappresentazioni* embraced subject-matter devoted to the apostles
and the early Christian fathers as being of equal importance to
material drawn from the Old and New Testaments. Both were
regarded as '*storia*' and of equal value to the establishment of
faith. How far much closer proximity to the Virgilian tradition of
epic narrative is responsible for this in the Italian language (and
thus in academic and ecclesiastical environments) is an open
question; but the intimate association of the aristocracy with
Italian guilds devoted to patronal saints must at least be taken
into account in this context. Plays relating to St Christine, St
Felicity, St George, St Eustace or St Christopher thus jostle plays
about the Magi, the Virgin or Christ himself for popular attention in the fifteenth century. Even in the sixteenth century it is
still possible to find a play entitled,

Rappresentazione di san Cristoforo ridotta
The mystery of Saint Christopher,
ad uso di Commedia, e la Gloriosa e
adapted for the theatre, and the
trionfante vittoria donata dal grande Iddio
glorious and triumphant victory granted
al popolo Ebreo per mezzo di Giuditta, ridotta
by the Almighty to the Jewish people
in Commedia . . .
through the person of Judith, adapted for performance . . .

In Italy too it was not unusual for a Corpus Christi Guild to concern itself with a play devoted to the Eucharist rather than with biblical subject-matter. One such is *Un miracolo del Corpo di Cristo* published in Florence *c.*1490. The plot of this play has close affinities with the English *Croxton Play of the Sacrament* of 1461.[34]

Spanish records parallel those from France and Italy in respect of the names of saints whose lives were thought to be worthy of dramatic treatment: they also supply many details of the staging techniques employed in the latter and more elaborate plays. Those originating in the eastern provinces (Barcelona, Mallorca and Valencia) appear to have been particularly spectacular. Up to four or five platforms were required in addition to the normal *platea*, each of which formed the base of one or more elaborate *loca*. A play devoted to St Crespin and St Crespinen (in Spanish *Crespinia*) demands that

Fer-se an z cadefals, y entre un y altre
Some scaffolds will be erected and between
aurà molts . . . El cap del cadefal sterà
each of them there will be much space . . .
un rey moro, y junt el palau aurà
On the top of the scaffold will stand a Moorish
una capella; aurà un Cristo crucificat.
king and next to the palace there will be a chapel;
En l'altre part del cadefal aurà una sglésia
there will be a crucified Christ. On the other side
ab una campeneta . . .
of the scaffold there will be a church with a small bell-
En l'altra cadefal sterà lo rey Maximà, y
tower. . . . On the other scaffold will stand King Maximilian
prop de se casa aurà un governador, quis.
and near his house will be a governor who is called
diu Ractioner.
Rationer.
Y al altre cadefal aura dos botigas, una ha a un cap, l'altra ha
And on the other scaffold there will be two shops,
l'altra cap. Y dos cases de ermitans;
one at one end and one at the other and two
a la una aurà un armità molt vell. En

hermits' houses, in one of which there will be a very
lo mateix cadefal aurà una caseta, en
old hermit. On the same scaffold there will be a hut,
què ey aurà dos de sabater, y una
on which there will also be two shoemakers' huts and a
taula y dos cadiras en lo mateix cadefal
table and two chairs on the same scaffold where the
que seran los sabaters.
shoemakers will be.[35]

Spectacular as this stage must have been, it was not more
demanding than the English play of *St Mary Magdalene*
(*c.*1500) in its scenic requirements. The play is constructed in
three distinct sections, although divided technically into two
parts. The action in Part I involves twenty changes of locality and
ranges over nine separate localities: Part II specifies at least
fifteen separate localities and thirty-two shifts of locality.[36] The
Cornish play of *St Meriasek* (1504) is also divided into two parts.

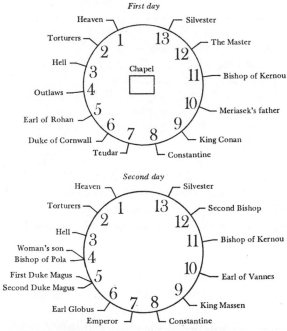

10   The Cornish play of *St Meriasek*: ground-plans of the stage arrangements
      for the first and second day as depicted in the original manuscript, 1504

The script is carefully orchestrated to facilitate staging on and within an earthwork 'round' and resembles the Cornish Corpus Christi Cycle in this respect. Provision is made for thirteen scaffolds on the circumference of the round on both days. Where principal characters appear on both days they retain the same scaffolds – the Emperor Constantine, the Bishop of Kernou, the Torturers, Heaven and Hell. Provision was made for a chapel to stand in the middle of the arena in Part I; not being required in Part II, it does not figure in the diagram in the manuscript.

The closer one studies this type of play the more amazed one becomes at the effrontery of their authors in daring to attempt to encompass so much within the necessarily restricting limits of a stage play. A saint will grow from youth to manhood and pass beyond the grave to salvation and a martyr's crown : in achieving it he will cross seas, traverse forests, engage in battles, escape ambushes, endure beatings and face torture before finally resigning his soul to God. Time and distance had no limits : anything which a man might encounter in the mortal world, no matter how sensational or horrific, found its counterpart upon the stage : yet all this was eclipsed in beauty in heaven and in bestiality in hell.

The paradox evident in all of this is that the graphic realism of each separate incident in these chronicles should be compounded with narrative of epic proportions and such apparently effortless continuity. Any reader of such scripts today is bound to wonder how it was ever possible to reconcile the actions prescribed by the stage-directions with a style of acting acceptable to audiences. One answer to this problem, as I have learnt from the experience of reviving parts at least of *Le Jeu de St Nicholas* and *St Meriasek*, lies in exploiting rather than suppressing the artificial and make-believe character of the performance. Saint Meriasek, for example, is required to sail from Brittany to Cornwall and calm a storm in the course of it : granted a toy-ship, meticulously made to miniature scale and fully functional in its sails, pennants, laniards, pulleys etc, with actors to assist choreographically as wind and waves, this scenic problem disappears and becomes instead a source of fun and pleasure to actors and spectators alike with the saint bringing comfort and renewed strength to the seasick and panic-stricken sailors. It is a game – elaborate, mimetic and effective. The second problem is less easy to solve : this lies in the difference of devotional response between audiences then and now to the title role in plays of this kind. No actor or director today can expect his audience to come and meet him half way in regarding early Christian saints and martyrs as heroic or romantic figures, although Thomas à Becket, as presented by T. S. Eliot in *Murder in the Cathedral*, has proved to be a notable exception. By contrast, for actors and audiences in the Middle Ages, all of them were far less distinctly defined as historical characters. That they were familiar in the pictured forms of stained-glass, fresco and statuary is undeniable: but far from breeding contempt, familiarity had served to elevate such figures in medieval minds above and beyond normal human beings. What they had achieved in the name of Christianity had set them apart from common men of whatever degree. And as with all heroes, the more local the saint, the keener the partisan interest in his life and works.

This is the common bond that links the massive *Mystère des Trois Doms*, devised and presented by the citizens of Romans in 1509 as the most appropriate form of thanksgiving for release from two years of plague, with the parishioners of St Olave's in Silver Street in London who in 1557 put on a short play about that saint to raise funds for their church. Personal patronage has gone out of fashion in our times and in doing so has led us to forget to what extent it dominated every aspect of medieval life. Every parish, every guild, every craft had its patron saint; so had every school; even pilgrims and travellers moved under the protection of St James or St Christopher. A chapel, a shrine and an image of the patron saint was an essential requirement for any institution or fraternity of consequence throughout the bounds of Christendom. Thus the great London livery company of Merchant Tailors was happy to be known as the Fraternity of St John the Baptist, devoted as much time and money to its chapel as to its hall, proudly displayed its patron's symbol, the lamb carrying a cross, in its livery badge, and expected due reference to be made to it in all civic pageantry.[37] Thus the Medici in Florence came to associate themselves with the *Compagnia del Magi* which for them served at once as a mirror image of their own affluence and their generosity as patrons, simplicity coupled with ostentation, humility with power.[38] The same fierce local pride elevated St George, St Ursula, and many minor saints whose names are now only remembered in terms of maps and road-signs in remote parts of Wales and Cornwall, into a dominant position in town and countryside alike. If we tend to forget this pervasive influence of the saints on all aspects of temporal life in the Middle Ages, we are also apt to ignore the importance of their role as intercessors between sinful mankind and God in heaven in the spiritual life of those times (see Plate 3).

St George provided the subject-matter of a play at Bassingbourne near Cambridge in 1511. Twenty-seven villages combined their resources on a federal basis to finance and present this play, and there are other East Anglian examples of this practice. Some villages, less adventurous or less affluent, only possessed a tabernacle and a statue which was paraded round the parish boundaries on the day in which their saint was commemorated in the Church Calendar: this was concluded by a banquet in the churchyard or in the nave of the church itself when the church had to do double duty as parish hall.[39]

At all levels of society therefore the local saint was a figure to be reckoned with in art as in religion. Male or female, the saint served as a focal point for celebrations in all matters of consequence to the community or to particular groups with common interests within that community. Their drawing power in the theatre can easily be verified by a glance at the accounts of income and expenditure in cases where these have survived (see pp. 183 ff. below). Veneration of the saint, when pursued with this degree of fervour and when fanned by the spirit of competition between groups or communities could easily pass beyond the bounds of devotion into idolatry. That this had occurred in many places by the start of the sixteenth century is evident enough from the reactions of Protestant and Catholic reformers alike who, divided as they may have been on many matters, united in condemning an adulation of the saints and martyrs that had clearly overstepped these limits.[40] One casualty of these reforms – at least in North-Western Europe – was the Saint Play which, by the middle of the sixteenth century, was everywhere being actively suppressed, or transformed into chronicles of kings and champions of more recent date and more questionable virtue. Even the drama itself rounded upon a type of play that formerly had nourished its own development so effectively. John Bale, writing for Lord Chancellor Cromwell's players in the

1530s, pours withering scorn on relics, miracles wrought with the aid of them and, indirectly, on the saints themselves. Thus 'Dissimulation' in *King Johan* says to 'Sedition',

> Than have we imagys of seynt Spryte and seynt Savyer.
> Moche is the sekynge of them to gett ther faver;
> Yong whomen berfote, and olde men seke them brecheles.
> The myracles wrought ther I can in no wyse expresse.
> We lacke neyther golde nor sylver, gyrdles nor rynges,
> Candelles nor tapperes, nor other customyd offerynges,
> Though I seme a shepe, I can play the subtle foxe :
> I can make Latten to bryng this gere to (th)e boxe
>
> (lines 708–15)

To sum up, Saint Plays were not a late development within an enfeebled tradition of religious drama. They embrace virtually the whole time-span of the theatre of worship itself, deriving their own strength and variety in part from liturgical music-drama (where they were confined in their subject-matter to the life of St Nicholas) and in part from the vernacular drama of Christ Crucified in the imitation of which they widened the scope of dramatic characterization and incident enormously. If, in doing this, their authors placed greater didactic emphasis upon faith and works than upon the call to repent which lay at the heart of Corpus Christi drama, they nevertheless extended not only the number of Calendar Festivals that could appropriately be celebrated by the preparation and performance of a play, but also opened the way to the recital in the theatre of the deeds, ideals, defeats, and successes of the heroes of secular legends and more modern history.

3

DRAMA OF MORAL INSTRUCTION

A. POPULAR EDUCATION

The Morality Play and the shorter Moral Interludes were self-evidently didactic in purpose. Unlike Saint Plays or Corpus Christi drama, however, they were not designed to edify through the example of others, but to illustrate in a much more personal and direct manner what traps the Devil set for the unwary; how they were baited; and how, with the aid of Divine Grace, the individual soul might recognize them for what they really were and still attain salvation. In short, such plays were primarily concerned with ethics, and the game upon which they were structured was that of war. They thus bear a close resemblance to tournaments in which the princes in the lists are God and Lucifer and the prizes for which they joust are the souls of men (see Plate 27 and pp. 152-7 below).

Morality Plays and Moral Interludes were tied neither to liturgy nor to Calendar Festivals in any strict sense. Being instructional in character their message, like that of a sermon, was appropriate at any time. On this account such plays were destined to become of particular interest to companies of actors that had banded themselves into semi-professional groups and needed a repertoire of plays to offer to audiences whenever and wherever they could be found.

Structured as combats, these plays were far more deeply concerned with argument and debate than with narrative or the portrayal of character. To be intelligible to popular and frequently illiterate audiences therefore, the arguments used had to be closely related to popular education.

The intellectual ideals which dominated the Middle Ages, and the institutions which enshrined them, had been inherited from classical antiquity and confirmed and strengthened by the early

Christian emperors. They were grounded in the well-organized libraries and in the teaching curriculum which passed into the care of the early monastic foundations. St Augustine bestowed the great weight of his authority upon the *trivium* (Grammar, Rhetoric and Dialectic) and the *quadrivium* (Music, Arithmetic, Geometry and Astronomy) as a suitable basis for Christian education. Known as the seven Liberal Arts they came to be personified as human figures in the Middle Ages, equipped with appropriate emblems to distinguish one from another. This group of ladies acquired a leader, Dame Sapience (Wisdom), the product of their collective benefits and graces (see Plate 29). And what St Augustine did for the curriculum in Christian society of the fifth century AD, St Jerome, Cassian and Cassiodorus did for monasticism. It was in the monasteries that rules of conduct were established governing the Christian way of life : and it was these rules which served first to define and then to animate figurative concepts of the eight Vices (later compressed into seven) and the corresponding Virtues. The Vices came to be popularly known as the Seven Deadly Sins – Gluttony, Lechery, Anger, Sloth, Covetousness, Envy and Pride – and became the principal agents of Satan in the fight for souls. The Virtues were split into two groups, the Four Daughters of God (Mercy, Justice, Temperance and Truth) and the Three Cardinal Virtues (Faith, Hope and Charity) (see Plates 24 and 28).

The monasteries of the sixth century served as forges in which the educational basis of classical civilization and the new moral code of Christian ethics were first welded together and then defended against the attacks of barbarian invaders. There the Latin language was assiduously cultivated and manuscripts constantly copied as a routine duty begetting in the course of time a Christian humanism that was to become the foundation not only of the Dominican and Franciscan Orders in the thirteenth and fourteenth centuries, but of the *chansons de geste* and the poetry of Dante and Chaucer.

No less important than language and literature in monastic culture were philosophy and theology, mastery of which were the ultimate goals aspired to. Until the twelfth century however, such advances as were made in both disciplines were handicapped by the spirit of localism which was an innate characteristic of a monastic foundation despite the common rule uniting all the houses that subscribed to it. The thirteenth century witnessed a great change, with the founding of universities outside and independent of the monastic schools. These new establishments stretching across Europe from Oxford and Paris in the west and Padua and Bologna in the south to Cracow in the east served to centralize knowledge and internationalize it. Interestingly enough the word *'universitas'* means 'group', 'guild' or 'corporation'; and indeed the early universities grew up on lines very similar to those of the religious and trade guilds which were discussed in the previous chapter (see pp. 66-7 above). Just as membership of a guild extended to embrace both masters and apprentices who worked under elected wardens, so the university linked its masters (the teachers) with its apprentice-teachers (the students). The University of Paris was subdivided into faculties, each characterized by special interests – Arts, Theology, Law and Medicine – and governing themselves under the presidency of a rector or chancellor. Oxford had no Faculty of Law. Students eager to make this their profession had in consequence to go to London to the so-called Inns of Court. The Faculty of Arts, incorporating as it did the old liberal arts of earlier times, was regarded as a preparatory school for study in one of the three other faculties and was thus characterized by its youthfulness. With no college system to establish discipline, in the fourteenth century the *pueri* and *clerici* of the Arts Faculties earned the universities a reputation for being centres as much of riot and debauchery as of learning. Many clerks eked out a precarious living as minstrels and entertainers to support themselves in their studies.

This must be considered as a factor of considerable consequence in the context of the transition from Romanesque to Gothic forms in all the arts, including drama. There is also a vital correspondence to be noted between the founding of the universities and the growth and influence of the new Orders of mendicant friars, the Dominicans and the Franciscans, in the course of the thirteenth and fourteenth centuries, since members of these new Orders quickly acquired an ascendancy in the government and thus over the curricula of these new educational establishments. This was destined to have profound effects upon the philosophical outlook of the late Middle Ages and to provide a synthesized philosophical and theological basis for the sociological principles advocated by the friars in their preaching. Pioneers in this movement include such famous names as Duns Scotus, William Occam, Stephen Langton, Vincent of Beauvais, Cardinal Ximenes of Toledo, Bonaventure and Thomas Aquinas. It was Thomas Aquinas who was destined to provide the Church with the liturgy for the celebration of the Feast of Corpus Christi.

Philosopher and preacher thus join hands to propagate the message that the only existing reality is individual reality, and that in consequence every individual must be himself and become responsible for his own salvation. He must be assisted to understand that Lucifer and all his devils will attack him constantly and in insidious ways in the hope of corrupting him, but that if he opens his heart to God he will be lent assistance – emotional and intellectual – that will protect him despite his own unworthiness. The methods adopted to communicate this message to literate and illiterate folk alike must be our next concern.

B. SERMONS, THE FINE ARTS AND THE DANCE OF DEATH

It is sometimes supposed that a peasantry that could neither read nor write in the Middle Ages must have been totally cut off from all philosophical, political and social discussion and thus incapable of understanding or communicating with their better educated and more affluent fellows in the social hierarchy: yet such evidence as we possess consistently argues to the contrary.

First there is the sense of community, so much stronger then than now, acting as a binding force in village, parish, guild, and walled city. This in itself permitted ideas to percolate freely as common property within the group. Next there is hierarchy itself with its own rules, its initiation ceremonies, its outward figurations of degree and responsibility in dress and blazon, and its coveted prospects of promotion which served to reinforce the sense of community. In addition, we have to include in our thinking the position of the priest in the community, and that of the fine arts when artists are working under the patronage of the Church and in the service of the people. Today we have our museums and art galleries visited by the few : then they had their churches, their taverns and their guildhalls festooned with frescoes, tapestries, paintings, wood-carvings, statues and stained-glass for everyone to gaze upon, almost obligatorily, week in and week out.

Popular stories from a wide range of sources thus found their way into pictures and became familiar to those unable to read them for themselves. Not only the Bible and the lives of local saints, but stories drawn from classical mythology and romance poetry were thus communicated to craftsmen in wood and stone and plaster who retailed them visually in an iconography that was at once common property yet distinguished by personal idioms and idiosyncrasies. The abstract personifications of the Deadly Sins, the Cardinal Virtues and the Liberal Arts found their way by similar means into the common stock of knowledge. Justice was as recognizable by her sword and scales as was Judas by his red hair: St Peter with his keys, St Catherine with her wheel, Prudence with her mirror and Envy with her snake were instantly identifiable: animals, birds, trees, flowers, and precious stones were all pressed into service as symbols to distinguish, to define and to reveal. The owl, fearful of the day and flying by night, came to symbolize Satan; so did the spider (see Plate 26). The scorpion became the emblem of Jews in Christian society, and the dolphin symbolized Christ's salvation of the soul; among flowers the lily and the iris were dedicated to the Virgin Mary, and clover to the Trinity; amongst stones and metals, gold symbolized idolatry, the carbuncle (because of its blood-red colour) Christ's Passion.[41]

If a continuous assault was made upon the eyes of men and women in the Middle Ages as part of a shared educational process, much of this process was directed at their ears and just as frequently. The principal instrument for this was the sermon. G. R. Owst in his *Literature and Pulpit in Medieval England* discusses in detail the subject-matter and oratorical techniques of the preachers who, in churches on Sundays and at market crosses on weekdays, made up for the lack of books and formal schooling in all matters of scriptural exegesis and the application of scriptural precept to personal conduct.

Dominican and Franciscan preachers (many of them schooled in the new universities, more especially in Paris) by recourse to parable, allegory and typology taught in the manner both of Christ himself and of St Paul, and found ways to make the complexities of Christian doctrine seem simple : with that achieved, they applied doctrine directly to daily life. The idea governing the allegorical *exemplum* of the medieval sermon is best paralleled, in modern parlance, by the 'cautionary tale'. By starting with an anecdote, whether historically true or fictitious, the preacher secured silence and the attention of his audience. The source of the anecdote, moreover, was immaterial: it could be secular or religious, ancient or modern, for what mattered was its relationship, by way of illustration, to the moral issue to be discussed. The *exemplum* provided the initial 'figure'. A nautical anecdote would thus provide the preacher with the figure of 'a ship on the sea' which he could then embroider and extend: if the sea is taken to represent the world, or life itself, then the ship can be equated with Christ, with Faith, with the Church. Similarly a drinking story could provide the preacher with a figure of 'a tavern and its keeper': by extension the keeper could be translated into the Devil and the tavern into Hell, and the inmates' loss of reason in the fumes of smoke and alcohol into the snares laid by the Devil in the guise of pleasures for all mankind. By the same token any story beginning with a lark, an owl and a dove in a wood at night would be more than likely to introduce a moral tale of a priest seduced into breaking his vow of chastity by the Devil.

Herein lay the critical link between Holy Writ and secular *geste* which, in the case of dramatic narrative, permitted interaction of one form of play upon another until, in the shape of Interludes, all are fused into a drama that remains essentially religious in tone however secular the text may appear to be in its outward characteristics.

At the heart of most sermons of the fourteenth century lay an exhortation to penitence coupled with injunctions 'to lay down the pomp of secular life', and reminders that eternal life, whether in heaven or hell, would last so much longer than life on earth that only fools would fail to prepare for it. On this topic the rhetoric of the preachers was skilled enough to stimulate many listeners into dressing themselves in sackcloth, smearing their hair and faces with ashes and equipping themselves with whips to redress the balance between their past self-indulgence and their present condition. In this the artists vied with the preachers in depicting a scene that came to be known as the Dance of Death. A magnificent if rather late example survives on the old footbridge at Lucerne. Originally, 63 panels of the roof carried a picture with explanatory verses portraying Death as a harvester and leading a procession of men and women from every walk of life to their inevitable graves. Battles remove some; childbirth, murder, accident, plague and disease remove others; all their finery, rank, power, strength and beauty fade into bones and dust. All these vivid images, conjured up in words by the preachers and in pictures by the painters and constantly re-iterated by both, joined up in the animate form of theatrical representation in the drama of crime and punishment (see Plates 19 and 27).

C. THE DRAMA OF CRIME AND PUNISHMENT

Unlike any other drama within the theatre of worship, Morality Plays were not tied to a particular Calendar Feast. They were not liturgical in inspiration, nor were they directly related to patronal saints. As a theatrical *ludus* therefore, a Morality Play was pos-sessed of a quality unique to itself, mobility : if successful in its own terms of reference, it could be repeated : and it could be repeated, moreover, not only on another occasion, but in another place. It thus invited the attention of any actor or producer who might have cause to consider placing play-acting on a professional basis as a means of earning a living. There can be no doubt that this thought occurred to many a troupe of minstrels in the service of the nobility in Western Europe during the last decades of the fourteenth century and the early years of the fifteenth century, and that some of them began to band themselves into small com-panies and to tour the neighbouring countryside with their plays. A good example is provided by the Account Rolls of the Obedien-taries of Selby Abbey in Yorkshire for the year 1479–80 :[42]

In reward to the players before the Abbot and convent at the feast of the Innocents	2ˢ
In reward given to the players of Sir John Conyers	12ᵈ
In reward given to the players of Sir James Tyrell	8ᵈ
In reward given to the players of Lord Scope	12ᵈ
In reward to the players of the Duke of Gloucester	6ˢ 8ᵈ
In reward given to the players of our lord the King	6ˢ 8ᵈ
In reward given to the players of the Earl of Northumberland	5ˢ

Professional exploitation of the Morality Play in the form of
Moral Interludes, however, was clearly a secular development
which owed its driving force to commercial rather than religious
inspiration and objectives. The growth of the Moral Interlude
therefore and the successes of the players of Interludes can be
more appropriately treated within the section of this book
devoted to theatres of social recreation. Nevertheless, these
developments could hardly have won the degree of popular
support that they achieved in the fifteenth and sixteenth centuries
had the ground not been thoroughly prepared for them by the
amateur initiatives that were first devised and formulated in the
three-dimensional presentation of sermons within the theatre of
worship.

To say that the Morality Play owed little to the principal
Feasts of the Christian year does not mean that it owed nothing to
the drama of Christ the King or to the drama of Christ Crucified :
it certainly adopted the ritual pattern of a fall from grace followed by a reversal that opened the way to the regaining of that
lost grace, and it took over wholesale the emblematic stage conventions of other forms of religious drama. Within that ritual,
however, there was a sharp shift of emphasis away from narrative
and towards argument with a corresponding stress placed upon
the personal responsibility of every individual in the matter of his
own salvation or damnation. Ideas inherited from classical antiquity about hubris, nemesis and the Goddess Fortune therefore
came to be coupled with the Christian concept of sin. If misfortune overtook a man, be he a prince or a peasant, the probability was that the root cause lay within his own nature : such
blows, however, need not be regarded as irreversible while there
was still time to recognize the fault, to repent and to pray for
grace.

If this was a constantly repeated message in the sermons of
Dominican and Franciscan preachers, it also found its way into
literature. In the English language these ideas find their fullest
expression in John Lydgate's *The Fall of Princes*. Lydgate however was not an innovator in this respect since he had been preceded by Laurence Priemierfait in France and by Boccaccio in
Italy : he was also deeply indebted to Chaucer's *Monk's Tale*.
There, the narrator says he will 'biwayle in maner of Tragedie'

tales of those illustrious men of high degree whose prosperity was
suddenly shaken and who were overtaken by calamity.

> At Lucifer, though he an angel were,
> And nat a man, at him I wol biginne;
> For, thogh fortune may non angel dere,
> From heigh degree yet fel he for his sinne
> Doun in-to helle, wher he yet is inne.

In the next stanza he tells of Adam's loss of Paradise and attri-
butes this to his own disobedience

> . . . he for misgovernaunce
> Was drive out of his hye prosperitee.

In this way, and with frequent repetition, the idea of the fall
from grace, regardless of a man's position in society, came to be
associated with moral weakness of character.[43] Thus, just as in
the Judgement Play of the Corpus Christi Cycles, popes,
empresses and lawyers figure among the damned as well as
among the saved, so in Morality Plays the Seven Deadly Sins are
given ample opportunity to batten upon the frailties of 'Mankind'
or 'Everyman' to bring about this fall from grace. Only when he
has awoken to the danger threatening his soul does this
generalized individual, be he 'Dux Moraud' or 'Humanum
Genus', come to realize what help God in his mercy can bring to
his aid if he will recognize the wickedness of his ways and repent.
Such plays therefore, although threatening a tragic conclusion,
are always capable of being transformed through the power of
God's redemptive love into reconcilement and a happy ending.
It is in this sense that Dante used the word Comedy as a title for
the poetic vision which he describes in *La Divina Commedia*.

If the use of the words 'comedy' and 'tragedy' brings the
Morality Play startlingly close both in spirit and in genre to
secular drama of the sixteenth century, it is necessary to recall
that the presence of allegorized personifications in the cast-lists of
German and Anglo-Norman plays of the twelfth century serves
to associate them just as closely with early liturgical music drama.
We have already had occasion to recall that Gothic Saint Plays
find early prototypes in the St Nicholas plays of the Romanesque
period, and it is no less important to remember that both Virtues
and Vices figured in the twelfth-century liturgical play of Anti-

christ from Tegernsee. This play with its battle scenes and its personifications of Heresy, Hypocrisy, Justice and Mercy warns us forcibly against categorizing Morality Plays as 'outgrowths', late in time, of Miracle Cycles or Passion Plays. So too do the brief dialogues attributed to Guillaume Herman and Stephen Langton on the subject of the reconcilement of the Heavenly Virtues (see also Plate 28). Nevertheless, when we talk about Morality Plays we are not talking about plays in Latin verse designed to be chanted, but about plays written to be spoken in vernacular languages; and if the surviving records are to be trusted these begin to make their appearance in the late fourteenth century and the early fifteenth in the Low Countries, France and England. In this Gothic context it therefore seems probable that the sermons of the friars provided a similar stimulus for the addition of this sort of *ludus* to the theatre of worship as the institution of the Feast of Corpus Christi had done in the formulation of the drama of Christ Crucified: indeed Wycliff in his *De Officio Pastorali* specifically connects the two when he remarks that 'herfore freris han tau(gh)t in Englond (th)e Paternoster in Engli(gh)est tunge, as men seyen in (th)e pleye of Yorke'.

Both begin to make an appearance in existing records at about the same time. In England the first is Wycliff's reference which I have just quoted, to the play in York in 1378: another is mentioned at Lincoln in 1397. No text of such a play has reached us, but we possess a descriptive note in respect of the York play and information relating to guild responsibility for the production of another in neighbouring Beverley in 1469. The Beverley play was divided into eight 'pagends': thirty-nine craft-guilds participated, using the same acting-areas as they normally employed for the performance of the Corpus Christi Cycle: the 'pagends' are named after the leading actor associated with each – i.e. 'Pryde: Invy: Ire: Avaryce: Sleweth: Glotony: Luxuria: Vicious'. Responsibility for the last pageant was allocated to the 'gentlemen, merchands, clerks and valets'. This again contradicts any notion that the acting of such plays was entrusted entirely to simpletons.[44]

The descriptive note on the York play states that responsibility for it rested with a special guild, *Orationis Domini*, and that 'all

1. Text and music of the St Gall *Quem Quaeritis*, tenth century

2. Text and music of the Lucerne Passion Play, as used in 1583

3. *left* Christ Pantocrator supported by the Virgin and Saints as intercessors; mosaic decoration of the walls and dome of the central apse, Monreale Cathedral, Sicily, eleventh century

4. Moses expounding the Law; manuscript illumination in the Bury St Edmunds Bible, *c.*1135

5. *above* Exterior of the
Roman amphitheatre
Arles, France

6. Roman mosaic of a bull-
baiting

7. Mosaic decoration in
St Mark's Cathedral
Venice, as depicted by
Canaletto

8. *above* Fresco of the patriarchs Isaac, Abraham and Jacob in the Coptic
rock Church of Gah, Ethiopia, fourth century AD

9. Apostles on the tympanum of the porch, Malmesbury Abbey, Wiltshire,
eleventh century

10. *above* Satan and Antichrist in Hell. From the Last Judgement in the Cathedral on the island of Torcello in the Venetian Lagoon, twelfth century

12. The Empress Theodora with her councillors. Mosaic decoration in the church of San Vitale, Ravenna, 547AD

11. *opposite below* Lucifer. Carved capital by Gisilbertus of Autun, Autun Cathedral, France, twelfth century

13. *below* Four Saints. Mosaic decoration in the Oratory of St Venantius, Lateran Baptistry, Rome, *c.*640 AD

14. The Resurrection. Illumination from the manuscript Sacramentary of St Etienne de Limoges, c.1100

15. The Three Marys visiting Christ's sepulchre. Illumination from the manuscript *Book of Pericopes* of the Emperor Henry II, c. 1010

16. King David with musicians and dancers. Manuscript illumination from the *Psalterium Aureum*, St Gall, *c*.900

17. The ascension of St Mary Magdalene. Manuscript illumination, Sforza Book of Hours, late fifteenth century

18. Self-portrait in stained glass of the Swiss painter and playwright, Nikolas Manuel, Cathedral Church, Berne, Switzerland, early sixteenth century

20. The building of Noah's Ark. Photograph of a scene from the production in 1969 of the *Cornish Cycle* in St Piran's 'Round'. Perranporth, Cornwall, by the Drama Department of Bristol University

19. *opposite* The Dance of Death. Detail from the fresco in the Campo Santo, Pisa Cathedral, Italy, late thirteenth century

21. The head of a pastoral staff of the late fourteenth century, carved, painted and gilded to represent the Adoration of the Magi

22. Visit of the Magi and the Nativity. Detail from 'The Triumph of Isabella', Brussels, 1615. This pageant-car is one of ten depicted in the painting by Denis van Alsloot, now in the Victoria and Albert Museum

3. The martyrdom of St Apollonia. Manuscript illumination by Jean Fouquet
o the Hours of Etienne Chevalier, fifteenth century

25. *left* Hell-castle. Manuscript illumination from the Hours of Catherine of Cleeve fifteenth century

26. The owl as a Symbol of Hell. Illumination in a fifteenth century manuscript of Ovid in the Bibliothèque Nationale, Paris

24. *below* The Seven Virtues. *Left to right:* Prudence, Justice, Faith, Charity, Hope, Fortitude and Temperance each being furnished with the appropriate emblems. Painting from the studio of Francesco Perellino, fifteenth century

27. *above* Battle between the good and the bad angel for the soul of the deceased. Manuscript illumination in the Hours of Catherine of Cleves, fifteenth century

EXVLERAVICTRIX LEGIO QVAR MILLE CO
Martiribus regina fides animarit inhoston
Hunc fortes focios parta plaude coronat
Floribus ardoruiq. ruber acstiner ostro

DEPVDICITIA ETES

28. *Below* Modesty challenges Lust, while *above* Faith crushes Despair (? Persecution) and offers the wreath of victory to four martyrs. Manuscript illumination in a copy of Prudentius's *Psychomachia*

29. Fortune and wisdom
with their emblems. An
early sixteenth-century
wood-engraving

30. Antichrist, alias the
Pope. An early sixteenth
century wood-engraving

32. A knight slaying a wildman. Enamelled, silver-gilt perfume case of the mid-fifteenth century

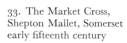

33. The Market Cross, Shepton Mallet, Somerset early fifteenth century

31. *below* A wildman and a wildwoman. Swiss tapestry of the mid-fifteenth century

34. Burlesque Tournament of Abstinence versus Gluttony, early fourteenth century

35. The Strife of Lent with Shrovetide. Painting by Peter Breughel the Elder c.1550

36. *above* Nigerian masquerade, photographed in Lagos, 1965

37. St George. Wall painting in the Chapel of Farleigh Hungerford Castle, Somerset, early fourteenth century

Dūs Galfridus louterelt me fieri fecit

9. Tournament: Sir Geoffrey Luttrel with his wife and daughter. Manuscript illumination to the Luttrel Psalter, 1340

38. *right* Tournament: Knights tilting before ladies. French, early fifteenth century

40. An 'entremet' representing the Conquest of Jerusalem performed before the
King of France and the Holy Roman Emperor in Paris, 1378. Manuscript
illumination from *Chronique de Charles V*, late fourteenth century

43. The Mummers'
Play photographed
at Marshfield,
Gloucestershire,
on Boxing Day 1970

41. The Court of Mirth.
Manuscript illumination
to the *Roman de la Rose*,
late fifteenth century

42. Biship Beckington's
Jester, Wells Cathedral,
Somerset, fifteenth century

44. Pageant-stage with mechanical rose and lily erected in Paris for the Marriage of Mary Tudor, daughter of Henry VII, to Louis XII of France, 1514.

manner of vices and sins were held up to scorn, and the virtues held up to praise'. That it was popular is proved by the fact that it was revived in 1399, 1488, 1558, and 1572. Responsibility for it passed during the fifteenth century into the hands of the Mercers in the Guild of Holy Trinity : in the sixteenth century it passed again, this time to the Guild of St Anthony. On the three occasions that we learn of it from 1488 onwards it is being performed on Corpus Christi Day, presumably as an alternative to the Cycle, and on one of them (1558) we learn that it was advertised by the crying of banns (see pp. 81-2 above).

In Lincoln similarly, although we possess no descriptive records, the Paternoster Play recurs as an alternative to Corpus Christi and Saint Plays between 1397 and 1521.

In this category must also be placed the Creed Play from York. It was bequeathed in 1446 to the Corpus Christi Guild : the prompt-book (*Originale*) described it as a play about 'the Articles of the Catholic Faith' : items of costume for St Peter, Christ and the apostles figure in an inventory of 1465 : King Richard III saw it in 1483, and it appears to have been revived every ten years from 1495 onwards until 1535. The deed of bequest states that it was to be performed 'in various parts of the said city', but from 1495 onwards performances seem to have been given only 'at the common hall'. After the suppression of the Guild of Corpus Christi in 1547 the play passed to the Hospital of St Thomas : attempts were made to revive it in 1562 and again in 1568, but it is doubtful whether these efforts were successful. In 1568 the prompt-book was submitted to the Dean of York for his approval. This was not forthcoming. His comment is highly informative.

> thoghe it was plawsible [ten] yeares agoe, and wold now also of the ignorant sort be well liked, yet now in the happie time of the gospell [i.e. the Reformation] I knowe the learned will mislike it, and how the state [i.e. the Government] will beare ite I know not.[45]

The costume items for this play suggest that it may have borne a closer resemblance to a sequence of Saint Plays or to the Corpus Christi Cycle itself than to the Paternoster Play : on the other hand it is hard to see how a play devoted to 'the Articles of the

E

Catholic Faith' could fail to be concerned with the defence of that faith against attack and thus to contain features that link it to Morality Plays.

The earliest text of a Morality to survive in England is that of *The Castle of Perseverance* which has been dated variously between 1405 and 1425. It was devised for performance, like the Cornish Cycle and the *Life of St Meriasek*, in a 'Round' and is some 3,500 lines long. The castle of the title stands where the chapel required for Part I of *St Meriasek* is placed, in the centre of the arena, and serves to illuminate visibly the close resemblance between the structure of the play and a particular form of tournament known as a *Pas d'Armes*.[46] The 'Pas' was an obstacle (originally a pass or narrow passage) to be defended by a single challenger or group of challengers against all comers. In this instance the metaphoric *Pas* to be defended is the soul of Humanum Genus. The point is made succinctly in the opening Proclamation.

> And God hathe gevyn man fre arbitracion
> Whether he wyl hym(self) save hy(s) [?soul.]

In this struggle he will be helped by a Good Angel who 'covetyth evermore man's salvation'; but he will be attacked by a Bad Angel who 'bysyteth hym euere to hys damnation'. The first round in this emblematic joust goes to the Bad Angel who succeeds within one hundred and eighty lines in introducing Humanum Genus to the World, the Flesh and the Devil. Later in the play the jousting will become fully realistic when Belial, assisted by Pride, Caro and the Deadly Sins gallop into the arena on horseback and charge the castle with lances: they are repulsed by a bombardment of red roses symbolizing Christ's blood and the redemptive power of His sacrifice (see Plates 27 and 28).

Richard Southern in *The Mediaeval Theatre in the Round* provides a detailed analysis of the staging of this play; but as he fails to notice the parallel so carefully drawn by the playmaker with this most popular and spectacular form of tournament and elects without much warrant to fill the *platea* with spectators, little confidence can be placed in this analysis. As one of the most elementary rules of any *ludus,* athletic or mimetic, is a well-defined *separation* of the areas reserved respectively for performers and spectators, it seems more prudent to read the

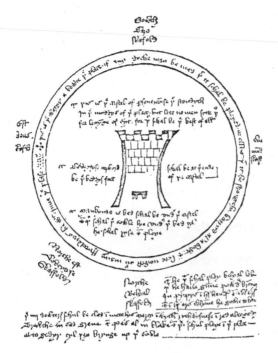

11 *The Castle of Perseverance*: ground-plan of the stage arrangements as depicted in the original manuscript, early fifteenth century

ground-plan of this manuscript, along with those of the Cornish plays, as meaning what they say, and thus accepting the lack of any provision for an audience *in* the ground-plan as indication that provision was made for it *outside* the acting-area. A recent production of the Cornish Cycle in St Piran's 'Round' has at least proved conclusively that with scaffolds set on the top of the bank and ladders connecting the scaffolds to the *platea,* ample room remains to accommodate spectators in an orderly fashion on terraces on the inner side of the bank and to supply them all with a full and unimpeded view of all the action both on the scaffolds and in the arena (see Plate 20). This arrangement has the additional advantage of ensuring that whatever spectacular effects may have been planned and provided for in the arena they are not set at risk by the presence in it of a large and unpredictable crowd. To suppose that the committees of management who took such meticulous pains to secure order and discipline in every other aspect of their preparations for large-scale open-air performances should have ignored this hazard and left it to a few ushers (stylers) to control crowds allowed to stand in the acting area is about as likely as to presume that the directors of top division football clubs today would admit supporters to the football pitch itself as well as to the stands.[47]

Bound together with the manuscript of *The Castle of Perseverance* are two other plays; one is known alternatively under the titles of *Mind, Will and Understanding* and *Wisdom* (i.e. the Wisdom that is Christ); the other is simply called *Mankind*. Both are much shorter than *The Castle* and less spectacular; but both follow the same basic pattern of construction. In the latter Mercy and Mischief serve as protagonist and antagonist respectively while in the former these roles are given directly to Christ and Lucifer.

Other notable plays in the genre in English that have survived to us are *Mundus et Infans, The Pride of Life* and *Everyman*.

12   The Castle for a *Pas d'Armes*, College of Arms manuscript, early
      sixteenth century

The second of these reaches us from Dublin and the third may be a translation of a Dutch original.

All five plays share several features in common. They are all of fifteenth-century provenance; they are relatively short, none of them taking much more than an hour to perform; they all have small casts, and, clearly, can as easily be acted indoors in a hall or on a simple booth stage in the open air. In short they are transportable and could form a useful part of the repertoire of a travelling company : on the other hand the instructional element and the emphasis upon repentance are so paramount as to make it seem probable that these plays were prepared initially for 'special' audiences of the sort that might be anticipated in a school, a university or a priory where it would be normal to assume that profit must be mixed with pleasure for pleasure to be justified, even on a holiday. They would thus be ideal for inclusion in the repertoire of companies like those of Sir John Conyers or the Duke of Gloucester when visiting Selby Abbey as they did in 1479-80 (see p. 111 above). When, a year later, 'the players of the town of Beverley' visited the Abbey a section of their Paternoster Play of the Seven Deadly Sins would have been appropriate, had they lacked anything newer or better.

Despite the essential seriousness of the themes which gave Morality Plays their name, their usefulness to quasi-professional groups of actors depended very largely upon their acceptability to the audiences of the banquet hall and the fairground who paid for them; and the nature of these environments, in both of which alcohol was readily accessible, made humour a desirable commodity. It is this factor which best explains the frequent association of Morality Plays on the Continent with plays of a farcical character. In France it is often difficult to distinguish with strict precision between *sotties, moralités, farces* and *entremets.*[48] Humour could be provided in situation, character, dialogue, or in any combination of the three. When the humour is confined to the dialogue we may think of it as wit : when it provides the fabric of the plot in the basic situations of the piece, it clearly approaches farce in our sense of that word : and when it informs character, the clown and the buffoon come into their own as the principal sources of entertainment. A fine example of a short play in which all these characteristics are blended within a story that points a serious moral is provided in the Dutch *Het Esbatement* *van den Appelboom* (The Miraculous Apple Tree).* It starts seriously with a dialogue between two peasants, Staunch Goodfellow and his wife Steadfast Faith whose tribulations resemble Job's. God appears and rewards them by offering to grant them whatever they ask for.

> *Staunch Goodfellow:*
> Praised be the Lord! Boundless in his Grace! Thus I pray, then, adoringly, that You might grant it of Your mercy that our apple tree may stay eternally fertile, bearing fruit throughout the year, winter and summer; and also that whosoever comes along and climbs it to our despite, that he shall stick fast in the tree till my own command releases him.

Suffice it to say that when Insatiabilty, Riotous Living, Loose Wanton, Death and the Devil appear the seriousness of the opening sequence gives place to farcical humour of both character and situation.[49]

German parallels may be found in the *Fastnachtspiel* with its extensions into the *Neidhartspiel*, where the *Narr* (Fool) and dancing are prominent features, and which culminated in the plays of Hans Sachs in the sixteenth century. Dancing was also important in Spanish plays of this sort, the *entremés, pasos, sainte* and *farsas* of the late fifteenth and early sixteenth centuries, a dance of the 'Seven Virtues and Seven Sins' being presented as part of the Corpus Christi Festival in Madrid as late as 1579. Of these dramatic forms the *farsas sacramentales* seem to have approached the Morality Play of Northern Europe most closely. These include a *Farsa llamada Danza de la Morte*, by a cloth-shearer named Pedrazza and published in 1551. It was out of such plays as these that the fully allegorical *autos sacramentales* of the late sixteenth and early seventeenth centuries were destined to develop.[50]

That a similar variety of dramatic entertainment existed in England early in the fifteenth century is made clear enough from a prohibition issued in London in 1418. This stipulates that

> . . . no manere persone, of what astate, degre, or condicioun that evere he be, durying this holy tyme of Christemes be so

* ed. P. J. Meertens, Leiden, 1965.

hardy in eny wyse to walk by nyght in any manere mommyng, pleyes, enterludes, or eny other disgisynges with eny feynyd berdis, peynted visers, diffourmyd or colourid visages in eny wyse . . .[51]

Two English pieces which in their message resemble Moralities but which in their melodramatic and near tragic narrative could just as fittingly be described as 'plays' or 'enterludes' are the so-called *Croxton Play of the Sacrament*, and the piece known by the name of the title role, *Dux Moraud*, since we only possess this actor's part.[52] The former, already referred to in the context of Uccello's predella in Urbino (see p. 90 above), foreshadows Marlowe's *The Jew of Malta*, and the latter concerns itself with incest and murder a century before these matters are treated in *Hamlet*.

The paradox, therefore, that is implicit in the sudden proliferation of words used to describe dramatic entertainments presented in the late fourteenth and early fifteenth centuries all over Europe coupled with the lack of descriptions or definitions to distinguish one precisely from another, indicates that social, commercial and artistic pressures were already exercising strong influences upon drama in a recreational context. By this time the ritualistic qualities and stage conventions of liturgical music-drama, the narrative techniques of vernacular Corpus Christi drama, the biographical approach to drama developed within Saint Plays, and the structural assets of physical combat and verbal argument formulated within Morality Plays were all available for imitation, adaptation, contraction or extension in secular and professional circumstances.

In my opinion it is this variety or possibility, covered with the novelty of professional as an alternative to amateur approaches to these possibilities, that best explains the advent of the Interlude and with it the inauguration of a new era in theatre history. There is thus a constant ambiguity about the English Interlude and its Continental equivalents throughout the fifteenth and sixteenth centuries. It was at once the property of amateurs and professionals, adults and children : in subject-matter it could be strictly religious and devotional, secular and recreational, or an amalgam of both : in tone it could as easily become farcical as tragic.

Part II:
Theatres of Recreation

4

DRAMA AND NATURE

A. CLIMATE, SEASONS AND AGRICULTURE

One may approach the subject of drama as a leisure recreation in medieval Europe from at least two standpoints. First, we may view it in terms of Celtic, Roman, Teutonic and Norse customs which had been absorbed into social life before the coronation of Charlemagne as Holy Roman Emperor: alternatively, we may view it in terms of the musical, literary and mimetic entertainments which troupes of minstrels were commissioned to provide in baronial halls at a later date.

Although the second of the alternatives appears at first glance to be the more obvious, the first should not be completely overlooked; for it is in the occasions for revelry within the agricultural year and in the places used for the mimetic games associated with them in a pre-Christian era that we may discover how a secular theatre, independent in origin from the theatre of worship, grew up in Europe in the course of the Middle Ages.

As we have seen in the preceding three chapters, all forms of drama in the theatre of worship, with the single exception of Morality Plays, were not only tied to Calendar Festivals but owed their very nature and quality to those of the festival itself: and yet, behind these Christian festivals – Christmas, Easter, Saints Days – lay other and much earlier festivals which the missionaries and their successors had endowed with new meanings. Thus in AD 601 Gregory the Great instructed St Augustine at Canterbury at the hands of Abbot Mellitus not to destroy the fanes [i.e. pagan temples].

> Destroy the idols; purify the buildings with holy water; set relics there; and let them become the temples of the true God. So the people will have no need to change their places of

concourse, and where of old they were wont to sacrifice cattle to demons, thither let them continue to resort on the day of the Saint to whom the church is dedicated and slay their beasts no longer as a sacrifice, but for a social meal in honour of him whom they now worship.

Herein lies the origin of those 'Church Ales' and churchyard banquets that were so to disturb Philip Stubbs and other Puritans in Elizabethan England; but the passage quoted also warns us to anticipate the survival of cult and customs as well as buildings and festivals. Within the new religion, as E. K. Chambers remarked,

> The chief thing required was that the outward and visible signs of the connexion with the hostile religion should be abandoned.

And as he went on to observe,

> It was of the customs themselves that the people were tenacious, not of the meaning, so far as there was still a meaning, attached to them, or of the names which their priests had been wont to invoke. Leave them but their familiar revels, and the ritual so indissolubly bound up with their hopes of fertility for their flocks and crops, they would not stick upon the explicit consciousness that they drank or danced in the might of Eostre or Freyr. And in time, as the Christian interpretation of life became an everyday thing, it passed out of sight that the customs had been ritual at all.[1]

In England, when Augustine came, these customs were in some districts Celtic, in some Roman, in others Norse and Teutonic; in some, an amalgam of two or more. All, however, had a common source in the climate, in the seasons, in food and survival, and thus ultimately in energy. Loss of energy terminating in death, and the renewal of energy culminating in procreation, provided the constants and the polarities linking the old religious beliefs of successive generations and cults with those of the Christian fathers who themselves preached life eternal beyond the grave in the person of a risen Christ.

It is thus to the routines of agriculture, to the sowing and harvesting of corn, to the insemination, birth and slaughter of pigs, sheep and cattle, that the peasant communities of the early Middle Ages returned year in year out when decorating their festivals with dances and mimetic games. The days and weeks chosen for these celebrations had come to be denoted in the Calendar by the names of Christian saints and commemorative Feasts, but the recurring cycle of the agricultural year still linked them with the winter and the summer solstices, 23 December and 23 June, the vernal and the autumnal equinoxes, 15 March and 15 September, and the attendant phenomena of nature – tides, rain, sunshine, frost – on the correct and continuing sequence of which survival so self-evidently depended. Ploughing, the gathering of hay, the shearing of sheep, the harvesting of corn, fruit and grapes, the slaughtering and salting of cattle, and the burning of offal and fallen leaves thus acquired a special significance which successions of primitive peoples learned to externalize in figurative rituals. With the blade of the plough and the maypole employed as phallic emblems, together with the flames, smoke and ash of the bonfire used as symbols of death, and with the sword, the garland and the circle serving the same purposes in both contexts, country people were possessed of objects that could form the basis of mimetic rituals designed to encourage fertility, growth and survival in the face of recurring threats of destruction and death.

> Room, room, brave gallants all,
> Pray give us room to rhyme;
> We're come to show activity,
> This merry Christmas time;
> Activity of youth,
> Activity of age,
> The like was never seen
> Upon a common stage.
> And if you don't believe what I say,
> Step in St George – & clear the way.

This introductory verse for the Presenter of what Chambers described as a 'normalized' version of the Mummers' Play preserves, in its stress upon the word 'activity', that concept of energy which was deemed to be so essential to survival and to stem in the final analysis from the sun.[2]

If the cult of energy and of its source, dimly descried in the sun, was at the centre of primitive religions in Europe, the ritualized forms of this cult ranged widely through every conceivable magical incantation and charm which climate, seasonal phenomena and the local landscape suggested as a means to evoke its blessings. Sword-dances, scarf-dances, stick Morrises, King-games and May-games survive to remind us of these charms and incantations: truncated and mangled as the forms may be in which they have reached us, vestiges at least of the original rites and their purposes are sharply enough defined to be recognizable still.

The Sun-King that conquered winter and ruled in summer is still to be descried behind St George of the Mummers' Play and Robin Hood of the May-game, the one owing his place to Christianity, the other to romantic songs and ballads. St George's adversary, the Turkish or the Moorish Knight, survives from the Crusades : sometimes both have been replaced by more topical heroes from the Napoleonic or other wars : local history also adds its details, and serves to shift date and occasion backwards or forwards in the Calendar, dislocating one custom from another and attaching it to a different festival. Strolling players bring new disguises and new jokes; dialect blurs vowels, elides consonants and corrupts old texts. Drunkenness, brawls and alleged rapes provoke injunctions and prohibitions which in their turn cause breaks in tradition; and when customs come to be revived failures of memory and inexperienced newcomers between them account for further changes.

It is in this state that the customs that were once an organic part of primitive religions in rituals acknowledging changes in the seasons and the climate have reached us today. It is thus necessary to approach them all with great caution, for it is as easy to jump to false conclusions about the origin of each of them as it is tempting to endow them all with a significance to drama and theatre that they never actually possessed.

B. FOLK FESTIVALS

The number and variety of medieval folk festivals is as intimidating as it is astonishing. How was it possible for such relatively unsophisticated communities to support so many festivals? Why did they take so many forms, each with so many variants? Where can use of the word 'play' in the context of these festivals be interpreted as drama in our sense of that word, and where was it used to mean only a recreational game? Where should a historian draw the dividing line between a Plough Play and a sword-dance, between a sword-dance and a Morris dance, between a Morris dance and a May-game, between a May-game and the Mummers' Play? And, since so much of what recorded information survives about all these secular activities reaches us from ecclesiastical sources, how can they be properly regarded as manifestations of a wholly secular theatrical tradition rather than a religious one?

Answers to all these questions only begin to become apparent after it is realized that the customs in question represent some aspect or aspects of a primitive cult, and that most of them had long since become dislocated from their original places and purposes in the seasonal cycle of Celtic, Teutonic or Roman religious rites and had subsequently become attached to another festival within the much more highly organized Calendar of the Christian year.

This is no place to offer a detailed analysis of these progressive dislocations and attachments: it is enough to observe that behind all the folk festivals of medieval Europe at some point between the start of the Christian era and the development of human society lie four moments in the year that were recognized as critical to mankind : two in March and September when the balance between daylight and darkness were in exact equilibrium, and two more in December and June when the ever-increasing hours of darkness and of daylight respectively stood still and then moved into sharp and evident retreat.

It can be said with certainty that all the festivals of primitive religions in pre-Christian Europe took note of this dualism in nature and of the correspondences between darkness and daylight, cold and warmth, life and death. Whether these correspondences were observed in terms of the seasonal changes in the physical world of trees, plants and animals, or in the remoter world of the heavens, or in both, is an open question. What matters is that the changes manifest in the progress of winter towards spring, and of spring towards summer, or of those evident in the translation of summer into autumn and autumn into winter were all regarded as important enough to be worth celebrating. The festivals which resulted from these observations and the deductive thinking that accompanied them were thus rooted in December (mid-winter), March (spring), June (mid-summer) and September (autumn); but the dualism implicit in the occasion was also reflected in the rituals that grew up to mark the festivals. Thus the festivals were invariably Janus-like in character, being forward and backward looking simultaneously and contained features exemplifying both characteristics. Evergreens and children, were as much objects of veneration in the December festivals as were sacrificial rejection cults in March and April. It was this dualism at the heart of all four seasonal festivals which accounts for the shifting of particular customs from one festival to another when a new religion came to be imposed upon its predecessor. Several such dislocations and reattachments had already taken place by the time Christianity had established itself as the single religion of Northern and Western Europe : the substitution of a Christian Calendar, therefore, of universal application, only served to accelerate this process and to fulfil the hope expressed by Gregory the Great in the sixth century (see p. 125 above) that if Christians would not abandon venerated customs, they would at least come to forget the pagan idols and demons in honour or fear of whom the customs had originally been instituted.

i. WINTER FESTIVALS

The growth of the twelve-day Feast of Christmas in the Christian Calendar has already been examined in the context of theatres of worship (see pp. 41-51 above). By the time that the Easter Introit began to receive overtly dramatic treatment in the liturgy in the tenth century, this festival had already attracted to itself most of the customs originating in the earlier cults and associated with the period late October to early January. There was an exact correspondence between Christmas Day itself and the day dedicated in the Roman Calendar to *Sol Invictus:* there was a similar, if more approximate correspondence between the Roman Kalends 1–3 January and the Christmas Epiphany or Twelfth Night (6 January). The Roman Saturnalia with its *Rex Saturnalitius* (Winter King) had been celebrated on 17 December; the customs associated with this boisterous festival of inverted social status and folly had only to be advanced a week in time to find themselves absorbed within the Christmas festivities of the Christian world. Thus the *vota* (goodwill greetings to the emperor), *strenae* (gifts and offerings) and masquerades of the Roman mid-winter festivities all came to be transferred to the twelve-day Feast of Christmas, as did the Fool King in the context of relaxed and inverted social hierarchy already noticed in the Boy Bishop and the Feast of Fools (see pp. 50-1 above and Plates 41-3).

In so far moreover as the Christian vigil of Advent was itself a prologue to Christmas, so the November and early December festivals of Celtic, Norse and Teutonic religions became absorbed into Christian Feasts of the Advent and Christmas period collectively. Notable among the customs associated with these festivals were sacrificial rites, the cult of omens and prophecy and the veneration of trees and shrubs which defied snow and ice by retaining their leaves and fruits. These customs re-emerged in the group of Feasts within the Christian Calendar starting with Hallowmas on 1 November and continuing through All Souls (2 November), St Martin (11 November) and St Andrew (30 November) to St Nicholas Day (6 December) and incorporating Feasts particular to the Virgin Mary: they did so under such names as *Todenfest*, Wassail and Yule.

Yule with its logs, Wassail with its cakes, apples and cider, Martlemas (lit. St Martin's Mass) with its beef, and Halloween with its masquerades, ghosts and bonfires all reveal ideas originally derived from harvest, sacrifice and the death of the year, which found new forms of expression in the carols, mummings, sword-dances, banquets and 'potations' of Christian communities in medieval Europe. Another of these was the hobby-horse, an inanimate and vestigal survivor of the man who in wearing the head and skin of the newly sacrificed animal had formerly become the living image of a tribal God.[3]

ii. AUTUMN FESTIVALS

In the Christian Calendar the three-month period from the beginning of August to the end of October was the deadest and dullest of the whole year. Starting with Lammastide (1 August) and ending in Hallowmass (1 November) this quarter of the year contained many Saints' Days including those of the Apostles

Matthew and Luke, but only one major Feast, St Michael and All Angels (30 September).* This may be explained to a great extent by the fact that in the agrarian communities of the early Christian era the late summer and early autumn was one of the two busiest seasons of the year : the corn harvest, succeeded by the fruit harvest and the wine harvest, made heavy demands on labour both in the fields and in the markets, and with the coming of frost and snow, scarcity of pasture made it necessary to slaughter large numbers of sheep, cattle and geese.[4]

In the course of time some of the customs particular to this season of harvest became dislocated from their original source and were transferred to one or other of the winter festivals, notably those elements most closely associated with death. Others, however, survived within their proper season and coalesced around the great fairs which marked the successful completion of the harvest in the marketing and sale of ale, cloth, food, fuel, skins and wine against the winter. Many of these fairs came to coincide with a local Saint's Day and culminated in a carnival, the most outstanding feature of which was a torchlight procession. Many of the fairs continue to this day, having attracted to themselves in the course of time the additional attractions of fireworks and illuminated floats. In England these festivities are especially vigorous in the West Country where in villages like Priddy on the edge of the Mendip Hills the annual sheep fair in August reaches back in unbroken line for over six hundred years, and where in towns like Bridgwater the citizens claim the right to stage their annual carnival in early November, despite the traffic chaos and damage to property, by virtue of a charter received from King John. In the fifteenth century, Bath supported a *Rex Autumnalis*, and so did neighbouring Wells. This may have been a harvest equivalent of the May King in spring and thus a vestigial fertility figure; but it may also have been a corn-stook effigy due to be executed and burnt on a bonfire, and thus a survival from a time remote in the past when animal and even human sacrifice provided the rites with their *raison d'être*. In many places, however, a figure of this kind, constructed in autumn and crowned with a garland was carefully preserved through the winter to be rejected

---

* October 9 was dedicated to SS Simon and Jude, and this was destined to become important in England in the sixteenth and seventeenth centuries as the date chosen to celebrate the election of a new Lord Mayor of London (see pp. 168–71 below).

and destroyed in the spring, the head being cut off and used as a football.

The dominant feature of the autumn festivals distinguishing them from those of mid-winter was the essentially domestic aura of the customs. Centred on the home, the dances, games and songs look backwards to departed ancestors and forwards to children as yet unborn. In the Christian year the former came to be attached to the Feast of St Michael or that of All Souls, while the latter were absorbed in Feasts dedicated to the Virgin Mary and to St Nicholas between 8 September and 6 December.

iii. SUMMER FESTIVALS

Two dates repeat themselves in the context of summer festivals which eclipse all others in importance, until the start of the fourteenth century when a third came to rival them both. The first was that of the summer solstice, 23 June : for Christians midsummer night was also the vigil of the Feast of St John the Baptist, which was followed a week later by St Peter's Day : both were major Feasts.[5] For Christians, however, both of these Feasts were of less general consequence than the three-day holiday of Whitsuntide or Pentecost; but from 1313 onwards the new Feast of Corpus Christi, occupying the Thursday following Trinity Sunday, came slowly to take precedence over them all for reasons already discussed (see pp. 59 ff. above). Following the Reformation this Feast was suppressed in Protestant countries in the middle of the sixteenth century, after which time Whitsun and the summer solstice, or 'Midsummer Watch' as it was frequently called, resumed their former dominance as the principal festivals of the summer months.

The fact, however, that both Whitsun and Corpus Christi were 'movable' Feasts dependant in date on that of Easter in any year, and not fixed in the Calendar like St John the Baptist's Day or Midsummer Day, inevitably served to dislocate many customs particular to high summer, and to attach them to spring festivals instead, in much the same way that many autumn rituals of primitive religions drifted in Christian Europe towards the mid-winter Feasts. The strength of this drift and its effect is illustrated in this couplet from William Warner's *Albion's England* of 1586 :

At Paske [Easter] began our Morrise, and ere Penticost our May.
(v. 25)

Spring in any case is the season subject to maximum variation in Europe in relation to latitude and climate; for where in Spain or Italy almond blossom may be expected to appear in March, in Scandinavian countries no flowers are likely to be seen before April. It is thus both simpler and more convenient to consider the customs of the summer festivals as part of an extended spring festival beginning at the end of February and lasting until late May or early June.

iv. SPRING FESTIVALS

In Christian Europe, Easter Day was placed on the first Sunday following the first full moon after 21 March. Stretching behind it for forty days lay Lent, introduced by the festivities of Shrovetide; following Easter by five weeks were the Rogation Days which immediately preceded Ascension Day and which were succeeded two weeks later by Whitsuntide. Trinity Sunday was a week later still, and the Feast of Corpus Christi was allocated to the Thursday immediately following it. Thus the entire range of 'movable' Feasts linked liturgically with Easter spanned a period of slightly more than three months – fourteen weeks and three days to be precise. As always this period included its quota of Saints' Days; but only one of them acquired any special importance of its own; that was St George's Day, 23 April.

Perhaps the best way to approach the folk festivals is in terms of the varied moods of this extended sequence of liturgical Feasts since this has a marked bearing on the question of the attachment of the customs originating in primitive religions to new locations in the Christian Calendar. First, then, it should be noted that the long vigil of Lent with its obligatory fasting and penances corresponded with the tail-end of winter when stores of food and fuel were running dangerously low. Ash Wednesday, so called because of the penitential garments of rough sack-cloth and the faces disfigured with embers and ashes, introduced this six-week period of enforced abstinence which reached its nadir on Good Friday, commemorating Christ's crucifixion, deposition and entombment.[6] As if to stir up sufficient energy and zeal to face this prospect, the three days preceding Ash Wednesday, known as Shrovetide, were given over to festivities which encouraged and permitted indulgence in every form of pleasure that was about to be denied. Revels were the order of the day – and so was licence. Thus in many countries Shrovetide came to be better known as Carnival.

At the other end of Lent lay Easter and the joyful celebration of Christ's harrowing of hell and resurrection from the dead. Easter, however, was much too sacred a commemoration in a spiritual sense for Christian joy and thanksgiving to be allowed to degenerate into the revelry and licence of Carnival. If physical release from the restrictions of Lent was to be obtained, this had to accommodate itself to other occasions and opportunities in subsequent weeks : chief among these were St George's Day, the first day of May and, several weeks later, Whitsuntide, when Ascension Day and the days of supplication known as Rogation Days immediately preceeding it were safely past.

The customs which this frame of Christian liturgical practice had to absorb were, broadly speaking, twofold : customs figuring the rejection of winter and customs derived from fertility cults welcoming spring. With the date of Easter being calculated from the datum point of the vernal equinox this was not difficult to accomplish. Sacrifice and sexual intercourse had formed the basis of the rites from which most of the customs had originally derived; both remained so explicitly self-evident within the customs as to arouse the implacable hostility of all Puritan sects in the sixteenth century and to give Ben Jonson the chance to ridicule the latter in *Bartholomew Fair*.[7]

The principal customs in which the original sexual and sacrificial ceremonies were still blatantly apparent in the sixteenth century included the processions associated with the dressing of holy wells and the beating of the parish bounds, the rough games of football, tug-of-war, and hocking (involving the capture of a victim), dances centred on swords, staves and maypoles together with mimetic games employing disguise and dialogue devoted to the Lord and Lady of May, Robin Hood and Maid Marion, wildmen and women and giants. One or more of these elements obtruded through the customs associated with every major festival from Shrovetide to the Midsummer Watch : and behind them all lie the love lyrics of the wandering scholars of the twelfth and thirteenth centuries. For these, as Helen Waddel put it, '. . . are the poets of February, when this year's birds begin calling in the twilight trees, of January itself, those days of incredible sweetness, the first stirring of the blood, the first mounting of the sap, so much more poignant than the full burgeoning.'

Three of these customs warrant special attention – mumming, sword-dances, and the May- or King-Game.

Mumming

Mumming was the name given in England to the masquerades of Shrovetide and New Year's Day. Like all disguise, that of the early mummers served simultaneously to conceal the identity of the individual and to release his (or her) inhibitions. In the early Middle Ages, however, there is no evidence that permits us to suppose that women were ever included in the mummers' ranks: men frequently enough dressed themselves as women, but never women as men. Although the costumes adopted were no longer the skins of sacrificial victims, the environment of Carnival encouraged those disguised to indulge in sexual, criminal or seditious activities that they would never have undertaken at other seasons of the year when easily recognizable by their neighbours and acquaintances. Church and State both took strong exception to the practice which appears to have been easier to suppress at Shrovetide than at New Year when the principal object of the mumming was either to present gifts or to raise money for food and drink.

The importance of mumming to drama lay not in the custom of mumming *per se*, but in the basis which it provided for development into drama in a more sophisticated and strictly secular environment. Given disguise and processional visitation in conjunction, a need could arise quite naturally for a Presenter or Expositor to explain the purpose of the visitation and to introduce the silent visitors according to their rank, names and station within the chosen masquerade. His simple, explanatory prologue or epilogue could in turn be extended into a running commentary in dialogue form. This happened both in town and country during the fifteenth century; and whenever it did so mumming survived the formal prohibitions of ecclesiastical and civic authorities, and adopted for itself new names particular to the place, the occasion and the nature of the game devised to celebrate it. Among the nobility mummings ornamented with music, song, dance, scenic decoration and simple texts developed into Disguisings which in the sixteenth century were translated into Masques.[8] In country districts mumming survived in the simpler contexts of folk-dance, athletic trials of strength and processional games.

Sword-dances

Essential to the sword-dance as it has survived to us is a fiddler or piper, a singer and dancers equipped with swords or staves. A hobby-horse, a man dressed as a woman (the Bessey) and a fool (the Tommy) are frequently present in addition, together with a collection-box.[9]

It is virtually certain that the sword-dance developed out of sacrificial rites signifying the expulsion of winter; but that it could also figure the death of summer followed by its magical resurrection is also clear. Thus the sword dance has survived in two distinct forms. At the simpler level of children's games and fairy-stories, the shorter version lingers in 'Oranges and Lemons' which concludes with the symbolic chopping off of heads, while the larger version forms the basis of such stories as that of the Sleeping Beauty which, not surprisingly, has found its way back into dance in the most famous of all classical ballets.

In its folk form, however, the sword-dance is reminiscent of war-dances, wooing ceremonies and sometimes both : it can also contain an execution and a revival or cure. In some cases it is provided with a substantial, if often incomprehensible, text : in others it has lost all semblance of mimetic ritual and survives only as a piece of relatively elaborate choreography.

Historically, references to dances of this kind can be traced back to Tacitus and his observations of such customs among German peoples in Roman times.

> *genus spectaculorum unum atque in omni coetu idem. Nudi*
> ... a type of game is invariably played at every assembly
> *iuvenes, quibus id ludicrum est, inter gladios se atque infestas*
> object of which is for naked youths to jump over and
> *frameas saltu iacient. Exercitatio artem paravit, ars decorem,*

between sharp swords and threatening spear-points. The
non in quaestum tamen aut mercedem: quamvis audacis
lasciviae
purpose of this feat is to execute it gracefully, not money or
pretium est voluptas spectantium.
other gain: the reward lies in the fun of the risks taken and in
the pleasure of the spectators. (Tacitus, *Germania,* 24).

From the middle of the fourteenth century onwards, when we hear of it as a folk *ludus* in Nuremberg, references to such customs became widespread in Europe in the context of festivals between Shrovetide and Whitsun : in England their special habitat was, and still is, the North and North Midlands.

Astonishing as it may seem, the swords which characterize this dance or game may well not have belonged to the original ritual from which the dance-ceremonies are derived. That the basic ritual took the form of a linked circular dance around a sacrificial victim seems certain; but the links could as easily have been sticks, staves or strips of cloth in the first instance. As it became necessary to explain the ritual, the sword or dagger that was used both to kill the bull, goat or other sacrificial beast and as an emblem of the male sex-organ, came to be adopted as the link itself in the circular dance. Further rationalizing of the ceremony in the interests of comprehensibility led in time to a representational performance or *ludus* (play, game) which externalized and made explicit the significance of the ceremony. Thus in some places the swords were used as links in the circular, clockwise dance symbolizing the movement of the sun, were locked round the neck of the dancer (the clown, 'lack wit' or weakling), and then withdrawn with a loud grating sound figuring his execution. Some scholars have argued that the lock represented resurrection rather than execution, interpreting the circle of the lock itself as a female emblem : placed over the head of the chosen male dancer it is thus made to symbolize union in the sex-act.[10] However this may be, surviving texts make it clear that much stress in the mimetic game was laid on the sexual prowess of the leader or 'King' and his companions compared with the lack of it in their victim. The latter dropped to the ground, once the swords were released from the lock, and was then buried. In the extended version of the game, a doctor is summoned who then supplies the victim with an elixir which revives him. In one English play, as the victim rises, he says,

> Good morrow gentlemen, a-sleeping I have been;
> I have had such a sleep as the likes was never seen;
> But now I am awake and alive unto this day,
> And now we'll have a dance, and the Doctor
> must seek his pay.[11]

The final dance and the passing round of the collection-box among the spectators conclude the ceremony.

Considerable variations are to be found in the character of the sacrificial victim. For instance there are the feeble-witted clown and the epicene woman-man (the Bessey) of modern survivals: behind them lie the nameless victims of Jack o'Lent (sometimes associated with Judas Iscariot) and Jack in the Green who, in their turn, are transformations of the 'woodwose', wildman or green man. The latter of course found his way into literature – most notably in *Sir Gawain and the Green Knight* – as well as into drama, and still survives today in the signboards hanging above many pubs of that name unrecognized for what he is by the customers[12] (see Plates 31 and 32).

Of the texts accompanying the sword-dance game which survive to us none can be dated earlier than the eighteenth century. From these it is evident that on to such narrative as may have existed in earlier times have been grafted the names of heroes and enemies of modern wars and corrupted texts of scenes from playhouse comedies scavenged from strolling players. Nevertheless the recurrent and predominant features of the anti-clockwise circular dance, the swords, the heroes and their combats, the epicene victims and their deaths and resurrections proclaim clearly enough the dramatic origins of these customs in rituals celebrating the rejection of winter and the greeting of spring. It is not surprising, therefore, that many of these elements are to be found repeated in the dances, games and plays associated with Hock-tide, Plough-Monday and, above all, with the month of May.

Hock-tide was widely celebrated on the Monday and Tuesday, a fortnight after Easter; but only in Coventry does a text appear to have accrued to the strange game incorporating a sword-fight of men capturing and binding women who must then sue for their freedom, the roles being reversed on the following day.[13] By contrast the Plough Play was confined to Nottinghamshire and Lincolnshire. A plough is dragged round the village by boys harnessed to it : with them go the Bessey, St George and a number of other characters including a Lady, a young lover and a doctor : the theme of the play, however corrupt the text, is invariably a wooing. Some plays interpolate a combat between the courtship and the wedding, others do not. Plough Monday itself fell on the Monday after Epiphany and thus well before Shrove-Tuesday. It was accepted by the Church, the plough itself being blessed and the collection which the gamesters had formerly gathered in their own self-interest being turned to the benefit of the church. Those who refused to contribute ran the risk of finding that the ploughboys had revenged themselves by turning their plough to its proper use on the offender's lawn and garden.[14]

Mayings

By the sixteenth century the Church had in many places come to terms with May-Day customs as it had done with those of Plough-Monday. By 1445 'pageants, plays and May-games' had become the responsibility of the Guild of Holy Cross at Abingdon in Berkshire. Churchwardens' accounts from East Anglia, Shropshire, Somerset, Surrey and Kent include frequent and fairly regular entries for both expenditure and income in connection with May-games. By this time such games had come to acquire alternative names such as 'King-game' or 'Robin Hood-game'. Nevertheless, in none of the customs associated with folk-festivals is there such ample evidence of the innate conflict between Christianity and the rites of earlier heathen religions; and although an accommodation of sorts was arrived at in many places during the fifteenth and sixteenth centuries, the hostility of the more serious-minded clergy towards these customs manifested itself with increasing force as Puritanism began to attract followers in the early decades of the seventeenth century, and finally succeeded in suppressing them.

There is not the slightest doubt that the principal cause of this hostility was rooted in the seuxal licence which these customs celebrated and actively promoted. Puritan preachers of Elizabethan times like Philip Stubbs and Stephen Gosson were so certain in their minds what the principal cult-objects of Mayings

– the maypole and the May-Queen's crown – represented as to equate them directly with Dagon, Baal and other Philistine idols.[15] Earlier Catholic bishops like Robert Grosseteste at Lincoln and Walter Chanteloup at Worcester in the thirteenth century had sought to ban these customs. Grosseteste specifically instructed the archdeacons in his diocese to forbid

> *alios ludos quos vocant Inductionem Maii sive Autumni ...*
> other games called the Induction of May, or that of Autumn.

Chanteloup was equally specific in telling his clergy to put a stop to

> *... ludos fieri de Rege at Regina, nec arietas levari, nec*
> King-and Queen-games, ram-raisings*, public
> *palaestras publicas fieri, nec gildales inhonestas.*
> wrestling matches, and indecent ceremonies.

In the fourteenth century the Chapter of Wells Cathedral was still trying to expel these games from within its own precincts : since dancing girls figured prominently in the games, as records from London, Oxford and other places testify, it is not hard to see why. Yet these injunctions appear to have had only sporadic effect, for it is precisely this custom which Philip Stubbs found it necessary to castigate in his *Anatomy of Abuses* of 1583 when he said,

> ... and in this sorte they go to the Church . . . dancing and swinging their handkerchiefs over their heads, in the Church, like Devil's incarnate, with such a confused noise that no one can hear his own voice. Then the foolish people, they look, they stare, they laugh, they fleere, and mount upon forms and pews, to see these goodly pageants solemnized in this sort. Then after this, about the Church they go again and again and so forth into the Church yard, where they have commonly their summer halls, their Bowers, Arbours and Banqueting-houses set up . . .

Much later still the young Milton in his 'Ode to the Morning Star' could still recognize the spirit that underlay this custom making it doubly offensive :

* Possibly ram-horns on the top of a Maypole.

Hail bounteous May that doth inspire
Mirth and youth, and warm desire.

Frequently – too frequently for the May-game's critics – warm
desire found its fulfilment when, as Beaumont and Fletcher put
it,

The morris rings, while hobby-horse doth foot it feateously;
The Lords and Ladies now abroad, for their disport and play,
Do kiss sometimes upon the grass, and sometimes in the hay.

They might well have added 'and sometimes in the woods at
night' when, on the excuse of gathering branches of may-blossom
and other flowers for the next day's revels, the youth of town and
village escaped for one night in the year from the watchful eyes
and gossiping tongues of their neighbours to enjoy personal freedom from the taboos of society, whatever the consequences, in
the privacy of darkness and the trees.

It is this association of the May-game with the forest that
served in many places to equate the Lord and Lady with Robin
Hood and Maid Marion. When this association of the *Rex et
Regina* of the traditional game was first made is unknown; but it
had attracted literary attention, at least in France, before the
close of the thirteenth century when it became the subject of a
short pastoral play by Adam de la Halle. *Le Jeu de Robin et
Marion* presents Marion as a shepherdess and Robin as her rustic
lover: their romance is challenged by a travelling knight who at
first outwits Robin but is later outwitted himself by Marion:
interpolated into the action are many songs and dances. This was
a play for courtiers, not peasants.[16]

In England a tradition of heroic songs celebrating Robin Hood
in his struggles with King John and the Sheriff of Nottingham
grew up independently of the French pastoral songs devoted to
Robin and Marion. Sir Edmund Chambers advanced the hypothesis that in the course of time these two traditions fused to
form a new legend of Robin Hood and Maid Marion, the Lord
and Lady of May: it seems a likely one and has not been
challenged. To this hypothesis I would add another, namely that
both traditions fused with a third – that of the 'woodwose' or
wildman or green man of the forest and his wild lady clothed only
in long hair and leaves and equipped respectively with a club

and a garland (see Plate 31). However that may be, by the close of the fifteenth century the corporation of Wells described this season of the year as *hoc tempus de Robynhode* and specified 'puellis tripudiantibus' (dancing girls) as part of it, while the Paston letters some thirty years earlier provide evidence of a play of Robin Hood in East Anglia. Three fragmentary texts of such plays have survived. One of them can be dated *c*.1475 and seems likely to be the play referred to in the Paston letters. It is an exceptionally interesting piece in that it relies for its structure almost entirely upon a sequence of athletic games. Robin meets a knight with whom he engages first in archery, then in stone throwing, then in wrestling and finally with swords. The Knight is killed and Robin decapitates him.

> *Robin:* Now I have the maystry here.
> Off I smyte this sory swyre;
> This knyghts clothis wolle I were,
> And in my hode his hede woll bere.

A battle follows involving Friar Tuck and the Sheriff of Nottingham and there the fragment ends.*

The other two fragments are of much later vintage. One is a play of Robin Hood's enrolment of Friar Tuck and the other of Robin Hood's exaction of tribute from a potter to the 'chiefe governoure/under the grene woode tree' : both involve challenges and fights. They were first printed by William Copland *c*.1560. Both employ Robin himself as a presenter who introduces each play as a recital of a particular story.

> Now stand ye forth, my mery men all,
> And harke what I shall say;
> Of an adventure I shal you tell,
> The which befell this other day.[17]

This is the most familiar formula of all compères' introductions and can be repeated *ad infinitum* as the ritual opening to an endless variety of short dramatic incidents. Several of them interspersed with songs and dances could thus be made into a full

---

* The editors of the Malone Society edition have provided this play with a speculative conclusion scripted from a contemporary ballad (see *Collections*, I, pp. 117–24); they have also reprinted the plays commissioned by Henslowe from Munday and Chetlle between 1598 and 1601 under the titles of *The Down fall* and *The Death of Robert, Earl of Huntingdon Otherwise Called Robin Hood of Merrie Sherwood* (Reprints 196415).

day's game : all of them could be as easily repeated or varied in subsequent years.

The dances were sometimes processional and sometimes rounds. Helston in Cornwall still offers an example of the former, while Painswick in Gloucestershire and South Petherton in Somerset provide examples of the latter. A particularly spectacular variant survives from Abbots Bromley in Staffordshire where the dancers are equipped with antler head dresses.[18]

The cult of neo-classicism in literature and drama in the first decades of the seventeenth century led by Chapman, Fletcher and Jonson provided yet another opportunity to embellish folk plays with sophisticated extension and ornament : this was deliberate imitation of the pastoral setting of 'Satyr' plays modelled on those that were supposed to have existed in the Greek classical theatre. Fletcher led the way in England with *The Faithful Shepherdess*, a pastoral tragi-comedy written for the King's Men in 1608–9. Jonson and Shakespeare both provided a dance of Satyrs for the same company shortly afterwards, Shakespeare in *The Winter's Tale* and Jonson in *The Masque of Oberon*. It was Jonson, however, who seized on the old English Robin Hood play and developed it into a full-scale tragi-comedy entitled *The Sad Shepherd*. The manuscript was found among his papers after his death and no date can be firmly attached to it. In the Prologue he states,

> His scene is Sherwood, and his play a Tale,
> Of Robin Hood's inviting from the vale
> Of Belvoir, all the shepherds to a feast :
> Where, by the casual absence of one guest,
> The mirth is troubled much, and in one man
> As much of sadness shown as passion can.[19]

The mood of this play is nostalgic; and Jonson shows himself to be as keenly aware of the attack being mounted on all rustic games and festivities by the Puritans (described in Act I Scene 2 as 'the sourer sort of shepherds') as he is in his defence of the fairground jollifications that provide the plot and setting of *Bartholomew Fair*. *The Sad Shepherd* can therefore be said to be an epitaph for all May-games as well as being the zenith of the genre.

C. THE MUMMERS' PLAY

Three full-length studies of this strange processional dance and mimetic game with dialogue have appeared in print during the past fifty years: R. J. E. Tiddy's *The Mummers' Play*, E. K. Chambers's *The English Folk Play* and Alan Brody's *The English Mummers and their plays*. This of itself shows what interest this play has aroused and still retains for anyone concerned with the development of drama in Christian Europe. However, it is far harder to pin down the precise influence that this play may have had upon more sophisticated types of drama, religious or secular, at any time from the tenth century onwards: indeed, an objective examination of the evidence suggests to me that it may have had very little, and that such traffic as there was between folk-plays and other dramatic entertainments flowed in the opposite direction.

The first fact that has to be faced is that while Mummers' Play texts have reached us from many parts of England, none of them can be given an earlier date than the eighteenth century. The lack of texts from any earlier period is normally explained away by recourse to the theory that illiterate peasants transmitted them orally from father to son and never wrote them down. Yet even if one accepts this rather dubious premise (and it is surely curious that no poet or diarist from Chaucer to Pepys should have even described such a play) one still cannot trace any of the named characters in any version of the play back beyond the Crusades.

The second fact that warrants equally serious attention relates to the special quality of the corruptions that litter the surviving texts making many passages incomprehensible. Since it has been proved that between the eighteenth century and the present day the play has continuously been absorbing names, jokes and even incidents from topical events and debased versions of recognizable metropolitan plays performed by strolling players on tour in the provinces, it seems likely that the texts received and written down by eighteenth-century observers had been equally roughly treated in preceding centuries.

On both counts therefore it seems necessary to make a distinction between content and form in any discussion of the possible influence of the Mummers' Play on other forms of drama. In my view it is also necessary to give much greater weight to the part

played by the 'gathering' or collection of money invariably associated with any performance of the play in keeping it alive over the
centuries than is normally the case in books about the play's place
in folk-lore and in drama.

i. THE PLAY'S FORM

The form of the Mummers' Play is familiar enough. A Presenter
– usually Father Christmas, Headman or Fool, but occasionally
a Devil or an old woman – calls out a Champion, having first
cleared a space for the action. This Champion's name is frequently St George or Prince George. He is followed by an antagonist –
sometimes the Turkish Knight, sometimes the King of Morocco,
sometimes Slasher. They fight and the Champion kills his boastful
antagonist. A doctor is called for who effects the corpse's resurrection. Characters equipped with musical instruments and
collection-boxes then appear to take money off the spectators
while a dance is performed. The central combat can be extended
and supplemented by subsidiary characters; and the dispute that
leads up to the combat can be related to rival claims to a woman,
frequently the King of Egypt's Daughter. The form is thus constant in essentials, and there is no reason to doubt that the
mimetic ritual is of itself of great antiquity (see Plate 43).

ii. THE COLLECTION

So great is the range and size of charitable foundations and
endowments in urban society today that it is difficult to realize or
recall how limited are the resources of country villages for raising
funds of any sort. Indeed it is extraordinary how money continues
to be found in sufficient quantities to repair the fabric of
churches, their organs, and their bells, or to furnish parish halls,
or to improve the amenities of the sports field and pavilion. In
these circumstances it is still the pennies contributed to sales of
work, whist-drives and so on that the villagers themselves donate
over long periods of time which make the difference between the
success or failure of such appeals to public generosity. Like the
annual harvest supper and the local flower-show, the Mummers'
Play, wherever it is performed, has long been used to raise funds.
The performers have themselves been primary beneficiaries in

that the collection taken from the spectators pays first for their own refreshments; it is the surplus that passes on to the local charity or charities in most need of support. Family pride plays its part in this and accounts for the fact that particular roles pass automatically from father to son rather than being open to public audition.

Once these commercial aspects of the play are understood, it is easy to appreciate how responsibility for organizing and arranging the performance becomes restricted to a small group of villagers resembling a guild, and how the Church could reach an accommodation with groups of this sort in respect of Christmas, May- or Whitsun-games. It is the games' usefulness as a fund-raising device that in many places protected them against the attacks of their detractors and ensured their survival. No less important were the social and competitive aspects of possessing a notable mimetic game; for this not only brought visitors from other parishes in the district into the village to see it (as flower-shows, gymkhanas and football matches still do), but gave the villagers a commodity that could be readily exported, thus making life more enjoyable for the performers while swelling their funds as well. Villages today that can mount a good darts or skittles team enjoy similar advantages. It is in this sort of context then that we must approach such expense accounts as the following recorded by the Churchwardens of East Harling in Essex :

1457 Paid for bread and ale when Lopham Game came to this town ij[d]. For bread and ale to Garblesham Game vj[d].

1463 Item, in expenses, when Keningale Game came to town at Wrights vj[d].

1467 Bread and ale to the Keningale Players.

1494 Received of a Church ale, made the Sunday before Mid-summer when Keningale and Lopham came hither xviij[s] ij[d].[20]

Thus the village of Blighborough in Suffolk visited the village of near-by Walberswick with its May-game on at least four occasions between 1489 and 1495 : Tilney, in Norfolk, celebrated Plough Monday from 1440 onwards and the Wardens of All Saints Church recorded in 1490 the collection of 'Pascal Silver' *in ecclesia* (5s. 10d), 'May Silver' *in villa* (7s) and 'Plough Silver', also *in villa* (6s. 5d). In the early years of the sixteenth century

F

the churchwardens of St Mary's, Bishop's Stortford, occupied themselves with both Hocking and May 'Ales'. And who, we may ask, were the men that earned xvj^d for playing before the Mayor of Dover in Kent on the last day of December, 1467, xx^d 'for a play at cristmasse' in 1470, and iij^s iij^d on 3 January 1476?[21] Neighbouring Lydd presented a play of St George in 1455–6 and paid xviij^s vj^d for it; in 1484–5 they gave v^d to 'the Players in the hyghe strete': New Romney gave iiij^s in 1532 'to Robyn hode players of Hythe'. The St George play in Lydd was a much larger and more spectacular drama than might be imagined at first glance; at least it had become so in the early sixteenth century. In 1526 it was substantially revised by a Mr Gybson of London and is described as 'the life of St George': by 1533 it occupied four days of performance. The town of Bassingbourne in Cambridgeshire also possessed a play 'of the holy martyr St George': this too was elaborate, and twenty-seven villages in the neighbourhood contributed towards the costs of production. This is a far cry indeed from the simple Mummers' Play; but the Lydd and Bassingbourne examples warn us explicitly that by the sixteenth century the Mummers' Play was no more immune from much more sophisticated literary and theatrical treatment than the Maygame in the guise of the Play of Robin Hood[22] (see Plate 37).

iii. CONTENT

Granted that almost everything to do with the Mummers' Play prior to the eighteenth century is speculative and hypothetical, I can see no reason why the texts that reach us then should all be in such chaotically corrupt form, or why the corruptions should vary as they do with locality unless what we are dealing with is what was left after the wholesale emasculation of the theatre in the provinces in the late sixteenth and early seventeenth centuries. The work of the Ecclesiastical Commissions, in suppressing local religious plays during the reign of Elizabeth I, followed by the steady withdrawal of touring professional companies between the accession of James I and the outbreak of the Civil War, succeeded in divorcing provincial towns and villages from all previously maintained standards of playwriting and play-production: and unlike London the provinces failed to regain a professional theatre at the Restoration. It took another hundred years before playhouses in the Georgian style began to be built as a new amenity in the wealthier provincial towns.[28]

When these facts are taken into account, it seems to me that the hypothesis which best explains the content of the Mummers' Play in the texts we possess is this. Like other folk-games derived from the rites of pre-Christian religions, the ceremonies associated with the figurative rejection of winter and the welcoming of spring that give the Mummers' Play its own particular form were deliberately allowed to continue by the Christian Church provided always that they were first purged of those elements that were wholly incompatible with Christianity, and then moved in the Calendar to the nearest and most appropriate Christian holiday. In this way the Mummers' Play, along with Plough Games, Hocking, and May-games, acquired a new lease of life in songs, dances and athletic trials of strength appropriate to the season of the year : the Church, in reaching this accommodation with local tradition and sentiment, had to remonstrate on occasion against abuse of its own tolerance, but it was also glad to share in the practical expressions of charity that these festivities stimulated in the participants.

With the passage of time and with the growth of both romance literature and religious drama many of these games came to be expanded and ornamented with texts, until, by the close of the fifteenth century if not before, the major religious festivals were celebrated in many towns and villages with the performance of a well-organized, scripted and rehearsed play with a Lord of Misrule as the Presenter, St George or Robin Hood as the hero and a Turk or an oppressive baron as the villain. All this while and until the Reformation it is the folk-festival that is in debt to literature, music and drama for its growing strength and energy in small communities, not vice versa : with the Reformation the tide began to turn. For a brief period the professional writers of lyrics and stage-plays, as they moved into the ascendant in Shakespeare's lifetime and as they became attracted to pastoral themes and plots, return the compliment and borrow heavily from country revels in both a nostalgic and a mocking vein. It is in this manner that 'Whitsun pastorals' find their way into *The Winter's Tale*, 'Pentecost pageants' into *The Two Gentlemen of Verona*, and theatrically minded clerks and artisans respectively into *Love's Labour's Lost* and *A Midsummer Night's Dream.* George Peele, Ben Jonson and Beaumont and Fletcher are equally indebted in their plays and masques to the plays and games of town and country fairs and festivals that were threatened with disappearance by the swelling tide of Puritan disapproval (see pp. 141-2 above). As this attack was spearheaded by the extremists within the reformed Church, so the traditional partnership between Church and folk-festival collapsed and the customs had either to survive on their own (frequently in the face of vicious opposition) or die out. In the hundred and fifty years between the start of this onslaught and the return of more tolerant days in the latter half of the eighteenth century, all such games withered from malnutrition, and those that emerged alive did so in a severely debilitated condition with the texts lopped and truncated, dialogue mangled, and characters degraded or translated into scarcely recognizable ghosts of their former selves. These are the sword-dances, Plough-Plays, Wassails and Mummers' Plays familiar to us. That they have survived at all is due as much to their abiding ability to provide their performers with free cakes and ale as to any other reason.

5

DRAMA AND NATURAL MAN

A. COURTYARD, HALL AND CHAMBER

Although most of the palaces, castles and monasteries of medieval Europe are now romantic ruins or so heavily altered by subsequent generations as to be virtually unrecognizable for what they once were, these buildings were designed and constructed on strictly utilitarian lines.

The life of their owners was conducted partly in public and partly in private; and this distinction is the first of several common factors to be noted about all such buildings. The private apartments of the sovereign, baron or abbot formed the heart of the building. These rooms included one known as 'the chamber', a large, open room furnished to allow the owner to relax in comfort with his family and friends. The official responsible for the upkeep of these private apartments was the chamberlain.

Adjacent to these rooms were those of a semi-public character that met the needs of everyone else in residence. Chief among these were the hall or refectory and the kitchen presided over by the steward. On all occasions of a ceremonial or festive character the owner would normally feed in the hall with his guests and retainers. Its size, moreover, made it the most convenient locality for any public entertainment provided for the recreation of the assembled company at night or in the winter months. Thus the hall of the palace, or castle, in Carolingian Europe was at least a potential rival to the cathedral or church as a suitable locality for mimetic entertainments, and communal singing and dancing.

Outside the protective walls of the private and public apartments lay the courtyard, designed to accommodate the needs of visitors, tradesmen and garrisons together with their horses. Responsibility for this area was entrusted to the marshall. He too, together with the steward, was normally responsible for such entertainments as were arranged in an open-air environment in the park or its neighbourhood.

All three of these areas – the chamber, the hall and the court-yard or park – offered opportunities for social recreation : the size and character of each imposed itself in turn upon the nature of the recreation provided and the audience admitted to it : thus entertainment in the park or courtyard was virtually a public spectacle while that in the chamber was almost as invariably intimate and domestic. The owner's personal jester or musicians could also be called upon to move out of the private apartments in order to entertain a wider public in the hall on festive occa-sions, while travelling minstrels could just as easily be invited into it from the outside world and earn a specific reward. The hall, therefore, by virtue of its position and function in the whole edifice and its environs, came to be by far the most important of the three in the subsequent development of entertainment of a specifically dramatic character, since it was there that all forms of strictly secular pastime, intimate and domestic on the one hand and public and popular on the other, fused into the wide range of sophisticated pleasures that Henry VIII, Machiavelli and Catherine de Medici regarded as the proper environment of a renaissance prince. Thus in the sixteenth century the hall emerged not only as the natural locality for singing, dancing and amateur masquerades, but as the forum for the presentation of Interludes, opera and ballet.

Paradoxical therefore as it may seem, it can fairly be claimed that where the theatre of worship moved steadily outwards in its development from the centre of the roofed and enclosed basilica to courtyards, streets and market-places, the theatre of social re-creation moved in the opposite direction, collecting and concen-trating its energies in the course of its development just as steadily upon the hall.

B. WAR-GAMES

The growth of tournaments both in number and scope during the tenth and eleventh centuries was not a matter of chance : it was an aspect of the deliberate antiquarianism of the age that placed the collection, study and imitation of Roman art high in its order of cultural priorities.

Sculpture and bas-reliefs of the Roman occupation were avidly collected in France, and museums were established to house them: the realism of Roman painting was admired and copied, thus leading to the creation of interesting tensions with Byzantine formalism within the Romanesque style of art and architecture.[24]

A similar interest arose in Roman *ludi*, mimetic and athletic, possibly as much derived from pictorial illustrations on vases, sarcophagi and mosaic floor-tiles as from literary descriptions. Where the nobility were concerned, athletic games – especially those of a military nature – took priority over the scenic ones. This interest was at first neither esoteric nor aesthetic, but strictly practical: it developed within the context of battle-schools to train young knights in the arts of war as understood and practised in the tenth century. The name given to these para-military exercises in Normandy was 'tournament'.[25]

It often happens, when one age self-consciously imitates another, that the product created, although echoing past precedent, is distinctively new: the tournament is a case in point. Central to this medieval *ludus* is the figure of the knight. In one sense this figure had as an ancestor the Roman *eques*, whose place in the social hierarchy of the old Empire lay between the senator and the plebeian: but in another sense he was something unknown to Roman imperial society – a landowner by virtue of his military service who fought as a cavalryman in time of war. By the tenth century, leadership in military technology had passed to the Franks and Normans; the Bayeux Tapestry supplies many illustrations of the knight on horseback armed with a heavy lance (the weight of which rested ultimately on his stirrups), and protected by a long, pointed shield.

If the knight's military equipment was French, his relationship to his social superior was German in origin: tied by a solemn oath to protect his overlord in arms, this vassalage earned him his land. By the eleventh century, this was regarded as a privilege, rather than as a demeaning duty, since by then knights were freemen and since force of arms virtually determined political power. Against this background knights themselves acquired a measure of independence and, within the local boundaries of their own territory, responsibility for law and order.

The custom of knighting reached England with the Norman Conquest and, with it, the idea that the knight should lead his troops into battle, the infantry being regarded as the support-troops for the cavalry. Skill in this art had to be acquired; and it was in providing this training that early tournaments found their justification. Understandably, these militaristic and frequently lethal exercises aroused the hostility of the Church and provoked a succession of Popes into trying to stop them : but, as with earlier heathen rituals, the Church found it more expedient to control them by acknowledging their existence while trying to inspire in the knight himself a sense of Christian idealism. The concept of the Church Militant, and that of the individual in arms to serve Christ, thus fused with a sense of privilege born of a long tradition of knighthood to make 'honour' the prime goal of the knight himself and 'chivalry' a word of extraordinary potency in medieval society.

> The realities of war, the ideals of the Church, the pride of noble families, the records of heralds, and the researches of lawyers all contributed to give the cult of knighthood an ardent following. Without the splendour of secular ceremonies and the flights of fancy of the romances, however, its flame would never have been so bright.

Here Richard Barber sums up his study (*The Knight and Chivalry*) of the status of the knight in the Middle Ages. It is this link between the knight himself and ceremony and literary romance that served to bring the *ludi circensis* of the tournament into conjunction with the *ludi scenici* of the banquet hall : the catalyst was woman, considered as an object both to be served and entertained.

Ladies began to attend tournaments in the latter half of the thirteenth century, by which time these battle-schools had been both regulated in the field by governments and associated with romantic aspirations in secular literature by poets. Slowly, single combat became fashionable, sometimes on horseback, sometimes on foot, and acquired the name of the joust. A competitor then had the choice of the tilt which was a joust on horseback with spears, or the barriers, which was a joust on foot with swords. Single combat of either type served to stimulate the competitive element in this rough sport, giving the knight that fame which he prized so dearly, a development which the presence of ladies as spectators could only encourage. In this way the arts of war became associated with those of love and courtship, that of self-protection and preservation with that of survival into the future through procreation; the Court of Chivalry with the Court of Love (see Plates 38 and 39). Remote though these barbaric games may seem to us, they were not greatly different either in spirit or in inspiration from those of teenage gangs in urban areas today, when the girls among them cast the taunt of 'chicken' at the boys and vandalism follows; only in their outward forms and in their social basis were they wholly different; for tournaments were restricted to the nobility. Thus the participants – the knights and the ladies in whose honour the violent and dangerous feats of daylight hours had been enacted – together with the judges, all moved into the palace or castle in the evening to celebrate outstanding victories and feats of bravery with feasting, singing, dancing and the award of prizes.[26] The ceremonial character of these proceedings quickly acquired a ritual quality, ornamented with martial and visual pageantry. Granted the vivid nature of the combats at the centre of this ritual, the outcome of which was always uncertain, each tournament resembled an epic drama acted out in real life. In the course of the fourteenth century a new dynamic was given to the dramatic quality of tournaments in these sophisticated circumstances by the addition of a new form of combat, the *Pas d'Armes*. This consisted of some obstacle which a spirited challenger could offer to defend against all comers. In the wake of this development followed an allegorical preamble, or prologue, to explain the obstacle and the presence of the knight or knights defending it. The obstacle was usually some tower, gateway or other artificially constructed object which was made to house a lady or ladies in whose service the knight or knights had pledged themselves to accomplish deeds of unprecedented valour. In England a special variant of the tournament was that social gathering of knights and their ladies known as a Round Table.[27]

The direct imitation of chivalric literature in Round Tables and in *Pas d'Armes* led naturally to the elevation of ladies from the role of mere spectator to that of initiator and presiding genius; and in such circumstances gallantry came to eclipse skill and the costs of participating came to restrict participation to the few who could still afford the privilege. Even so, tournaments continued, in some measure, to fulfil their original function as

F*

training schools in cavalry warfare until the end of the fifteenth century when the invention of gunpowder made the knight in armour an anachronism on the battlefield. From then until the early years of the seventeenth century tournaments lingered as a Court prerogative and were translated into 'soft and silken wars' conducted in the tiltyard by day and in the banquet hall as the climax to a masquerade by night[28] (see Figure 12).

The implications of these remarkable war-games for the development of mimetic games, both secular and religious, were many and important. They encouraged the growth of spectacular ceremonial in a strictly secular context and helped to formulate a code of identification devices within the conventions of heraldry that rivalled those of the Church in Christian iconography. Carefully regulated auditoriums had to be constructed surrounding the lists, some circular, some rectangular.[29]

Perhaps most importantly, they created forms and images that fired the imagination of society at large and served in consequence to feed literature, the visual arts and drama with stories, emblems and actions, both enriching composition and construction and ornamenting style with lively detail in the process.

Thus the Wakefield Master depicts Christ on his cross as a knight on horseback about to enter the lists (see p. 90 above); the author of *The Castle of Perseverance* sees the Castle of his title as the obstacle to be defended in a spiritual *Pas d'Armes;* and Henry Medwall entertains Cardinal Morton's guests with a bawdy parody of a joust in *Fulgens and Lucres.* A little later, when professional impresarios want an auditorium for the baiting of bulls and bears they have only to copy the example of the organizers of tournaments to know how to construct one. Costumes and scenic devices derived from pastoral and chivalric literature, together with pageant cars imitative of Roman triumphs and replete with the iconography of classical mythology, paraded the lists by day and entered the banquet halls at night to rival the spectacle which the promoters of the theatre of worship were providing for their audiences in monastic courtyards, market squares and earthwork arenas. Like the customs derived from the early religious rituals of the folk, tournaments provided patterns derived from a variety of types of combat that were dramatic in form and thus liable to attract the attention of men of letters required by their masters to provide sophisticated masquerades, interludes and plays to distinguish festive occasions from working days. By these means they came to exercise an influence upon the professional theatre of the sixteenth and early seventeenth centuries both for their spectacular quality in plays like Shakespeare's *Richard II* or *Pericles*, and as short dramas in their own right like Ben Jonson's Masques at Barriers.

C. SEX-GAMES

The devotion so ostentatiously displayed by a knight towards his lady in the organizing of tournaments may suggest to modern minds that medieval chivalry and marriage were related by romantic bonds never rivalled since. The fact is that love had little if anything to do with the selection of a marriage partner : such partnerships were arranged by parents and firmly geared to property and its inheritance in the parents' own interest. Marriage at fourteen was not unusual and the engagement of bride and groom could take place when they were less than half that age. Christianity had failed abjectly to civilize society in this respect since clerics were vowed to celibacy themselves and viewed women either disinterestedly or as the bait by which Lucifer could most easily bring a man's soul to hell. Marriage was regarded as a state that was permitted to laymen in part because laymen were, by definition, too weak in a moral sense to take and keep vows, and in part because it did something to reduce and control the lawless violence of lust while permitting the begetting of children.

Love, nevertheless, was an emotion experienced so widely and so deeply as to be impossible to ignore. In a society that placed marriage as an institution on the same level as a business transaction, it is scarcely surprising that love was treated as something at once instinctive and to be valued in a context outside and above marriage.

The late Professor Trevelyan in discussing this subject in his *English Social History* observed :

> Since, therefore, love was not the normal basis of marriage, the Troubadours of Languedoc at the end of the Eleventh Century, and the French and English poets who succeeded them in chanting the service of a pagan 'God of Love',

regarded the passion of love as being under no obligation to respect so irrelevant a thing as the marriage bond.

He went on to add,

> The great gift of the mediaeval poets to the Western world was this new conception of the love of man and woman as a spiritual thing – the best of all spiritual things, raising men and women above their normal selves in all gentleness and virtue.[30]

Nevertheless, in a Christian society (and notwithstanding the Church's condescending attitude towards marriage contracts) a glaring discrepancy existed between this idealized view of love as irrelevant to marriage and the seventh commandment: 'Thou shalt not commit adultery.' It thus became one of the principal preoccupations of the Court of Love to discover means to bridge this gulf: one answer was found in secrecy, another in constancy between lover and beloved, and a third in zealous protection of the personal reputation of all parties involved. This of course included not only the lovers but their husbands and wives and their respective families. The involvement of families could thus bring sex-games perilously near to war-games where honour was at stake.

The difficulty of maintaining this delicate balance produced codes of conduct that were very elaborate and carefully observed. The need for decorum brought with it a language of emblems, signs and tokens. In personal attire, ribbons, jewelry and flowers acquired special meanings; portrait-miniatures, gloves, rings and other personal adornments were exchanged, worn as favours and cherished above all other possessions; even colours acquired an emblematic significance of their own. Constancy, in its turn, provoked feats of daring and endurance, especially in the knight, in part to keep devotion alive and in part to secure devotion's rewards. Honour, since secrecy and constancy in extra-marital attachments were its mainstays, came into a different category: its ultimate protector was the joust *à outrance*, or duel to the death.

The fact that the knight, in pursuit of fame and honour, was more often an absentee from his own home than in it made the fulfilment of *amour courtoise* much easier than might otherwise have been the case; but the penalties for breaches of the code were harsh. Divorce was difficult; but social ostracism and virtual incarceration were not. In such conditions festivities that permitted a relaxation and even a reversal of normal codes of conduct and social hierarchy were welcome, none more so than the masquerade or mumming : for not only did disguise conceal identity and release inhibition, but it encouraged secret flirtations that would otherwise have been an obvious affront to honour. Mummings and Disguisings therefore swiftly attained recognition as a formal pastime within courtly revels and proved far too precious in that environment to fall a victim to the injunctions and prohibitions which crippled and destroyed civic mummings in the early decades of the fifteenth century. Further encouragement was provided in romance poetry which succeeded in justifying courtly love by idealizing it. Thus Robert of Brunne could write in *Handlying Synne*

> There is no such solace under heaven of all
> that a man may have, as the true love of a good woman.[31]

Héloise and Abelard, Tristan and Iseult, Arthur and Guinivere were only the most famous of the romantic lovers that fired the imagination of the twelfth century : for it became the fashion for the scholar poets, then and in succeeding centuries, to sing the praises of their own ladies in lyric verses. Set side by side with the epic poetry of the *chanson de geste* lauding the exploits of crusading knights, a new and intoxicating vision of the world was born in Provence that owed as much to the sagas of the Northern scôps and gleemen, and to the views and language of Horace, Ovid and Virgil on love and heroism, as it did to the aspirations of contemporary Christian society.

The growth of this new poetry has already been discussed in the context of language (pp. 57-9 above). Here therefore it suffices to add that in France, the poets acquired the name of *trouvères*, and that during the thirteenth century they both aspired to the status of gentlemen in society and surrounded themselves with musicians, acrobats, jugglers and other entertainers who travelled as troupes under their leadership. It was to the advantage of both to stick together; for the entertainers (known collectively in France as *jongleurs* and in England as *tregetoures*) depended on the social standing of the *trouvère* to gain entry to the homes of the nobility, while the *trouvère* himself gained and maintained his prestige through the reputation of his troupe. Known as minstrels they entered the service of the larger land-owners as household servants and became entitled to wear their lord's livery. Queen Eleanor of Aquitaine, the wife of Henry II, introduced them to England, and the fashion which she set was quickly followed. By the close of the fourteenth century minstrels were both sufficiently numerous and strongly enough entrenched to claim guild status both in Paris and London.[32] This pattern was copied in Germany and Austria, but with differences of emphasis; here the singers and poets acquired the name of Minnesingers. And just as it had proved possible for the most joyous miracles of the Christian faith to be commemorated by physical re-enactment in drama, so it was possible for these minstrel troupes to attempt translation of these visions of mortal love and courage from recitals by a single poet into mimed action by a group of *lusores* or players. That this process had begun before the close of the fourteenth century is amply documented in contemporary prose and verse. The Siege of Troy and the Conquest of Jerusalem by Geoffrey of Boulogne were both presented as dramatic entertainments in Paris in palace halls in Chaucer's lifetime. The way was thus wide open before the fifteenth century began for the rapid growth of entertainments devoted to love, war and honour, that were secular in content and dramatic in form.

Both plays and masquerades, however, despite their popularity, yielded pride of place among the sex-games of the aristocracy to dancing. Ordered as it was with extreme formality and decorum, it nevertheless brought the sexes directly together, permitting eyes to exchange looks, hands to touch and words to be spoken: in the dance therefore genuine courtship could start from physical contact in households so designed and ordered as to make segregation of the sexes the normal order of the day. It is thus by no accident that even in the sixteenth century Romeo should meet Juliet or Benedict court Beatrice within the stately measures of a dance. Indeed, I would myself go so far as to assert that as the nucleus of drama within Christian worship was song, so in the secular environment of social recreation the nucleus of dramatic entertainment was dance.

D. MUMMINGS, DISGUISINGS AND MASQUES

The practice of masquerade and mumming, so popular at New Year and Shrovetide, proved firmly enough entrenched in medieval society to survive the formal prohibitions of Church and State as effectively as it had already deflected the hostility of Christian missionaries in earlier centuries. It simply changed its skin like a snake, and re-emerged in new guises, both civic and aristocratic.

A description of an English mumming in the old style survives from 1377 when the Lord Mayor and the citizens of London rode across the bridge to Kennington to visit Richard II. On this occasion the mummers assumed the disguise of popes, cardinals and African princes carrying gifts: the visitation, coming at this season of the year, has an obvious association with the Calender Festival of the Epiphany and is reminiscent of the activities of the *Compagnia de Magi* in Florence (see p. 102 above). On this occasion they rode to the palace on horseback by torchlight carrying their gifts with them: on arrival they were given audience by the young king, played a game called 'mumchance' with loaded dice with him, thus ensuring that he would win the gifts as a prize: they then danced among themselves on one side of the hall, the courtiers dancing just as formally on the other. They left as mysteriously as they had come.[33]

No other descriptions of civic mummings as vivid as this one have survived to us; but that this practice enjoyed wide popularity is clearly established by the survival of several texts of official prohibitions, from the fifteenth century. One of these, issued in London in 1418, I have already quoted (see pp. 120-1 above): another issued in Bristol in 1479 requires '... that no maner of personne of what degree or condicion that they be of at no time this Christmas goo a mommying with close visageds ...' The reason is made obvious enough since this command is linked with orders forbidding walking in the streets at night without a lantern, candle or torch, and prohibiting the wearing of any weapon 'wherbye the Kinges peas may in any manor wise be broken or hurt ...' The penalty for any infringement of these orders was a fine or imprisonment.[34]

The Court however was above its own laws; and so one

suspects were the nobility when immured in their own castles. Required by the archbishops to abandon the Feast of Fools as a liturgical ceremony in churches, they did so; but they continued to maintain and encourage a personal fool and a Lord of Misrule in their own domains. Likewise required by the king and his sheriffs to abandon mummings that permitted subjects of whatever degree free entry into these homes with both their identity and intentions shrouded in cloaks and masks, they obliged; but they kept the practice alive among their own friends who could use disguise to *pretend* to be strangers; and this they did (see Plates 36 and 40).

As a formal entertainment the Disguising enjoyed a brief lifespan. It arose as an answer to the prohibition of popular mumming early in the fifteenth century, and was itself superseded by the Masque a century later, thanks to another shift of emphasis coupled with the adoption of an Italian name, *maschere*. It is from Ben Jonson, himself the supreme librettist of Court Masques, that we learn the Masque was formerly known as a Disguising; and it is the historian Edward Hall who tells us that the Venetian custom of permitting the disguised dancers in their special cloaks and head masks to take partners for the final dance from among the spectators was first followed in England by Henry VIII.

> On the daie of the Epiphanie at night, the Kyng with xi other were disguised, after the manner of Italie, called a maske, a thyng not seen afore in England, thei were appareled in garmentes long and brode, wrought all with gold, with visers and cappes of gold . . .

The dancing over, 'thei took their leave and departed'.[35]

In point of time and character, therefore, the transition from Disguising to Masque can be charted with some precision. What, unfortunately, neither Hall nor Jonson tells us is whether the Disguising possessed a text, or if it did of what sort. To acquire some sort of answer to that question one must turn, paradoxically, to the earlier transition from Mumming to Disguising. When that is done, the likelihood emerges that the word Disguising came to replace Mumming as the title for this form of entertainment in conjunction with the addition of a Presenter and a text. Some evidence for this hypothesis is available in the sequence of seven poems by John Lydgate written between 1427–35, which he himself entitled variously and which in abbreviated form read as 'A Mumming', 'A ballad for a Mumming', 'A disguising' and 'A Ballad in wyse of Mummers Disguised'.[36] In its full form perhaps the most interesting title is the following one.

> And nowe fillowethe a lettre made in wyse of balade by Lede-gate Daun Iohan, of a mommynge, which the goldesmythes of the Cite of London mommed in right fresshe and costele welych desguysing to theyre Mayre Eestfeld, upon Candel-masse day at nyght, affter souper; brought and presented unto the Mayre by an heraude, cleped Fortune.

This title describes vividly what actually occurred. A member of the Goldsmith's Company, dressed as a herald, arrived with a letter which he read to the assembled Company at dinner in their Livery Hall in London. The letter was in fact a ballad in fourteen stanzas composed by Lydgate. It serves to introduce thirteen other members of the Company, dressed as King David and representatives of the twelve tribes of Israel, who carry a model of the Ark of the Covenant into the Hall and present it to the Lord Mayor. Inside this ark is a scroll telling him,

> Where yee shall punysshe and where as yee shal spare,
> And howe that Mercy shal Rygour modefye.

In other words, as the Herald reads the ballad to the assembled guests, the disguised mummers mime the actions as specified in it verse by verse.

With one exception the other 'Disguisings' take a similar form: this is *The Mumming at Hertford*. In this instance two distinct groups of people are presented to the King (Henry VI) and his guests on New Year's Eve – six peasants in one group and their wives in the other. The peasants are spoken for by the Presenter: the wives speak for themselves in *oratio recta* through one of their own number. Most of them have names: Robin the Reeve is married to Beatrice Bittersweet, Colin Cobler to Cicely Sourcheer, Bartholomew the Butcher to Pernelle, Tom Tinker to Tibot Typster and Colle Tyler to Phyllis. The King is asked to arbitrate in the quarrels between them and to determine who is to have mastery in each household. Prudently, the King, through his Chamberlain (or some other official) postpones judgement telling them all to return in a year's time to hear his verdict. This is a high-spirited comedy that trembles on the brink of dialogue.

The *Mumming at Bishopswood* is also notable; for this is a sophisticated May-game presented to the Sheriffs of London at an open-air banquet. In this instance the disguises are drawn from classical mythology; the mummers are led by Flora who presents Ver and May. Lydgate drew again on classical mythology for a Mumming for the King when keeping Christmas at the Palace of Eltham: this time the mummers represented Bacchus, Juno and Ceres, either directly or through merchants acting as their ambassadors. The number three, together with the gifts of wine, wheat and oil presented to the King, sound suspiciously like a remoulding of the old Epiphany mumming with Roman deities substituted for the Magi. A similar mutation of the parable of the miraculous draught of fishes within a neo-classical frame was devised by Lydgate for the Mercers of London in yet another Mumming for Twelfth Night. This Disguising required three elaborately dressed and painted ships together with fishing nets.

Such a ship is illustrated in a French miniature [Plate 40] depicting a no less interesting *entremet*, or 'mime without words', devised (in all probability by Philippe de Mézières) for King Charles v of France in 1378. This was presented on Twelfth Night for the entertainment of the King's uncle, the Emperor Charles iv, and depicted the Conquest of Jerusalem by Geoffrey of Boulogne. Jerusalem is represented in the miniature by a castle with scaling-ladders set against it. Christians and Saracens are clearly distinguishable by their respective costumes and make-up. There are grounds for believing that this *entremet* was intended to stimulate interest in launching a new Crusade. A detailed description of it survives in the elaborately illustrated MS *Chronique de Charles V* preserved in Paris in the National Library.[37]

Eleven years later, in 1389, the French Court witnessed another such *entremet*, devoted this time to incidents from the Siege of Troy. Froissart described it in his *Chroniques*. The scenic items were large, ornately decorated and placed on wheels hidden from view: they included a pavilion, a ship, and a castle representing the city of Troy.*

* A plan of the layout of the hall on this occasion is printed in *Early English Stages*, vol. I, p. 214.

Thus in both France and England there is ample evidence of sophisticated secular entertainments presented indoors and at night as the fourteenth century ended and the fifteenth century began. That spectacle was an important aspect of these entertainments is made obvious by the descriptions and texts which survive. From this point in their development such entertainments could just as obviously expand in two directions: either they could follow the already clear-cut example of the religious Miracles and Moralites towards extended narrative in dialogue form, or they could increase and improve the singing, dancing and scenic spectacle while restricting the literary component to an introductory and explanatory preamble.

In the course of the fifteenth century both courses of action were adopted. The former resulted in a succession of short plays, known in England as Interludes, presented by small companies of quasi-professional actors who were paid for their efforts: these will be discussed in section F below (pp 171-7). The latter retained both its popularity and its largely amateur status throughout Europe, and was rapidly developed in Italy, most especially in Venice, to allow the disguised mummers to take partners from among the spectators. With this step taken, the old Disguising acquired the new name of Masque.

Spectacular examples of both styles of entertainment before and after the change of name survive from the English Court in the first two decades of the sixteenth century. An opportunity for unusually lavish entertainments was provided in 1501 when Catherine of Aragon arrived in London to marry Henry VII's elder son, Prince Arthur. Although no texts survive for the Disguisings on this occasion, the official description of them dwells at length on the elaborate costumes and scenic devices, and makes it clear that the latter bore a close relationship to those used for the jousts on the same occasion. For the Disguisings the scenic devices were placed on wheels so that they could be easily removed when the central floor-space of the hall was required for dancing. Already the spectacular qualities of lighting were beginning to be exploited. One of the devices was a gigantic lantern. This was

cast out with many proper and goodly windows fenestered [i.e. paned] with fine lawn, wherein were more than an hundred great lights: in the which lantern were XII goodly ladies

> disguised. . . . This lantern was made of so fine stuff, and so
> many lights in it that these ladies might perfectly appear and
> be known through the said lantern
> (College of Arms MS 1st M. 13, f 55 : spelling modernized).

Henry VIII, some three years after his accession in 1509 encouraged the disguised performers to take partners from among
the spectators. In the course of the next twenty years Court entertainments became increasingly spectacular, not least the new
Masque. In 1528 Cardinal Wolsey and Henry himself entertained the French Ambassadors lavishly in London and at
Greenwich. The revels on this occasion incorporated a debate on
the relative merits of love and riches which, like Lydgate's
Mumming at Hertford, proved inconclusive.[38] This time, however, that matter was pressed to physical combat with the inter-
vention of six armed knights who proceeded to fight a joust at
barriers.

> Three of them would have entered the gate of the Arch in the
> middle of the Chamber, and the other three resisted, and sud-
> denly between the six Knights, out of the Arch fell down a bar
> all gilt, at the which bar the six Knights fought a fair battle,
> and then they departed, and so went out of the place (Hall's
> *Chronicle*, pp. 722 et seq : spelling modernized).

The debate was finally resolved by the arrival of 'an old man with
a silver beard' who claimed that princes needed both com-
modities, 'love' in order to be obeyed and served, 'riches' to
reward lovers and friends. This opened the way for the entertainment to develop into a double Masque of Lords and Ladies, the
Lords presenting themselves on a mountain 'set full of roses and
pommegramates', the Ladies issuing out of a cave. When the
formal dances were at their height,

> suddenly entered six personages, apparelled in cloth of silver
> and black tinsel satin, and hoods on their heads . . . and these
> persons had vizors with silver beards so that they were not
> known : these Maskers took Ladies and danced lustily about
> the place (Ibid).

This last phrase conveniently demonstrates that notwithstanding the political undertones of the entertainment, and the

fact that the visual spectacle was entrusted to an artist of the calibre of Hans Holbein, its principal attraction, at *human level,* lay in the dancing and the direct confrontations which that provoked between the sexes within the old rules of the Courts of Chivalry and Love.

Medieval traditions and renaissance innovations are here depicted in a delicate balance that the forward march of time would not permit to remain static for much longer. Shakespeare records that one of the causes of change was itself a Court Masque, and the prime instrument Anne Boleyn. It took the traditional form of mummers disguised 'as great ambassadors/ From foreign princes' visiting Cardinal Wolsey at York Place. Wolsey asks his Chamberlain to find out what they want:

> *Hautboys. Enter the King and others, as masquers, habited like shepherds, ushered by the Lord Chamberlain. They pass directly before the Cardinal, and gracefully salute him.*
> *Chamberlain:*
> Because they speak no English, thus they pray'd :
> To tell your grace, that, having heard by fame
> Of this so noble and so fair assembly
> This night to meet here, they could do no less,
> Out of the great respect they bear to beauty,
> But leave their flocks, and under your fair conduct
> Crave leave to view these ladies and entreat
> An hour of revels with 'em.
> *Wolsey:*
> Say, Lord Chamberlain,
> They have done my poor house grace : for which I pay 'em
> A thousand thanks and pray 'em take their pleasures.
> *They choose. The King chooses Anne Bullen.*
> *King:*
> The fairest hand I ever touch'd! O beauty,
> Till now I never knew thee!
>   *Music. Dance.* (Act i, Scene iv. 62-76).

The King's decision to divorce Catherine of Aragon and to marry Anne Boleyn with or without the Pope's approval changed the course of English history, religious and political, dragging the drama in its wake.

E. CIVIC PAGEANTRY

The growth of the merchant class, and with it the power of the cities, in the course of the thirteenth and fourteenth centuries has already been considered in the context of vernacular religious plays (see pp. 64-7 above). The support which wealthy merchants gave to the Church in helping both to organize and finance Corpus Christi drama, Saint Plays, and the larger Moralities was great. That they imitated the nobility and landed gentry in employing professional entertainers to amuse themselves at banquets on Feast days in their Livery Halls and in their own homes in also incontestable. Their function and achievement, however, as promoters of dramatic entertainment to celebrate specifically civic occasions is less familiar : yet these self-assertive gestures possessed a quality and character of their own, since they were at once secular and political rather than religious or social, which warrants attention.

The principal occasions that generated civic pageantry were the installation of a new mayor or Burgomeister, and visits to the city of Heads of State and their relatives. In both instances City Fathers recognized that such occasions provided an opportunity to enter into a dialogue between the citizens and the person or persons honoured that would spell out visually and verbally the significance of the occasion for both parties. The basic form of such celebrations was invariably a procession which in all probability was self-consciously imitative of ancient Roman 'triumphs'. As the procession wound its way through the principal thoroughfares of a city it encountered a variety of architectural monuments which, without much difficulty, could be transformed into platform stages from which clerks and children could address songs and speeches to the chief dignitaries in the procession passing below them. It was always open to the person thus honoured to pause and reply, or at least to show some mark of interest and appreciation before passing on.

Castellated gates in city walls, market crosses, and the larger water-storage tanks and fountains offered opportunities of this kind, and were pressed into service to this end in almost every European city large enough to possess them and important enough to warrant visits from emperors, kings and queens, or to wish to impress its own wealth and achievements on the attention of outsiders for political or commercial purposes (see Plate 33). Such stages were clearly of a temporary nature and limited in their resources: nor could processions afford to stop for long before each of them. These entertainments, therefore, usually took the form of tableaux, the emblematic iconography of which was very highly developed, and in which the speeches were normally confined to brief explanatory monologues. The personages presented in these tableaux had to be relevant to the occasion and their remarks pertinent to the expectations of the citizens who had financed them. Historical correspondences and topical allusions figure largely (and frequently laboriously) in these demonstrations. Invariably complimentary in character, the tableaux could however be sharply critical also.

In England, for example, when Richard II returned to London in 1392 after having transferred the Court to York, the citizens welcomed him generously with three pageants on the Great and Little Water Conduits in Cheapside and on Temple Bar in Fleet Street: but they also made it clear that their welcome, continued friendship and financial help would depend on his restoring to them their wonted liberties which he had rashly abrogated when deserting London for York. The message was clearly read and the desired action taken.[39] A hundred years later, when Henry VII visited Bristol, he was told by the legendary founder of the city, King Bremius, that the city needed help in restoring its cloth-making and ship-building industries after the depression of the Civil War. Again heed was taken of this message.

> After Evensong the King sent for the Mayor and Sheriff, and part of the best Burgesses of the Town, and demanded them the cause of their poverty ... The King comforted them ... so that the Mayor of the Town told me they heard not this hundred years of no King so good a comfort (BM. MS Cot. Jul. B XII. ff.19–21).

These street pageant theatres, despite the severe restrictions of space, were frequently very ingenious and even incorporated machinery. Barcelona in 1481 devised 'three spheres turning the one against the other', while in 1514 Paris provided 'a rose bush ... out of the which there projected a stem carrying a red rosebud which grew upward towards the throne of honour'. This rosebud symbolized Mary Tudor, the bride of Louis xɪɪ of France, who was himself represented as a lily growing in front of 'the throne of honour'. Then

> the lily descended from above midway to the ground (i.e. *to the lower stage*). Then, lily and rosebud ascended together up to the said throne where the said rosebud opened to reveal within itself a little girl gorgeously dressed who spoke . . . (BM MS Cot, Vesp. B II ff.g & gb).

The illustrated manuscript which provides this description also contains a picture depicting this very scene (see Plate 44).

Machinery at least as ingenious as this had of course long been in use on the religious stage and must not be regarded as an original contribution of civic pageants to the drama. However, in one respect, at least, the street pageants did add an important new dimension to the development of the theatre : this was the presentation of characters from modern history on their stages. When these are added to the saints and martyrs of the Christian era on the one hand, and to the heroes of the *chansons de geste* and classical mythology on the other, who had already joined the cast lists of medieval plays and entertainments, the maker of Interludes for professional players in a secular environment could claim to be equipped with a sufficiency of characters from modern as opposed to scriptural history to be able to regard any subject-matter as suitable for treatment in dramatic form. It did not require a renaissance to make this possible.

Civic pageants were by nature rare occurrences. Nevertheless they were community events and all the more memorable because of the festive atmosphere which accompanied them. They thus played an important part in keeping the conventions of theatrical representation – allegory, emblematic scenic devices and stage properties and colour symbolism in costume – vividly alive in a context closely allied to real people and contemporary life.[40]

It is in another form of civic spectacle or pageant however that realism was carried into actuality in the Middle Ages – the gruesome, pitiful and awe-inspiring rituals of public execution. Raised scaffold, gibbet, hangman (or masked headsman with axe) magistrate, priest-confessor and convicted felon combined to proclaim the processes of justice (at least as interpreted by mortals at that time) to the world at large in an outward figuration that was at once emblematic and realistic. The presence of a public audience provoked from the sacrificial victim the customary scaffold speech which, whatever its content and however it was delivered, was automatically endowed by its frightening finality with a violent theatricality. The burning of heretics was carried out no less publicly and with even greater ceremony.

Such spectacles inevitably made a vivid impression on the public imagination : and just as the spectre of Death summoning pope, emperor, merchant and peasant alike in the wake of plague and pestilence found its outward expression in art and literature, so the scaffold with all its grisly rites entered the drama as a scene calculated to arouse terror and pity in the highest degree or, in the wake of a rare last-minute reprieve, a corresponding joy in the hearts and minds of the beholders.

F. INTERLUDES

'The Tudor Interlude has the double interest of being itself a rigorous dramatic form, and of providing a basis for the greater works of dramatic poetry which followed.' So wrote M. C. Bradbrook in her foreword to T. W. Craik's notable book, *The Tudor Interlude.*

Few of us have much difficulty in recognizing what is meant by a Tudor Interlude : we think immediately of a short play in dialogue, of a small company of actors (sometimes schoolboys, sometimes adult professionals) frequently required to double roles, and of small stages backed by a screen or booth in a banquet hall or at a fair. We associate the preparation of such plays with choir-masters and academics – John Heywood, John Redford, Nicholas Udal and so on – and the subject-matter with secular concerns of a broadly farcical character. It has thus become habitual to regard Interludes as a product of renaissance humanism derived in part from the study and revival of Roman comedies in schools and universities, and in part from the coarse humour of countrymen, artisans and their apprentices in Tudor society. We are less sure of the relationship of this type of English play to the plays of a similar character that were being presented during this same period in France, Germany, the Netherlands and Spain : we are disconcerted to discover that Interludes could be serious and devoted to religious subject-matters : and when we are required to explain, in the light of these critical assumptions, how the word Interlude entered the English vocabulary in the context of dramatic entertainments a hundred years before John Heywood wrote any of his plays, most of us are so seriously put out to find an answer as to prefer to take refuge in disbelief.

Yet when the Mayor and Aldermen of London issued an Edict in 1418 forbidding mumming in the Christmas season of that year, the wording extends to 'any manere mommyng, pleyes, enterludes, or any other disgisynges . . .'

The word 'entyrludes' is also coupled, at almost the same date, with singing, wrestling and summer games by Robert Mannyng of Brunne in *Handlyng Synne* (lines 8989–96); earlier still, *c.*1385, Wyclif, in his *Tretise on Miriclis*, asks 'How thaune may a prist pleyn in entirlodies?'[41] The word also reaches us in its Latin form in the title of an early fourteenth-century manuscript, *Interludium de Clerico et Puella,* and again from New Romney in Kent in 1463 when Agnes Ford was paid 6*s.* 8*d pro ludo interludii Passionis Domini.*[42] Moreover, by the middle of the fifteenth century payments in account rolls to 'Players of enterludes' have to be reckoned with.

There is no getting round these facts. They oblige us to revise habitual critical judgements about the nature and origin of Interludes and force us to view them as a dramatic genre that developed alongside of vernacular Corpus Christi drama, Morality Plays and Saint Plays in the course of the fifteenth century. This would be easier to do than it is if any texts representative of the genre in English had survived to us; but they have not. We are thus left to speculate what sort of repertoire those groups of actors, described as players of Interludes and in the service of the nobility, presented in banquet halls at night which normally earned them the sum of 6*s.* 8*d.* as a reward.

In the latter half of the fifteenth century, and before the accession of Henry Tudor in 1485, we hear of players belonging to the King, the Dukes of Buckingham, Exeter, Gloucester and York, the Earls of Essex, Oxford, Northumberland and Westmorland, the Queen, the Duchess of Norfolk, the Archbishop of Canterbury and the Bishop of Carlisle, and to many lesser lords and knights. This list is representative and not exhaustive. The proliferation of quasi-professional acting companies cannot have come about suddenly in 1450 or thereabouts: it must have developed gradually and taken time to do so. Fifty to a hundred years, in my opinion, is not too long a span for a practice, initiated by the sovereign, to have been copied (under royal license) by the nobility, and to have spread through society to the point that the surviving records of payments prove it to have reached in the latter half of the century. Such reasoning takes the process back to a date at least contemporary with the French *entremets* of 1378 and 1389 already described (p. 164 above) and substantially earlier than the London ban on 'mummings, plays and interludes' of 1418. Thus Wyclif's use of the word, *c.*1385, as a dramatic genre unsuitable for priests becomes less shocking and more readily intelligible.

Another fact deducible from the records of payments to these players (*lusores, histriones, mimes*) is that they travelled extensively. The Duke of Gloucester's players, for example, can be traced between 1479 and 1480 in places as far apart as Selby Abbey in Yorkshire, and Canterbury and New Romney in Kent.

Clearly, then, these men were not participating in Disguisings, nor were they presenting Miracle Cycles on Corpus Christi Day, nor were they performing extended Moralities and Saint Plays. What then were they offering to their sophisticated audiences of an evening in the hall or chamber? In the present state of knowledge any answer to this question must be hypothetical; but more clues to the provision of a satisfactory answer exist than is often supposed.

The most direct of these is supplied by the titles of plays described as Interludes. I have already referred to the fourteenth-century 'Interlude of the Clerk and the Girl', and those of 'The Passion of Our Lord' of 1463 in New Romney: to these must be added the *Interludium de Corpore Christi* of 1389 at Bury St Edmunds in Suffolk, *The Jewess of Abbingdon* and *Jack Travail and his Companions* of 1427. The clear inference is that distinctions between religious and secular subject-matter had little or no bearing on whether or not the word 'Interlude' was used to describe it. Just as clearly, the choice of a word other than Mumming or Disguising suggests that it was desired to distinguish a dramatic entertainment scripted in dialogue throughout from an explanatory ballad or prologue the subject-matter of which was then represented in silent mime and dance. Another factor of consequence is that while Calendar Festivals provide the occa-

sions for festivities including 'revels', Interludes do not appear to
have been tied, like liturgical music-drama, Corpus Christi Cycles
or Saint Plays, to particular Feast Days. In this respect then the
Interlude of the fourteenth and fifteenth centuries shared the
freedom that distinguishes Morality Plays from other drama of
the period, being as suitable for performance on one day as
another and at any time indoors or out. If, in addition, as the
payments to players of Interludes indicate, the plays were short
and the number of parts small, it is obvious that a repertoire of
such plays would be of more use to a company that was forced to
travel to earn its keep than any other. This argument does not
preclude the writing and performance of Interludes by amateurs,
but it does suggest that without a stock of Interludes the idea of
deriving a regular income from acting as a profession could not
have developed very far. If this reasoning is accepted, then I
think we are entitled, by the last decade of the fifteenth century,
to regard play texts such as the anonymous *Everyman*, or Henry
Medwall's *Nature* and *Fulgens and Lucres* as Moral Interludes.
By that time we know something of the way of life of at least one
company that performed such plays.

The *lusores regis, alias, in lingua Anglicana, les playars of the
Kyngs enterluds* maintained by Henry vii were four in number
and led by John English. From their master they received a basic
retaining fee of five marks each together with their liveries. In
addition they received a gratuity in reward for every performance
given at Court. When not required there they travelled, receiving
similar gratuities for performances before the nobility in their
halls and from mayors in their guild-halls and city merchants in
their livery halls. In summer they could add to their earnings by
performing their plays to public audiences in town-halls, on fair-
grounds and in other places of public resort in the open air, either
charging admission at the door (where one existed) or circulating
a collection-box when it did not. The hall was thus the natural
home of the professional player. In that environment he was
already supplied *in advance* with a sense of occasion, a screen
provided with convenient entrances and exits and leading to
dressing-rooms and refreshments in the vicinity, a roof against
inclement weather, the warmth of a fire, and the incandescent
magic of candlelight. His fee, moreover, was guaranteed, or could
at least be secured by controlled admission to the hall. In the open

air everything was against him – the hazards of the weather, the makeshift character of stage, auditorium, and changing-room, and the perennial disinclination of casual spectators to pay for the show if they could escape without doing so. The single advantage of the open-air theatre – and it was a compelling one as the organizing committees of amateur Miracle Cycles and Saint Plays knew well – was the size of the audience that could be accommodated. It was the lure of this prize which, late in the sixteenth century, persuaded professional companies to simulate the conditions of the hall in arenas open to the sky (but so constructed as to control admission and secure a financial contribution from every spectator in advance) to which they gave the name of public playhouses.

The amateur 'player of Interludes' was under no such pressure to secure large public audiences. In choir-schools, grammar schools, universities, as at Court or in noble houses, the hall sufficed to accommodate the local community. It is thus in the hall that a succession of choristers and students, throughout the sixteenth century, presented Interludes for the entertainment of their fellows, whether in English, Latin or Greek, written for them by their masters, and frequently devised as much with a view to training them in the felicities of rhetoric and the techniques of oratory as to providing audiences with entertainment. Such was their success that in the latter half of the century William Hunnis, John Lyly and others felt confident enough to imitate the adult professionals in presenting their Interludes to public audiences by private invitation. It was in these circumstances that the so-called Private Theatres came to be established in halls at St Pauls, Blackfriars and Whitefriars.[43]

Interludes invariably sought to point a moral. The method, however, could be serious or farcical, the difference depending as much on the sort of audiences whose attention the actors sought to secure as on the status of the actors themselves. Religious subject-matter was as legitimate as source-material as secular life, at least until the Reformation. With that change, both in Germany and in England, the Moral Interlude became a weapon of propagandist polemic that was destined to shake the whole fabric of theatrical *ludi* that had been so laboriously built up over some six hundred years of consistently expanding experiment and community enterprise. This is discussed in Chapter 7, Church and State.

Where the staging of Interludes is concerned there is no reason to believe that the layout of the hall in the fourteenth or fifteenth centuries differed substantially from that for other indoor revels. With the dais occupied by the high table accommodating the master of the household and his guests, the players used the other end of the hall adjacent to the screen with the minstrels in the gallery above it for their play. The play-place was flanked with tables so that space was at a premium and contact with the audience extremely intimate. In essence the conditions resembled those for cabaret in restaurants today. Scenic units of the kind familiar in the theatres of worship, tournaments, civic pageants and Disguisings – ship, castle, pavilion, mountain, cave, arbour or clouds – were available to identify locality should this be necessary : but it is to be doubted if the texts of Interludes surviving from the closing years of the fifteenth century and the early decades of the sixteenth are a fair guide, whether anything as elaborate as that was called for. A painted cloth, hanging on or near the screen, supplemented by portable stage properties – chairs, tables, stools and so on – could normally meet the simple requirements of such plays, and all these items were readily transportable to other places when the company took to the road.

Since actors were required to play two or three different roles in most Interludes, costume was simple, making quick changes as easy to accomplish as to identify. The style of costume was normally that of contemporary fashion, making it possible for actors, on occasion, to appear to be members of the audience. A case in point occurs with the two servants A and B in Medwall's *Fulgens and Lucres* where the author uses this confusion of identity to considerable comic effect.[44] Nevertheless costume was carefully controlled not only to ensure swift identification of character but to figure in outward and visible manner the dominant features of the character's inner identity. In this way the makers of Interludes succeeded in forging a subtle instrument to contrast mask and face, physical appearance and spiritual reality. Notable cases of this technique are to be found in Redford's *Wit and Science,* and Bale's *Three Laws.*[45] Abstract personifications of Virtues and Vices were of course standardized and instantly recognizable from constant repetition in tapestry, stained-glass and frescoes :

thus Justice carried her sword and balances and was normally dressed in red, while Truth was dressed in white and carried a book. In this respect stage-conventions had not advanced materially on those first adopted in liturgical music-drama. Variety was provided by word-games, physical combats and songs and dances. Actors, uncertain of their reception at the hands of an audience in festive mood, defended themselves with apologetic prologues and epilogues : given the proximity of the spectators and the strictly subservient nature of the player in relation to his employer this is understandable, and indeed it would have been extraordinary if frequent *ab lib* exchanges were not a common occurrence in the course of performances which relied so heavily upon direct address with its many rhetorical questions and asides.

The player of Interludes thus had to be quick-witted, skilled in repartee and a versatile mimic, singer, dancer and acrobat. As a household servant society expected him to respect his station in the social hierarchy; yet his profession often required him to mimic and sometimes to parody the manners and behaviour of his social superiors. As a critic of grasping merchants, pretentious lawyers and pedants, and corrupt clerics, he endeared himself to their victims, yet was feared by the objects of his ridicule. Possessed of the financial means to secure a measure of personal freedom and mobility in strictly regulated and largely static communities, he was at once admired and envied. No wonder Wyclif thought it improper for priests to join their ranks; yet players of Interludes flourished and multiplied. No wonder Henry VIII chose to increase the number in his troupe from four to eight; yet it was his Parliament that first described them in the Statute Book as rogues and vagabonds.

Part III:
Theatres and Commerce

6

AMATEURS AND PROFESSIONALS

Latent within the festive music-drama of Christian liturgy was the seed of a larger and more self-consciously didactic drama of worship. While this seed was germinating in the thirteenth and fourteenth centuries and blossoming into the still festive *ludi* of the Feast of Corpus Christi, of Patron Saints' Days and into those exhortations to amendment of life dramatically conceived and formulated as Morality Plays, another type of drama, independent of worship, was developing simultaneously that took its life as we have seen from the rituals of agriculture, of war, of courtship and of civic ceremony. This second form of drama that linked the holiday spirit with the secular pursuits of social recreation came to be ornamented in sophisticated society by all the arts that leisure could invent and that wealth could provide in the private apartments of the palaces of Europe. Yet within these revels too – choreographic, melodic, poetic and spectacular as taste, occasion and space permitted – there lay the embryo of another drama, the short scripted play known as an Interlude devised for small companies of professional actors that they could detach from the initial environment of their master's hall and carry with them to other places and other audiences. It might be claimed that this was the limit of medieval dramatic initiatives and that there was accordingly yet another theatre still to be born, the strictly commercial theatre so familiar to us today; but I believe such a claim would be a false one. Rather is the professional and commercial theatre of the modern world (with its extensions into films and television) a parasitic growth which battened upon both the theatres of worship and the theatres of social recreation during the late Middle Ages and then developed its own strength from those elements within the parents on which it fed that openly invited commercial exploitation.

G*

In making this claim I wish to avoid any suggestion that the change from a predominantly amateur-based theatre to a largely professional one during the sixteenth century in Europe was brought about by some sort of conspiracy among financial speculators to debauch art for private gain. On the contrary, the involvement of the world of medieval commerce in that of dramatic art was just as gradual and natural as the evolution of dramatic art itself out of Christian liturgy and the varied social *ludi* of parish, park and banquet hall : for, as the drama in all these environments grew more elaborate, so it came to rely more heavily upon the trappings of physical presentation. It was these external elements of dramatic art – costumes, properties and scenic devices to identify persons and place – which themselves forced the first questions to be asked about production budgets and rewards for services rendered. Both questions came to be answered in financial terms as the evidence of countless account rolls, ecclesiastical and civic, amply testifies from the thirteenth century onwards. These questions were naturally referred to persons whose primary interests were not necessarily centred upon the drama at all, but upon commercial common sense and administrative efficiency – churchwardens, town clerks and the treasurers of guilds and colleges. It was thus the growth of the drama that first provoked the concern of its begetters with money matters, and this interest in its turn which suggested that overtures might be made to engage the practical help of men whose chief skill lay in commerce.

Nowhere in Europe has any evidence reached us to lead us to believe that the Church could not handle its own plays in the early Middle Ages. Musicians, scribes and actors could all be recruited from within its own ranks : acting-area, auditorium, costumes and scenic accessories could all be provided with little effort from its own resources. And granted the strict, liturgical context of Latin music-drama, there was no incentive to enlist assistance from outsiders. Once, however, a positive decision had been taken by the clergy to permit the nascent art of drama to pass beyond the formal boundaries of a liturgical *Officium*, and to exist in its own right as a *ludus* or entertainment, or to be used as an instrument of education in an evangelistic cause, self-sufficiency ceased to possess any particular virtue : for at once sound reasons presented themselves for encouraging laymen to participate in as active a manner as was compatible with a Christian way of life. To admit this was to do no more for drama than the Church had already been doing for centuries with all the other aspects of life – to endow the mundane and pagan with a new spiritual and strictly Christian significance.[1] This is not to 'secularize' a drama that was uniquely religious, but the reverse; to seize upon each new secular manifestation of dramatic vitality as it presented itself, and to remould it into a form that was capable of a Christian interpretation and could be firmly tied to a Christian festival. It was in this way, as we have seen, that the agricultural and seasonal rituals of village communities were purged of their offensive qualities by the early missionaries and given a new lease of life as folk customs on appropriate Calendar holidays of the Christian year. It was in this way that the *juvenes* (young deacons) of Beauvais were encouraged to occupy their leisure-time in writing a *ludus* about the Prophet Daniel, that a scholar-poet like Hilarius found his way to writing plays about Lazarus and St Nicholas, or the Nun Hrostwitha approached the plays of Terence when composing her own about the Church's martyrs. I would not wish to deny that each and all of these extensions of dramatic possibilities brought the drama into ever closer touch with secular life; but I must equally insist that this traffic also flowed the other way, bringing ever more aspects of secular life as imitated in dramatic games firmly into the patterns prescribed by the controlling hand of the universal Church throughout the length and width of Christendom. Thus, even in the case of the most 'secular' of farces and Interludes of the fifteenth century and the early sixteenth, the ethic informing their structure and moral conclusion was firmly Christian.

Where commerce is concerned, the Church's involvement with the costs of dramatic representations had begun by the start of the fourteenth century as may be observed from the account books of monastic establishments like Durham Priory where rewards were given to *Histrionibus domini Regis* (minstrels of our Lord the King) in the years 1300–3, and money was laid out in 1310 *In scissura tunicae stulti* (for the cutting of a fool's surcoat)[2] (see Plate 42). This of course does not mean that such payments had not started much earlier; only that no written records of an earlier date have so far been found. Even so, all such payments, then or earlier, must be regarded as in the nature of gifts or honorariums, that is to say as 'largesse' or bonuses voluntarily bestowed, rather than as an obligatory payment exacted for a service professionally rendered. If, in less sophisticated environments, the Mummers' Play, May-games or other folk *ludi* had by that time acquired a formal enough shape and sufficient content to warrant description as dramatic entertainments, then any collection of money taken from bystanders must also be regarded as optional gifts and not as obligatory levies. The dividing-line between the two is admittedly a thin one since in small communities the performers could readily revenge themselves upon individuals who were known to have refused to exercise the option to make the expected and time-honoured gift. Nevertheless the principle is important, and it is not until quite late in the fourteenth century that the character of the financial transactions recorded in account books changes sufficiently to allow us to be sure that dramatic *ludi* had developed to a point where considerations of a strictly commercial nature had to be faced and met.

There can be little doubt that the institution of the Feast of Corpus Christi in 1311 marks the start of this change. In England the Feast was universally observed from 1318 onwards, and from that time forward at least once a year every man, woman and child throughout Christian Europe, whether literate or not, was reminded that Christ's Church embraced him in his daily living as well as in his church-going. Before the end of the century this included the drama, since *The Play called Corpus Christi* had been pressed into service to provide an explicit and externalized confirmation of God's relationship with his creation. The development of plays depicting the heroism and steadfastness of the saints and martyrs, and of others explaining ultimate salvation or damnation as the personal responsibility of the individual, alongside of the Cycles and Passion Plays of Corpus Christi could only serve to enhance the Church's wish to secure the willing co-operation of laymen of all sorts and conditions. This co-operation included the provision of money to finance production.

By 1390 the craft guilds of the Yorkshire town of Beverley were being threatened with a fine of 40 shillings for failing to perform their plays: conversely in 1385 the chamberlains of King's Lynn in Norfolk record payments to actors who did perform a play on Corpus Christi Day.[3] By 1406 the clergy of Lincoln Cathedral were paying for costume materials for a play of the prophets and the Annunciation; these materials are specifically stated to have been bought (*emptis*). Some fourteen years later this same city allocated 8 shillings and 8 pence out of tithes to buy things for a play.[4]

From this time forward, almost wherever records of dramatic performances exist, money matters figure in them with increasing prominence. York and Coventry levied a special tax known respectively as 'Pageant-silver' and 'Pageant-pence'. At Romans, Valenciennes and Lucerne audiences were required to buy their seats. In small country parishes funds were raised by 'Church-ales' and the sale of local dairy and vegetable produce. Money for plays becomes an increasing preoccupation of cathedral chapters, city councils and churchwardens of parish churches in town and country alike. At Valenciennes, Lucerne and New Romney actors had to enter into specific financial recognizances that were legally binding upon them, paying deposits from which fines and forfeits were liable to be deducted before they were returned. By 1531 the Cardmakers and Sadlers Companies in Coventry found it necessary to appeal to the Mayor and City Council (Leet) to release them from their obligation to finance their Corpus Christi Pageant on the grounds that the '... charge is, and like to be, more ponderous and chargeable to them than they may conveniently bear or sustain in short time to come unless provision for a remedy may be speedily had.' It is to be noted that these companies' complaint does not arise from disenchantment with such plays or from an unwillingness to remain associated with the particular play allocated to them : it stems directly from an inability to meet the production costs.[5]

Nor, by this time, was money a matter of much less consequence to those responsible for presenting civic pageants, tournaments and Disguisings. The tableaux mounted in the City of London for Catherine of Aragon's reception in 1501 had to be paid for by a special tax levied on every ward of the City. The average cost of each pageant had by then risen to approximately £120. Tournaments had become so expensive as to debar all but the wealthiest members of the nobility from participating in them and Disguisings (judging by the Privy Purse Accounts of Henry VII cost up to 20 a time excluding the special costumes provided and paid for by the individual participants.[6]

What was this money needed for? Where Corpus Christi plays

and other large-scale religious *ludi* were concerned, the cost of parchment and the copying of actors' parts had to be met before rehearsal could begin. Thus at New Romney 3 shillings and 4 pence was paid, 'to buy paper for the writing of the parts of the play'. The author, depending on his status, frequently had to be paid, and so did the copyists. On a more modest scale, the Parish Church of St Mary at Hill in London 'paid to Mr Densell for making and drawing out our play 4 shillings', and a clerk 'for writing of our play 12 pence'. At Romans in France, the author of the *Mystère des Trois Doms*, Canon Pra, received 255 florins for the text; his co-author M. Chevalet received 27 florins for supplementary dialogue, and the copyists about 15 florins. Many indigent university students earned part of their subsistence in this way, especially in France.[7] From Lincoln and New Romney in England come instances of payments to individuals in connection with rehearsals conducted in their homes. Similar private rehearsals were encouraged in Lucerne.[8] By far the heaviest item of expenditure, however, was the stage, auditorium, stage machinery and the large quantities of costumes and scenic accessories. Unlike a monastic community, the craft-guilds and Corpus Christi or other religious fraternities were not self-sufficient when the need arose to provide, make or do things outside their normal specialities. Shipwrights could make an Ark for Noah; but why should the Mercers be able to provide craftsmen capable of constructing Heaven and Hell for the Last Judgement? Or why should a guild dedicated to the Holy Trinity be expected to create the machinery needed to stage the Ascension? Work appropriate to a guild, as the making of crowns for the Magi would be to the Goldsmiths, could be handled by the guild itself at small cost beyond that of the materials. Other work, however, of a constructional kind had to be farmed out to those capable of giving the work a professional finish consistent with its function and the aesthetic standards set by the committees of management responsible for the performance. In general, therefore, the more elaborate the accessories became, the greater the expense became too. It only needed a competitive element to enter in between one guild or organizational group and another for these construction costs to mount rapidly and to create a situation that neither the Church nor the civic authorities could control without the help of the other. In the fifteenth and sixteenth centuries situations arose from time to time which bankrupted their collective resources and forced them to appeal to private benefactors to pay off the creditors. Such was the case in Rouen in 1491.[9]

It is impossible to establish with any certainty whether the large and authoritarian committees of management encountered in England, France, Germany, Italy, Spain and Switzerland in the sixteenth century came into existence because of the Church's desire to involve the laity in its *ludi* or because of the wish of the laity to participate in them, or as a means of meeting spiralling production costs. The most probable answer is that all three causes played a contributory part and in that order of precedence. Once, however, plays of epic narrative dimensions and elaborate visual spectacle had come to be accepted as normal, no better alternative method of organizing and financing them was likely to present itself. The Church claimed and retained an absolute right over the script since matters of doctrine were always in question : the civic authorities could and did claim, with equal justification, that the public assemblies in public places which these plays attracted were matters that brought the King's Peace into question : responsibility for that rested with them. By the start of the sixteenth century therefore the economic problems of capitalizing the plays in the first instance and of obtaining an adequate return on the investment thereafter served to define and to separate in a potentially dangerous way the major areas of ecclesiastical and civic responsibility in the administration of them. Thus in practice, whatever the theoretical assumptions governing vernacular religious *ludi* had been, the Church came to regard itself as ultimately responsible for solving specifically dramatic problems while town councils came to look upon themselves as the final arbiter in specifically theatrical matters. The Church therefore retained its power to order the text, to authorize additional plays, to excise or vary others and, eventually, to forbid future performances by the expurgation or outright suppression of existing prompt-books and by refusing to supply new ones or to permit any other individual or corporate body to supply alternatives. Town Councils on the other hand, wherever laymen had been encouraged to accept responsibility as actors and for the provision of costumes, scenic accessories, the stage, tiring houses, auditorium and advance publicity, were likely to have obtained effective control over the means of production, however inadvertently, and were thus able to defy the Church if they wished to. This they could do either by refusing to provide any of the facilities required and thus forcing the Church sharply to curtail the scale of its plays and take them back into consecrated precincts; or, despite the Church's expressed wish to the contrary, they could organize performances when and where they liked for so long as they could retain copies of the prompt-books and rely upon the support of the central government.

This division of responsibility had many practical advantages so long as both Church and State shared a high opinion of such performances; but it was also one that could swiftly prove fatal to the continuance of them if ever a situation arose where one party or the other chose to change its mind about the value of such plays. Just such a situation did arise shortly after 1530 in the wake of the Reformation. The resulting discord between Catholics, determined either to press home their advantage by retaining the old plays or by reforming them with judicious cuts and modifications, and Protestants (just as determined to turn such plays into vehicles of propaganda or to suppress them outright) was catastrophic. The consequences of these disputes for the committees of management will be examined in the next chapter.

The point to be grasped now is that the startlingly swift collapse of the medieval theatre of worship during the middle years of the sixteenth century derived from the fact that control of it rested with the management committees rather than with the actors and producers. The feud between Catholics and Protestants did not have the effect of creating a uniform divorce between the ecclesiastical and civic sections of these committees : rather did it divide each section against itself, and thus replaced trust and confidence with mutual suspicion and antipathy at best and with outright anarchy at the worst. In some towns the Catholic faction proved strong enough for performances to continue : in others the Protestants outnumbered the Catholics and performances ceased or changed their nature. In short the struggle for survival became political : and once this had happened the central government acquired the power to usurp the authority formerly exercised by the committees, to regulate plays, players and places of performance.

Nowhere do the actors and producers, still less the playmakers, appear to have exercised any significant influence on the fate of the Cycles, Saints' Plays or lengthy Moralities. The reason is plain enough : as amateurs they lacked the capital needed to finance such undertakings, they lacked the executive authority needed to administer them, and they lacked the sense of purpose needed to make a success of collective bargaining with either the clerical hierarchy of the local area or the mayors, councils, sheriffs and magistrates in their own districts when confronted with threats of fines, imprisonment, and even a trial for heresy or sedition with execution as the penalty on conviction. The point at issue is that these plays did not die through any loss of religious faith or through any wish on the part of the performers to abandon acting or other aspects of play production : they collapsed and dis-appeared because the economics of play-production on so lavish and extended a scale had become too unwieldy for performances to continue without strong management at the centre.

The steady decline in the fortunes of the amateur theatre of worship after 1530 was matched in England, if not elsewhere, by a spectacular increase in the number of professional or semi-professional actors, and of shorter plays with smaller casts, that could be toured, either within the bounds of the local county or shire, or in London and other major cities. Most if not all of these actors had first acquired some other recognized craft or skill : this they could and did exercise to earn a living at times when plague, bad weather, hostile mayors and mean barons reduced their profits from play-acting to a pittance.

These then were the linkmen between the great professional actors of Elizabethan and Jacobean times like Edward Alleyn and Richard Burbage, who earned huge sums of money sufficient to endow a school or to provide capital for the building of play-houses, and the modest players of Interludes of the fifteenth century who pioneered a form of dramatic art that made profes-sional acting a viable way of life.

Like the amateur actors of the theatres of worship, the player of Interludes had another and more mundane basic trade or profession : he was servant to a knight or nobleman. As such he had his own menial, appointed tasks within the household year in year out as a hewer of wood, drawer of water, kitchen-hand or ostler. As such he wore the livery of his master, thus establishing himself in the eyes of the law as gainfully and legitimately

G**

employed. In addition he had a talent to amuse which received official recognition on feast-days in the banquet hall, more especially during the twelve-day Feast of Christmas when the normal rules of social behaviour were relaxed and the Lord of Misrule was required to recruit a team of entertainers from within the household.

Thus initially, he was at best an occasional performer and in receipt of occasional largesse. This situation was still familiar to Samuel Cox late in the sixteenth century when he wrote a letter to a friend in which he said,

> I could wish that players would use themselves nowadays, as in ancient former times they have done, which was only to exercise their interludes in the time of Christmas, beginning to play in the holidays and continuing until twelfth tide . . .

Some of these men, he says,

> . . . were such as pertained to noblemen, and were ordinary servants in their house, and only for Christmas times used such plays, without making profession to be players to go abroad for gain . . .[10]

Samuel Cox, of course, would not have had to write as he did if all players had continued to 'exercise their interludes' in the manner he describes: clearly some of them did not. With the example of the professional musicians before them and that of the travelling *trouvère* and his troupe of *jongleurs*, both precedent and incentive invited them 'to go abroad for gain': the fact that they had 'other trades to live off' was irrelevant. What counted was freedom; freedom of movement, freedom from the monotony of servile occupations, freedom above all to earn more money in one hour than they could normally hope to do at home in a whole year.

The translation from amateur to professional status was thus gradual and barely noticeable in fifteenth-century society since the player of Interludes at that time continued to receive largesse from the master of the house whether that house was his own or belonged to someone else: it was the multiplication factor that translated individual largesse into a regular income. Since these players were liable to arrest as vagabonds if they lacked a livery badge and letters signed by their masters authorizing them to travel, they inevitably publicized the fact wherever they went that their master maintained a company of players: this in its turn came to be regarded as a symbol of status encouraging other noblemen either to grant similar privileges to their own players or to recruit a company of their own for reasons that more nearly pertained to personal vanity and status within their own shire or at Court than to any special love of dramatic art. With increasing financial independence of the patron the players might be expected to have severed the old links with their masters and their original homes. This however they could not do since at no time during the fifteenth or the sixteenth century was society at large prepared to admit that acting should be recognized as a full-time occupation on a par with other crafts or professions. By the middle of the sixteenth century the professional status of many companies of players of Interludes had come to be accepted on a *de facto* basis; but officially they continued to be regarded as houshold servants, branded as such by their liveries and the letters patent without which they possessed no right to act at all and, indeed, would quickly find themselves clapped into prison as beggars.[11] To speak therefore about players of Interludes as 'professional actors' in our sense of those words is incorrect; yet at the same time these players followed a way of life, even during the fifteenth century, that was altogether different from that of the actors of epic religious dramas, thanks to an income directly earned from acting. That these earnings were erratic rather than regular is probable, but no more erratic than those of that large proportion of members of Actors Equity today who are so frequently declared to be 'resting' as opposed to 'in work'. What is certain is that they cannot be described as amateurs.

This distinction is an important one in the context of the quality of their performances: for the player of Interludes was stretched *as an artist*, both by the relative frequency of his performances and by the versatility required of him, in ways that the actors of religious *ludi* were not. Singing, dancing, fencing, wrestling, acrobatics were all essential skills required of him in addition to those of mimicry, rhetoric and repartee. Instant character was still the order of the day as it had been for generations in the theatres of worship; but in a company of four actors in which each player must double several roles in every play, it was just as important for a player to be able to change his identity from one character to another frequently and at speed.[12] Verbal 'asides', facial grimaces, and soliloquy accompanied these needs as essential technical devices to keep audiences informed of the character behind the disguise, the face behind the mask, the actor behind the character. This was the nature of the *ludus*, 'game' or 'play' – the experience shared between the player of Interludes and his audience – and one which grew in subtlety as old possibilities were refined and new variants tried out. Professionalism thus served to reinforce age-old habits of redaction both among playmakers and players. If a device worked – that is, if it provoked laughter as desired or some other notable effect – then it was retained, repeated and reworked from one play to the next. In this way the repertoire of stage business expanded and developed in parallel with the stock of plots and characters at the disposal of the playmakers. A particular physical game or routine became an item of dramaturgy on which a variety of verbal patterns could be superimposed, just as a particular confrontation of characters or juxtaposition of arguments could be used as a basis for varied physical interpretations. At the heart of this dramaturgy lay the actor's *experience* of his audiences – how to obtain their attention in the first instance, how to maintain it thereafter, knowledge of how to make them laugh or cry, knowledge of what would distract or bore them, how not to lose their sympathy and how to avoid arousing their active displeasure. At their hands the theatre of social recreation thus became imperceptibly but inexorably an actor's theatre, a theatre in which the poet was indispensable but always the servant or the partner of the actor, never his master.[13] A curious link with the religious stage survived in the prayer for the monarch at the close of an Interlude occupying the place always accorded to *Te Deum* in the theatre of worship.[14]

It was one thing for companies of four or even eight actors to acquire a large enough repertoire of plays and to give enough performances to earn their keep : it was quite another to save enough out of these earnings to amass the capital required to take a long-term lease on a hall or build an auditorium : that only became practicable in the 1570s and even then only with the help of commercial speculators. Players of Interludes therefore in the fifteenth and sixteenth centuries, as in preceding years, had perforce to lead a nomadic existence seeking short leases of halls and other places where public assemblies were permitted in which to

present their plays.[15] Such a life militated against large stages
and elaborate scenic equipment or machinery which was difficult
to handle and awkward to transport (see Plate 40). Shakespeare
provides us with a vivid picture of such a company seeking royal
patronage and hospitality at Elsinore. Its actors are entirely self-
sufficient. They have their repertoire of plays, but no writers are
with them : the master-actor, or first player, readily interpolates
new speeches into an old play and may well write some of the
company's plays himself. They adapt the great chamber of the
royal palace as their auditorium and acting-area: needing to
identify the acting-area as an orchard, they carry a painted cloth
or a three-dimensional tree and bench with them along with their
costume skips, but no architect, painter or mechanical engineer.
An apprentice boy plays the woman's part. Production costs are
minimal. Yet provided that there is 'no offence in it', King,
Queen and Court are ready to honour this company by watching
their play, and to provide its members with bed and board and
the customary largesse. Hamlet, a talented amateur himself,
knows them personally and thinks highly of them : Polonius, also
an amateur actor in his youth, is contemptuous of them.

Having established, as I hope, the essential distinction between
the professionalism of those players of Interludes whose repertoire
and artistry was controlled by their determination to earn a living
from acting in the late Middle Ages, and the amateur nature of
all other acting, something needs to be said about the commercial
aspect of secular as opposed to religious performances in this
context.

In the letter which I have quoted from Samuel Cox to his
friend of 15 January 1591 about acting, he draws an interesting
distinction between those players of Interludes who 'go abroad for
gain' and another sort whom he describes as,

> certain artisans in good towns and great parishes, as shoe-
> makers, tailors, and such like, that used to play either in their
> town-halls, or some time in churches, to make the people
> merry.

These players resembled the amateur dramatic societies of our
own times in the nature of their interest in drama and the quality
of their efforts; but they enjoyed a measure of subsidy rarely

known today. Audiences, says Cox, could attend in the knowledge that the players would admit them,

> without exacting any money for their access, having only somewhat gathered of the richer sort by the churchwardens for their apparel and other necessaries.[16]

Shakespeare again obligingly supplies us with a vivid portrait of this type of company in his Athenian mechanicals of *A Midsummer Night's Dream* who find themselves so unexpectedly required to bring their 'brief interlude' of *Pyramus and Thisbe* to Court. They themselves stress the importance of the financial difference separating such a company in its normal circumstances from one maintained by a nobleman. Flute, the bellows-mender, laments Bottom the weaver's misfortune in being translated into an Ass and losing his chance to act before Duke Theseus.

> O sweet bully Bottom! Thus hath he lost sixpence a day during his life; he could not have scap'd sixpence a day: an the Duke had not given him sixpence a day for playing Pyramus, I'll be hang'd; he would have deserved it: sixpence a day, in Pyramus, or nothing (IV.ii. 19–24).

Shakespeare, of course, was parodying his own *Romeo and Juliet*, as well as amateur dramatics, when devising *Pyramus and Thisbe* as a play within his play: even so, scripts of that character probably represent the peak of what was attempted by 'artisans in good towns and great parishes . . . to make the people merry'. At the other end of the scale lay the May-games complained of by Philip Stubbs in the passage from *The School of Abuse* quoted on page 141 where dance and song would appear to have taken precedence over dialogue.

As has already been noted many of these 'plays' and 'games' were closely associated with fund-raising activities. Surviving churchwardens' accounts reveal that these were profitably managed, substantial sums being raised from a relatively modest outlay. A case in point is the annual Hocking at the parish Church of St Mary Hill in London. The gatherers employed to collect money for this (usually the wives) were remunerated with a dinner of beef and ale costing between twelve and twenty pence; this investment brought in around twenty shillings from what they gathered. From 1523 onwards this church ran a school and arranged on occasion for the children to present a play.[17]

Another means of financing production costs was to allocate the rent or income received from individual properties to this specific purpose. Forty shillings a year was raised in this way in Ipswich (*c*.1450) from the grazing rights on the common marsh and 'the portman's meadow'. The churchwardens of Heybridge in Essex raised funds by collecting farm produce and then selling it to obtain the necessary capital with which to meet production costs. In Bishop's Stortford the collection taken at a play (*c*.1490) was supplemented by a gathering at St Michael's Church Ale which followed it. This principle was extended in some places to visiting players. Thus in Maldon in Essex in the latter half of the fifteenth century the actors of 'Stowe play' and the players of Lachyndon received eleven pence and ten pence respectively to cover their expenses (and doubtless a free meal as well) for presenting their plays in the market-place (*inforo*): there is no mention of a gathering or collection in the chamberlain's accounts; but, since the players claimed and received their expenses, the assumption is that the balance of the collection went into the town's funds.[18]

In still other instances a large parish acted as a focal point for all the smaller parishes in the district. Thus Bassingbourne in Cambridgeshire, Blighborough in Suffolk and Dunmow in Essex became responsible for festivities including the production of plays for which other adjoining parishes made specific financial contributions on a basis proportionate to respective size and population.[19]

It is only very rarely that records are sufficiently complete to provide us with either a full list of the actual production costs for this sort of play or a final balance sheet. A rough and ready indication of the former, however, can be gleaned from those of the parish of Holy Trinity, Bungay, in Essex between 1550 and 1570. They included the usual modest payments for paper and to the author and the copyist for writing out the parts. Costumes were hired on one occasion from Great Yarmouth (at a cost of twelve pence) with shoes, wigs and visors being obtained from other sources, while on another they were borrowed from Wymondham: the men who fetched and returned them had to be paid as well. This also applied to scenic accessories, some of which were borrowed or hired from Norwich and Great Yarmouth: other items, including a cloud and an unspecified number of painted cloths, were made locally. These accounts include two items of special interest : the first is provision for the hiring of a professional comedian 'for his pastime before the play and after the play both days – 2 shillings' The second is a payment to a night security guard 'for watching the scaffold for saving all things.'[20]

Curiously it is the neighbouring parish of St Michael at Braintree that supplies the well-nigh unique example of final balance sheets. These belong to the years 1523, 1525 and 1534. Three different plays were produced in these years all of which were performed once in the church itself.

The play of St Swithin in 1523 cost £3.1s. 4d. The collections totalled £6.14s.11½d., leaving a profit of £3.13s.7½d. In 1525 the play of St Andrew cost £4.9s.9d., but succeeded in making a profit of £3.19s.9d. Doubtless encouraged by these successes, the outlay on the play of St Eustace in 1535 was increased to £6.13s.7½d.: nevertheless, boldness was rewarded with substantially increased takings of £14.17s.6½d.[21]

It would be foolish to try to use these fragmentary records and others like them extending over more than a century to postulate formal conclusions about production costs and the methods adopted in amateur and professional circles for meeting them. What they do admit, however, is unequivocal proof that by the end of the fifteenth century the decision to present a dramatic entertainment of any kind anywhere automatically confronted the sponsor, the author and the performers with financial problems that had to be faced and met before production could begin. The longer the play, the more elaborate the production requirements and the greater the costs on the one hand, the more imperative was the need on the other for stringent managerial control. As this happened, aesthetic and commercial interests in the drama became inextricably mixed. And here, although sophisticated Court *ludi* including tournaments and Disguisings remained predominantly amateur and privately financed, the increasingly ostentatious displays of dramatic spectacle provided by those revels set standards for others to envy and emulate which, if copied, must inflate production costs still further.

All the evidence available to us both from English and continental sources suggests that the idea of professionalism in acting, and in costumes and settings, grew up at Court and worked its

way outwards into society through the lords spiritual and temporal who sought to provide their own tenants and dependants with
fashionable replicas of Court models. From there the desire to
enhance the visual aspects of dramatic entertainments and to
reinforce the technical skills (more especially the comic ones) of
individual characterizations spread naturally to the merchant
princes whose wealth, if tapped, could swiftly translate these
desires from aspiration into actuality. By the start of the sixteenth
century therefore some aspect of professionalism in dramatic art is
everywhere in evidence : in European Courts – whether those of
the Medicis, the d'Estes, the Valois or the Tudors – it is to be
found in the maintenance of professional musicians, actors, and
painters employed to design costumes and scenic spectacle : in the
larger cities – whether in Spain, in the Netherlands or in German-
speaking countries – ecclesiastical and municipal leaders join

13   Sketch of professional actors performing on a trestle-stage erected in
front of a village inn and with a curtained booth to serve as a dressing
room

forces to raise capital on a large scale to finance the employment of producers on long-term contracts and the payment of the best authors and artisans in the region.[22] Those employed and those rewarded came thus to realize that sufficient money could be earned from these activities, if undertaken frequently enough, to provide a regular income. It was the actors who first learnt this lesson, making themselves masters of their own destinies instead of the slaves of occasion, by travelling abroad with their Interludes and learning to handle audiences of the fairground and market-place as firmly as those of the banquet hall. To this extent at least the Italian *Commedia dell'Arte* and the English 'Players of Inter-ludes' resemble each other as pioneers of a new era in the annals of dramatic art. In this they were followed shortly afterwards by certain fraternities dedicated to charitable work in Spain (*Confradiás*) and, rather later, in France (*Confréries*). In the Low Countries the Chambers of Rhetoric (*Rederyker Kamers*) and in Germany the Guilds of Mastersingers, with their respective *landjuweel* or 'Carnival' competitions and prizes would almost certainly have developed similarly had not the bitter conflicts accompanying the Reformation retarded growth by denying them both opportunity and financial security.[23]

At the start of this chapter I remarked that the professional and commercial theatre of the modern world was a parasitic growth which battened upon both the theatres of worship and the theatres of social recreation during the late Middle Ages and then developed its own strength from those elements within the parents on which it fed that openly invited commercial exploitation. If this opinion struck the reader as contentious, the evidence set out in the rest of this chapter should help to convince him of the truth of it : for the English 'players of Interludes' and their equivalents on the continent *invented* very little, even if they took great risks, on their long journey towards fully professional status. Their *platea,* or acting-area, and its relationship to the audience was essentially still that of liturgical music-drama in Christian basi-licas of the eleventh and twelfth centuries and of the mummings and *entremets* of banquet halls in the thirteenth and fourteenth centuries. So too was the relationship of the *platea* to the vesting- or changing-room and to the scenic devices used to identify the locality of the stage action : nor were the conventions employed in dress and speech to equate the actor with the character repre-

sented notably different. Indeed in some respects the new professionals were incapable of even attempting what amateurs could
still achieve in the early years of the sixteenth century either in
the open-air playing-places of Corpus Christi Day or in the
courtly Disguisings in banquet halls at Christmas or Shrove-tide.
Where then did their advantage lie? The answer, I think, rests in
three factors denied to the amateurs. The first of these was their
infinitely wider experience of audience response and reaction
acquired from the obligation to travel widely and to repeat a
small repertoire of short plays very frequently. The second
advantage was derived from the first; a rapidly developing self-
confidence (closely linked to artistic technique) assuring them
that spectators would respond in the manner anticipated and
giving them the time needed always to be mentally several steps
ahead of their audiences and thus physically in control of both
stage and auditorium. The third was the need imposed upon
them to keep production costs down to a minimum and thus to be
masters of their art and fortunes rather than puppets manipulated
by committees (however well intentioned and disposed) of clerics,
burghers or academics.

These advantages they recognized and exploited to the full : in
doing so they displayed an imaginative initiative, took considerable risks, earned remarkable rewards and, ultimately, changed
the course of theatre history. At the same time what they offered
their audiences was seldom more than a *ludus*, 'game' or 'play',
compounded from the rituals of liturgical music-drama and
chivalric combats, the narrative techniques of Corpus Christi vernacular drama and the *chanson de geste*, the title role of Saint
Plays, the allegorical debates of the Morality Play, and the pastoral charm of folk games, together with all the representational
devices created and developed within all these genres over some
five hundred years of amateur initiative and experiment in
churches, town halls, market-squares and village streets.

7

CHURCH AND STATE

After Martin Luther had nailed his ninety-five principles to the door of the castle church in Wittenberg in 1517 and Henry vιιι had married Anne Boleyn in 1533 without having secured Pope Clement vιι's consent, religion in North-Western Europe became inseparable from politics : the drama, as a child of the Roman Catholic Church, was automatically sucked into this whirlpool of national and international strife with no hope of extracting itself until after the political conflict had been settled.

In parts of Germany, Switzerland and the Low Countries drama at once became a vehicle for Protestant polemic. In England papal claims to authority over audiences, players and plays were jettisoned shortly afterwards : nor was it long before German and Swiss example was followed in adapting Moral Interludes as propaganda for the Reformation. With the dissolution of the monasteries, the severe curtailment of the number of Calendar holidays and the abolition of the Feast of Corpus Christi, drama as it had been known in England for the past century or more was thrown into so chaotic a state as to require statutory legislation to control it from a Parliament nervous lest partisan riots among spectators at a play might spark off more serious uprisings[24] (see Plates 30 and 35).

In France, by edict of the Parliament of Paris in 1548, all religious plays were banned in the capital : provincial cities followed suit, piecemeal, over the next fifteen years. That the Protestant spirit contributed largely to these injunctions is certain, but in France at that time Catholics were themselves sensitive to the attacks mounted against the superstitious, indecorous and idolatrous aspects of many religious *ludi*. Being anxious therefore to remove such weapons from the armouries of their opponents, they were ready to accept rather than oppose the suppression of the *Mystères*.

In both Spain and Italy a similarly defensive spirit led the Church itself to promote an active policy of reform, either by means of stricter censorship of texts or by the withdrawal of production subsidies, *before* satirical attacks on aspects of the drama could be developed into a wider and more serious form of propaganda for secession from Rome. In Spain, heresy as actually experienced through direct contact with the Moorish invaders from the Islamic South was of far more concern than that threatening from Protestant factions in the more distant North. The Inquisition had thus already been strengthened during the last decades of the fifteenth century to unite national opinion in defence of the Catholic faith, and was ready to serve as a reforming agent long before the Protestant spirit to the North could constitute a threat of any consequence. Thus guarded and protected, Spanish religious *autos* acquired fresh support from ecclesiastical and civic authorities alike in the course of the sixteenth century and continued to develop as nowhere else in Europe.

The threat of heresy was no less real in Italy than it was in Spain, but it came from a different quarter. Since Italy possessed a common frontier with German-speaking peoples in the Tirol, and in Switzerland, at first Lutheran and then Calvinist views penetrated swiftly and deeply into the Northern provinces from Milan to Venice. Strong pressure was thus brought to bear on senior clergy to ensure that the *sacre rappresentazioni* did nothing to weaken orthodox positions in these debates. Purged of offensive comic business and reinforced didactically and artistically, the plays succeeded in obtaining a large measure of support throughout the country from Sicily and Naples in the south to Bergamo and Venice in the north until quite late in the seventeenth century. A much more serious threat to their survival in Italy developed from a succession of princes, dukes, cardinals and popes steadily switching their patronage and financial support to new forms of dramatic entertainment grounded in classical theories of play-construction and theatrical presentation. It thus became fashionable to make a clear-cut distinction between sacred and secular dramatic activity, encouraging development of

the latter within the environment of Court festivals and relegating
the former as devotional exercises to popular patronage.

Thus in varying ways all theatres of worship inevitably suc-
cumbed to change in the political aftermath of the Reformation
and the Counter-Reformation. In Spain and Italy a smooth and
gradual transition from distinctively medieval forms to new ones
conforming with humanist theories of the drama was effected
during the course of the sixteenth century. In France the transition was abrupt. In the North and West of Europe, however, it
was also gradual, but often violent and frequently unpredictable
in many of its twists and turns depending more on local circumstances and expediency than on any theoretical principles. Commercial, sociological and academic factors all came to play some
part in the nature and pace of change in the North as well as
strictly religious and political ones.[25]

In a book devoted to the medieval stage an attempt to dis-
entangle all these factors, each a complex one in itself, in respect
of the *pace* of change would be inappropriate; but it is necessary
to examine the *nature* of the change since this is the feature above
all others that determines why, how and when this period of
theatre history ends, and a new one can be said to have begun.

In Italy the seeds of change were sown early, and were
academic and linguistic rather than religious or theatrical. Of all
the vernacular languages of modern Europe, Italian, for obvious
reasons, was the closest to Latin as spoken and written by the
Romans : awareness of this simple fact led Italian scholars, from
the thirteenth century onwards, into self-conscious efforts to
purify their own language as a vehicle for composition and criticism by retrospective analysis of models surviving from classical
antiquity.[26] At first they had to rely on examples stored in their
own libraries, but by the beginning of the fifteenth century
wealthy merchants in maritime cities like Venice and Genoa
began to import manuscripts bought in those countries which had
formerly lain within the frontiers of the Eastern Empire centred
on Byzantium. Latin was itself still a living language – notably as
that of the Church, diplomacy and law – and was thus as worthy
of refinement as Italian : indeed, the refinement of Latin was an
essential prelude to the latter. Greek was a dead language in the
West, but it lay behind Latin and thus began to attract attention
in its own right : nor were the claims of Hebrew and Arabic on

scholars' attention overlooked. By the start of the sixteenth century Latin studies of this humanist kind were securely established in all the major schools and universities of Europe; Greek lagged behind, but steps were being taken in most universities to employ scholars to edit Greek manuscripts and to translate them into Latin. Erasmus is a case in point who, where the drama is concerned, found time both at Cambridge and at Leiden, to translate Greek plays. In Italy these studies attracted the attention and support of sophisticated courtiers including clerics of the highest rank who vied with one another in founding academies devoted to research and experiment. This support of literary and linguistic studies was extended to architecture and painting at an early date.[27] Before the close of the fifteenth century the possibility of combining the fruits of literary and architectural research, and of giving expression to both in performances of play by Plautus and Terence, had been realized. Scholars from France, England and German-speaking countries were not slow to take advantage of opportunities to study in these new academies, the most important of which in terms of drama was that established in Rome under papal patronage by Pomponius Laetus. An alternative form of secular dramatic *ludus* and an alternative manner of presenting it in theatres of social recreation thus existed long before the first rumblings of the Reformation began to disturb the foundations of the traditional religious *ludi*. Nevertheless, no sooner had Protestantism established itself as a cause commanding substantial popular support than the respective claims of Latin and Greek on the time and energies of scholars was opened to question.

Latin had been and remained the language of the liturgy, of the Vulgate, of the Roman Church: yet, as Protestant reformers never ceased to point out, the Old Testament had been written in Hebrew and the New Testament in Hebrew and Greek. Thus, as the Pope came to be equated with Anti-Christ, it was argued that the continued use of Latin had been and still was an obvious device designed to ensnare and enslave the unwary. Greek and Hebrew, by contrast, were the languages of original inspiration and thus to be espoused as those of the new enlightenment. In such circumstances as these the progress of the new humanist drama outside Italy was bound to shudder to a temporary standstill while scholars came to terms with the implications of this

clash of interest between Latin and Greek, and while politicians
debated what penalties should attach to too open a devotion to
either of them. Devout Catholics had to defend Latin against the
attacks of their opponents in standing up for their own faith : yet
to do this in the face of a Protestant government could easily be
interpreted as treason : no less self-evidently, men whose
championship of Greek under a Catholic regime suggested that
they might be heretics ran similar risks of arrest, imprisonment
and death. From the fifteen-thirties onwards therefore, changes in
the general tenor and direction of plays and performance in
North-Western Europe could not follow those taking place in
Italy under the influence of revivals of Latin plays and Roman
theatre architecture either smoothly or directly : where the will to
initiate still existed, it could at best proceed in fits and starts and
without calling attention to itself. This it succeeded in doing in
some schools and in most university colleges, usually disguised
as a requirement of the curriculum in Rhetoric, and thus serving
only as a very slow leaven upon the attitudues of future
generations.[28]

　　This then was one of the more important if unexpected cross-
currents working upon the drama in the countries where Protestantism established itself securely. Another is to be seen in the
attempts made by Protestants to make religious *ludi* serve their
own cause. The instrument chosen for this purpose was the Moral
Interlude and the method adopted was to translate the perennial
abstract characters of representative Human Being, supporting
Virtue and opposing Vice into the body politic, or Common-
wealth, supported by the reformed Church and attacked by Anti-
Christ in the shape of the Pope (see Plate 30). This weapon
proved to be double-edged since Catholics could just as easily
reverse the roles and present a Republic defended by the expo-
nents of the true faith from the ravages of envious and greedy
hypocrites styling themselves as Reformers.[29] It also served to
arouse passionate responses among spectators. Ridicule from the
stage provoked laughter and applause in one section of the
auditorium while arousing resentment and indignation in
another : injured feelings expressed themselves in hard words, and
hard words were answered in their turn by blows. The resulting
breaches of the peace forced mayors, sheriffs, deans and heads of
colleges to take action against the offenders and seek assistance in

preventing recurrences of such conduct from higher authority.[30]
Thus, almost imperceptibly, riots led to legislation, legislation to
censorship and control, and censorship and control to suppression. In Germany and the Low Countries these processes were
speeded up by civil war: in England they took a full century to
work themselves out, but at the end of the line the result was the
same – the disbanding of the acting companies followed by the
closure and then the demolition of the theatres.

That such an outcome was far from the minds of the original
reformers is made clear by their early attempts to rewrite the
Cycles, Passions, and even plays of eschatology to conform with
Protestant beliefs. In England, Martin Bucer, sometime tutor to
the boy-King Edward VI, argued strenuously that for the composition of tragedies,

> ... the scriptures constantly offer an abundance of material in
> almost all the stories of the Holy Fathers, the Kings, the
> prophets and Apostles, continuously from Adam, the first
> parent of the human race.

Bucer was a humanist as well as a Protestant; as well read in
Aristophanes as in Terence, in Sophocles as in Sencea and in
Aristotle as in Horace. Style mattered to him as did the provision
of public entertainment, 'which is not without value in increasing
piety'.[31] Yet the passion for public edification which he shared
with the Protestant playwrights who heeded his advice so far
outstripped their understanding of human nature (a liberty
which their Catholic predecessors had never permitted themselves), that they succeeded in boring their audiences rather than
entertaining them, and drove them into the arms of the professional players of Interludes who, in their own economic interests,
had to refrain from making so crass a mistake. This in its turn
inspired the jealousy of 'common players' which in Elizabethan
times was to provoke Stephen Gossen, Philip Stubbs and other
Protestants of Calvinist persuasion into pouring vitriolic scorn on
actors, plays and playhouses of all descriptions in a wave of
sermons, pamphlets and books. It was this spirit that led Edmund
Grindal, as Bishop of London, when asking the Privy Council to
stop all plays for one year on account of the plague, to add in
parenthesis, 'and if it were for ever, it were not amiss'.[32]

A third cross-current of Reformation politics in relation to the drama was commercial. This has already been referred to in the preceding chapter. So great was the inflation of production costs accruing to Corpus Christi drama in the early years of the sixteenth century that religious *ludi* on this scale could only be financed by the corporate efforts of ecclesiastical and municipal leaders in the region. The committees of management which they established could function efficiently so long as both parties shared a good opinion of the ultimate benefits of these undertakings within the communities for which they were responsible. No such unanimity of opinion could be maintained in the face of the Reformation for very long : and as that foundered the money needed to finance production dried up. Neither in Germany nor in England is there any real evidence of repressive policies designed by governments, cathedral chapters or city councils to exterminate such plays in the early years of the Reformation era. Where plays founder it is due either to uncertainty about the desirability of proceeding with performances in troubled times, or to unwillingness to underwrite production costs out of taxes that might prove unpopular, or to the withering of private benefaction, or to new regulations that fortuitously destroyed former opportunities and incentives for play production.

An example of the last comes from Lincoln. In 1537 the Bishop issued copies throughout his diocese of Henry vm's decree abolishing the majority of annual festival days on the grounds that 'the number of holydays is so excessively grown' as to have become prejudicial to the pursuit of agriculture and actively to promote idleness and riotous behaviour. Accordingly all clergy are to ensure that, 'the Feast of the Patron of every Church within this realm (called commonly "the church holiday") shall not from henceforth be kept or observed as a holiday, as heretofore hath been used. . . .' Four days only are to be generally observed as holidays in future – Christmas Day, Easter Day, and the Feasts of St John the Baptist (Midsummer) and St Michael. No holidays are to be observed in harvest time or during the Law-terms at Westminster : St George's Day, together with Feasts of the Apostles and the Virgin are excepted.[33]

There is no suggestion in this decree that Saint Plays or any other form of drama should be banned; but what is the point of celebrating such days with a performance of a play about the life and works of the patronal saint if neither the actors nor the former audience have the liberty to celebrate it at all? It is almost certainly on this account therefore, that references to performances of Saint Plays cease abruptly at the close of this decade. The exception is plays relating to St George. Could it be therefore that many villages, denied their own patronal plays, substituted a St George play instead at about this time, the vestigial relics of which in corrupted form have descended to us in the form of the so-called 'Mummers' Play'? No firm answer can be given to this question in the light of the evidence presently available : but were this to have been the case, many of the difficulties surrounding this and the other folk *ludi* discussed in Chapter 4 would admit of much easier solutions than they do now.[34]

Another example of the fortuitous disappearance rather than deliberate suppression of religious *ludi* comes from Hereford in 1548. In that year the Clerk to the City Council recorded in their Great Black Book that the funds formerly raised and devoted to the production of *The Play Called Corpus Christi* were to be diverted to finance maintenance work within the city. Only when it is noticed that the Feast of Corpus Christi was itself universally suppressed in England in that year does it become clear why this Cycle ceased to be performed then.[35] Many others must have been dropped at the same time and for the same reason. The probability is that these included plays in London, since these were well enough remembered to be revived eight years later in 1557 under Mary I. Detailed records survive from New Romney in Kent of the preparations for similar revivals in 1555 and on several other occasions up to 1568. Ipswich on the other hand appears to have dropped its Cycle as early as 1531.[36]

In the West Midlands and the North production of the Cycles continued virtually without interruption, and it was only after the Northern Rebellion of 1569 and the excommunication of Elizabeth I in 1570 that Church and State finally agreed that production must stop. Yet even as late as 1600 serious, if abortive, efforts were being made in Chester to revive that Cycle.[37]

To argue that the medieval theatres of worship and social recreation only became involved with politics as a result of the Reformation would be untrue; for there is evidence, as we have seen, of plays like the Tergensee *Antichristus* and the French *entremets* depicting the Conquest of Jerusalem and the Seige of Troy in 1378 and 1389 having been devised at least in part as propaganda to promote crusades.[38] Much later, in Tudor England, a play by John Roo presented at Grays Inn in 1526–7 so displeased Cardinal Wolsey as to occasion Roo's arrest and imprisonment. Edward Hall discussing this incident in his *Chronicle* says,

> ... the effecte of the plaie was, that Lord governance was ruled by dissipacion and negligence, by whose misgovernance and evill order, Lady Publike wele was put from governance: which caused Rumor Populi, Inward grudge, and disdain of wanton sovereignetie to rise with great multitude, to expell negligence and dissipacion, and to restore Publik welth again to her estate, which was so done.[39]

Two years later, in 1529, some representative of the City Council in Chester felt it necessary to write to London to seek advice on whether or not to proceed with a revival of a play about King Robert of Sicily lest it be thought 'unfit or unwise at this time'.[40]

Nevertheless, no evidence exists to suggest that the drama of medieval Europe ever found itself in serious trouble on account of its political content before the start of the sixteenth century. Trouble began in earnest when the Church elected to extend its own role from that of censor, and thus protector, of the drama, and adopted the more active posture of sponsor and promoter of anti-papal polemic. This initiative was German in origin but was rapidly developed in the free cities of Switzerland, notably Basle and Berne, and assumed more dangerous dimensions than might otherwise have been the case as copies reached the new printing presses that were rapidly being established in major European cities. Among the most striking of these early polemical plays are two by the painter Nikolas Manuel of Berne (see Plate 18), *Vom Papst und seiner Priester schaft* (1521) and *Der Ablasskrämer* (1525): in the former he contrasts a magnificent ecclesiastical procession with the simplicity of Christ's entry into Jerusalem, while in the latter he depicts a seller of indulgences, recognized and set upon by his former clients, and forced, under a spirited sequence of indignities, to disgorge the monies taken from them on an earlier visit to Berne.[41] Similar in character is the *Totenfresser* (1521) by Pamphilus Gegenback who was by profession a printer working in Basle in which not only the Pope, but bishops, monks and nuns are all depicted as ruthless exploiters of the poor and needy (see Plate 35).

German and Swiss precept met with a ready response in England in the next decade at the hands of Wolsey's successor as Lord Chancellor, Thomas Cromwell, and of Thomas Cranmer, Archbishop of Canterbury. Cromwell possessed his own company of players and commissioned 'sundry and divers fresh and quick wits' including an able Catholic priest converted to Protestantism, John Bale, to write polemical religious plays. Some of these plays were then performed in Canterbury with Cranmer in the audience.[42] It was to Cranmer too that the German playwright Thomas Kirchmayer dedicated his *Pammachius* in 1538. Originally composed in Latin and then translated into German, this play about a Pope of that name was acted in the original Latin at Christ's College Cambridge in 1545 where it created such a stir that Bishop Gardiner in his capacity of Chancellor of the University pronounced it to be 'too pestiferous to be tolerated'.[43] Such protests were by then too late to be effective. Only by legislation, supported by stiff penalties for infringements, could control of the situation be regained by either Church or State. It was these new controls in the final analysis, affecting actors, acting-places and times of performances, and the production and printing of plays that extinguished the medieval theatre.

What survived still resembled its antecedents in many important respects, especially in the mechanics and techniques of play-construction and the conventions of theatrical representation : but a new spirit was needed to face the dangers and to overcome the difficulties of the times – a spirit that was professional rather than amateur, metropolitan rather than provincial, and broadly academic rather than narrowly clerical. This spirit was forthcoming as soon as the professional players of Interludes and men of letters in the schools and universities realized that it was in their common interest to cultivate each other's acquaintance and work together to capture the large popular audiences that were losing their own plays of former years, but not their appetite for entertainment, with new plays that were cast in moulds that were still familiar and intelligible.

Because of the survival well into the seventeenth century in many countries, Catholic as well as Protestant, of techniques of play-construction and conventions of play-production that are so distinctively medieval in character it is very difficult to draw any firm line in point of date that accurately represents the close of this period of theatre history. Yet it does seem legitimate to conclude that once the Church found itself in conflict with itself, it lost both the inspirational and executive control over all aspects of drama and theatre that it had formerly exercised directly or indirectly throughout Christendom from the tenth to the sixteenth century; and that once this schism had spread from being a doctrinal conflict into a political one the Church was steadily forced to yield more and more of its authority to others better able to exercise it in the changed political, academic and commercial climate of the times. Even then the Church retained control over its own plays; but as these dwindled in the middle decades of the sixteenth century into minority status, and a largely provincial one at that, so it can be fairly claimed that the words 'medieval theatre' as a descriptive concept covering plays, players, theatres, stages and audiences ceases to be meaningful in any European country with the possible exception of Spain. Inspirational and executive control thus passed initially to academics and professional actors but was soon to be firmly and strictly subordinated to aristocratic control, a subject that will occupy the next volume in this series.

NOTES

I: DRAMA OF PRAISE AND THANKSGIVING

1 On this difficult subject see Otto Demus, *Byzantine Art and the West* (Weidenfeld & Nicolson 1970). *The Larousse Encyclopaedia of Byzantine and Medieval Art*, ed. René Huyghe (Paris 1958), supplies useful documentation on other influences from the Near and Far East including Persian, Egyptian, Indian and Chinese Art of earlier periods.

2 Christ as King and Christ as Man are discussed at length by Colin Morris in *The Discovery of the Individual, 1050–1200* (SPCK 1972).

3 On iconoclasm, see p. 28 above: also, for a more detailed examination, David Talbot Rice, *Art of the Byzantine Era* (Thames & Hudson 1963), pp. 74 et seq.

4 Some of Plautus's plays may possibly have been preserved in this way; but, unlike the works of other writers quoted, they were seldom if ever read. Revival of interest in Plautus's plays, both as literary and dramatic models, thus had to wait until the latter half of the fifteenth century when a much wider range of Latin literature became generally available following the seizure and export to the West of manuscripts hitherto preserved only in the libraries of the Eastern Empire. See Ch. 7 pp. 202–3 above.

5 On the Benedictine reform and liturgical music-drama see pp. 39–41 above. On the origins and development of the Church vestments used as costumes in liturgical music-drama see W. B. Marriot, *Vestiarum Christianum*, 1868.

6 On the musical development of liturgical texts see W. Smolden, 'The Origins of the *Quem Quaeritis* Trope and the Easter Sepulchre Music Dramas as Demonstrated by their Musical Settings' in *The Medieval Drama*, ed. Sandro Sticca (SUNY Press, Binghamton 1972), pp. 121–41, subsequently reprinted in changed and enlarged form as 'The Melodies of the Medieval Church Dramas and Their Significance' in *Medieval English Drama: Essays Critical and Contextual*, ed. J. Taylor and A. H. Nelson (University of Chicago Press 1972).

7 For the development and distribution of the Canonical Offices see p. 31 above.

8 The original Latin text was printed by E. K. Chambers in *The Mediaeval Stage* (1903) vol. II, Appendix O, p. 309: the English text given here is

that printed by Professor A. M. Nagler in *Sources of Theatrical History* (New York 1952) pp. 39–40.

9 For the full Latin text of this drama and the others which follow it (pp. 46–50) see Karl Young, *The Drama of the Mediaeval Church*: for the Dublin *Visitatio* see Chambers, *The Mediaeval Stage*, pp. 315–18: I am especially grateful to my colleague, J. M. Tester, for his help in checking my translations.

For illustrations of the costumes prescribed for Isaiah, Jeremiah and Moses see Plates 8 and 13.

2: DRAMA OF REPENTANCE

10 On the early history of Provençal and the growth of the *chansons de geste* see F. Mandet, *Histoire de Langue Romane (Roman Provençal)* (Paris 1840); on the itineraries of the early *trouvères* see Raimon de Loi, *Trails of the Troubadours* (New York 1926); for their English connections see J. Audian, *Les Troubadours et l'Angleterre* (Paris 1927); for their German and Spanish connections see A. R. Nykl, *Hispano-Arabic Poetry and its Relations with the Old Provençal Troubadours* (Baltimore 1946), and Theodor Frings, *Minnesinger and Troubadours* (Berlin 1949).

11 See Sandro Sticca, *The Latin Passion Play: its Origins and Development* (New York 1970), and Colin Morris, *The Discovery of the Individual, 1050–1200* (SPCK 1972). This change in philosophic and literary approaches to Christianity is no less apparent in fresco, painting and sculpture where it results in the substitution of the rood-screen as the dominant decorative feature of gothic churches for the figure of the Pantocrator (or that of the Virgin Mary as Queen of Heaven) in the domes and apses of earlier Romanesque basilicas.

12 See V. A. Kolve, *The Play Called Corpus Christi* (Stanford University Press 1966), pp. 33–56. The translation of Pope Urban IV's Bull given here is that supplied by Kolve (together with the Latin text) on p. 45.

13 The first play to bring together Advent, Christmas, Passiontide and Easter dramas appears to have been that presented in Latin at Cividale in North-Eastern Italy in 1298 and 1303. See Chambers, *The Mediaeval Stage* (1903) II, 77–8, n.3, and Sandro Sticca, 'The Literary Genesis of the Latin Passion Play' in *The Medieval Drama*, ed. S. Sticca (SUNY 1972), pp. 39–68.

14 See G. R. Owst, *Literature and Pulpit in Mediaeval England* (1933): Eleanor Prosser, *Drama and Religion in the English Miracle Plays* (Stanford University Press 1961), pp. 19–42, and Edward Peacock, *Instructions for Parish Priests*, ed. for EETS (1868). Also, M. C. D'Arcy, *Thomas Aquinas* (1930).

15 See Lucy Toulmin-Smith, *English Guilds*, ed. for EETS. (1870): G. Unwin, *The Guilds and Companies of London* (1908): Alice Stopford Green, *Town Life in the Fifteenth Century*, 2 vols (1894): R. Ehrenberg, *Capital and Finance in the Age of the Renaissance* (1928): J. Klein, *The Mesta: A Study of Spanish Economic History, 1273–1836* (Harvard 1920): G. Cross, *The Gild Merchant* (1890): H. Pirenne, *Mediaeval Cities, their Origin and the Revival of Trade*, trans. H. P. Halsey (1925): A. Luchaire, *Social France at the Time of Philip Augustus*, trans. E. Krebhiel (1912).

16 See F. M. Salter, *Mediaeval Drama in Chester* (Toronto 1955), pp. 72–80.
17 See M. Blakemore Evans, *The Passion Play of Lucerne* (MLAA 1943), and Elie Konigson, *La Représentation d'un Mystère de la Passion a Valenciennes en 1547* (CNRS, Paris 1969).
18 See M. Giraud, *Composition, mise en scène et représentation du Mystère des Trois Doms joué à Romans, les 27, 28 et 29 mai, aux fêtes de Pentecôte de l'an 1509* (Lyons 1848): also G. Wickham, *Early English Stages* (Routledge & Kegan Paul 1958), vol. I, pp. 164–7 and 302–6.
19 See J. P. W. Crawford, *The Spanish Drama before Lope de Vega* (Philadelphia 1922): W. H. Shoemaker, *The Multiple Stage in Spain during the Fifteenth and Sixteenth centuries* (Princeton 1935), and N. D. Shergold, *A History of the Spanish Stage from Mediaeval Times until the End of the Seventeenth Century* (1967).
20 Evans, op. cit., pp. 99–103. I am grateful to my colleague, George Brandt, for his help in checking the translation given here. Similar disciplinary orders of about the same date survive in England from New Romney in Kent. These are printed in Malone Society *Collections VII*, ed. Giles E. Dawson (1965), Appendix B, pp. 202–11.
21 In England banns and proclamations dating from both before and after the Reformation survive from Chester: on this subject see F. M. Salter, op. cit, and G. Wickham, *Early English Stages*, I, Appendix D, pp. 340–7. Some idea of the cost accruing from this item of production expenses can be obtained from the Chamberlain's Accounts of the Corporation of Lydd in Kent. These are printed in Malone Society *Collections VII*, ed. cit. pp. 89–112.
22 Readers interested in arrangements made for spectators and orderly attendance should pay special attention to those at Chester and York in England, Mons, Angers and Romans in France, and at Lucerne in Switzerland.
23 See G. Cohen, *Le Livre de Conduite du Régisseur et le Compte des Dépenses pour le Mystère de la Passion joué à Mons en 1501* (Paris 1925), and O. Jodogne, *Mystère de la Passion d'Angers de Jean Michel* (Gembloux 1959). I am grateful to my colleague, Dr T. Hemming, for checking these and other translations from the French.
24 See George Ferguson, *Signs and Symbols in Christian Art* (1954); Robert Hughes, *Heaven and Hell in Western Art* (1968); M. D. Anderson, *Drama and Imagery in English Mediaeval Churches* (1963); W. L. Hildburgh, *English Alabaster Carvings as Records of the Medieval Religious Drama* (1959); Emile Mâle, *L'Art Religieux de la Fin du Moyen Age en France*, 5th ed. (Paris 1949).
25 See M. A. Lavin, 'The Altar of Corpus Domini in Urbino: Paolo Uccello, Joos Van Ghent, Piero della Francesca', *The Art Bulletin*, XLIX, no. 1 (March 1967), pp. 1–24.
26 For readers of German the fullest accounts are given by W. Creizenach, *Geschichte des neueren Dramas* (1893–1903), vols I–III and H. Kindermann, *Theatergeschichte Europas*, 9 vols (Salzburg 1957–70), vol. 1.
27 See H. A. Rennert, *The Spanish Stage in the Time of Lope de Vega*, 1909 (reprinted by Dover Publications Inc., New York 1963) pp. 69–75. On

dancing in the choir of Wells Cathedral and in certain English parish churches see pp. 141 and 143 above.

28 The subject of performers in religious plays in Italy is discussed briefly by Alessandro D'Ancona in *Origini del Teatro Italiano* (1891), I, 401–25; French practice is discussed by Gustave Cohen in *Histoire de la Mise en Scène dans le Théâtre Religieux Français du Moyen Age* (Paris 1926), pp. 36–47, 57–61 and 196–243. On Spanish actors see H. A. Rennert, op. cit., Chapter VII and the Appendix to the first edition; on German actors see Kindermann, op. cit. Religious plays appear in Scandinavia and Czechoslovakia early in the fifteenth century, and in Poland shortly after 1470.

29 The so-called Digby Plays – (i) *The Conversion of St Paul* (ii) *St Mary Magdalene* (iii) *The Massacre of the Innocents* and *Purification* and (iv) *Mind Will and Understanding* – were printed by F. J. Furnival for EETS in 1896 from Bodleian MS Digby 133. The Cornish play of *Beunans Meriasek: The Life of St Meriasek* was edited and printed together with a translation by Whitley Stokes in 1872. The Bourges play, *Mystère des Actes des Apôtres représenté à Bourges en avril, 1536*, was edited and printed in 1854 by A-T. de Giradot. On the play at Romans, 1509, see note 18 above.

30 See Karl Young, *The Drama of the Mediaeval Church* (1933) vol. II, pp. 307–60; also Theo Stemmler, *Liturgische Feiern und Geistliche Spiele* (Tübingen 1970), pp. 111–14.

31 See G. Wickham, 'The Staging of Saint Plays in England' in *The Mediaeval Drama*, ed. Sandro Sticca (SUNY 1972), pp. 99–119.

32 On French Saints Plays see Grace Frank, *The Medieval French Drama* (1954), Chapters X–XII and XIV. See Fig. 10 p. 100 above.

33 See M. B. Evans, *The Passion Play of Lucerne*, pp. 138–40; and E. K. Chambers, *The Mediaeval Stage*, II, pp. 399–406.

34 On Saints Plays in Italy see D'Ancona, op. cit., I pp. 369 et seq. The *Croxton Play of the Sacrament* is printed from Trinity College Dublin, MS F.4.20 by J. M. Manly in *Specimens of the Pre-Shakespearean Drama*, vol. I, pp. 239–76, See also note 25 above.

35 See Shergold, op. cit., pp. 62–3. This text is Catalano.

36 See notes 29 and 31 above.

37 See C. M. Clode, *Early History of the Merchant Taylors' Company* (1888). Also G. Wickham, *Early English Stages*, I, pp. 64–70.

38 See Rab Hatfield, 'The Compagnia de'Magi', *Journal of the Warburg and Courtauld Institutes* (1971), pp. 107–61.

39 See R. A. Wright, 'Mediaeval Theatre in East Anglia: a Study of Drama and the Community in Essex, Suffolk and Norfolk, 1200–1580', M.Litt. Thesis, University of Bristol, 1971.

40 See p. 200-10 above·

3: DRAMA OF MORAL INSTRUCTION

41 See George Ferguson, *Signs and Symbols in Christian Art* (1954); also J. Evans and M. S. Sergeantson, *English Mediaeval Lapidaries*, EETS

(1933), and Sir William St John Hope and E. G. Cuthbert Atchley, *English Liturgical Colours* (1918).

42 See G. Wickham, *Early English Stages*, I, Appendix C, pp. 332–9.

43 See Willard Farnham, *The Mediaeval Heritage of Elizabethan Tragedy* (1930) and G. Wickham, 'Genesis and the Tragic Hero' in *Shakespeare's Dramatic Heritage* (1969), pp. 42–63.

44 See E. K. Chambers, *The Mediaeval Stage*, II, pp. 338–41 and 377–9.

45 Ibid., II, pp. 399–406; see also H. C. Gardiner, *Mysteries' End*, pp. 72 et seq.

46 On the *Pas d'Armes* as a form of tournament see G. Wickham, *Early English Stages*, I, pp. 22–30; and Richard Barber, *The Knight and Chivalry* (1970), pp. 173–5; also pp. 152–7 above.

47 See Southern, op. cit., and N. C. Schmitt, 'Was there a Medieval Theater in the Round? A Re-examination of the Evidence', *Medieval English Drama*, ed. J. Taylor and A. H. Nelson (Chicago 1972), pp. 292–315.

48 On this subject see Grace Frank, *The Medieval French Drama*, (1953), Chapters XIX to XXIV: for some English translations of some of these plays see Richard Axton and John Stevens, *Medieval French Plays* (1971).

49 The translation of the passage quoted is from that by N. Denny in *Medieval Interludes* (1972), pp. 73–95.

50 On German, Austrian and Swiss plays of this type see H. Kindermann, *Theatergeschichte Europas*, I, pp. 397–432: for Spanish examples see N. Shergold, *A History of the Spanish Stage*, pp. 50–1 and 87–9.

51 See E. K. Chambers, *The Mediaeval Stage*, I, pp. 390–419: Enid Welsford, *The Court Masque* (1927), pp. 37 et seq.: A. Nicoll, *Masks, Mimes and Miracles* (1931), pp. 171–5, and pp. 161–7 above.

52 The text is printed by N. Davis in *Non-Cycle Plays and Fragments*, ed. for EETS with a note on the Shrewsbury Music by F. L. L. Harrison, 1970.

PART II: THEATRES OF RECREATION

4: DRAMA AND NATURE

1 *The Mediaeval Stage*, I, 97–100.

2 *The English Folk Play* (1933, reprinted 1969), p. 6 et seq.; see also R. J. E. Tiddy, *The Mummers' Play* (1923) and Walter A. Donohue, 'An Investigation, from a Broadly Philological Standpoint of the Rebirth of Organised Dramatic Entertainment in Europe in the Early Middle Ages', M.Litt. Thesis, University of Bristol, 1970, pp. 136–50.

3 For Asian examples of similar festivals and associated customs see A. C. Scott, *The Theatre in Asia* (1972).

4 So great was this demand for labour in the summer and autumn months that the Christian religious festivals which occasioned public holidays at this time became an early object of government legislation in England following the Reformation. See pp. 206–7 above.

5 In churches it was normal to light a candle on Easter Sunday and to

H

keep this alight until Ascension Day. Following the Reformation, the Midsummer Watch was still celebrated with bonfires and pageantry in many English cities. See Robert Withington, *English Pageantry, An Historical Outline*, 2 vols (1918–20).

6 See O. B. Hardison Jnr, *Christian Rite and Christian Drama in the Middle Ages* (Johns Hopkins, Baltimore 1965), Chapter 3 'The Lenten Agon', pp. 80–138.

7 If Jonson's Zeal-of-the-Land-Busy is the most vivid of the stage caricatures of these 'sourer shepherds', Shakespeare's Malvolio provides a more human but nonetheless equally disagreeable portrait.

8 See Chapter 5, pp. 161–7 above.

9 See Chambers, *The English Folk Play* and Alan Brody, *The English Mummers and their Plays*. The latter provides a photograph of the Bessey and the Tommy at Goathland in Yorkshire (Figure 9).

10 For a fine picture of this 'lock' see Brody, op. cit., Figure 12.

11 Brody, op. cit., p. 77. On the variant in the Ampleforth Play with its corruptions derived from Congreve's *Love for Love* see Brody pp. 83–93 and Chambers, p. 149.

12 See R. Bernheimer, *Wild Men in the Middle Ages* (Harvard 1952).

13 See Chambers, *The Mediaeval Stage*, I, pp. 154, 187 and II, pp. 264–6: also pp. 148–9 above.

14 See Brody, op. cit., Figure 9. A complete recording in colour was made of this play for BBC TV in 1972 at Goathland in Yorkshire.

15 John Stockwood in a sermon at Pauls Cross on 24 August 1578 spoke of May-games in the following words. '. . . the Lords day . . . is horriblie prophaned by divellishe inventions, . . . in so much that in some places, they shame not in ye time of divine service, to come and daunce aboute the Church, and without to have men naked dauncing in nettes, which is most filthie: for the heathen that never hadde further knowledge, than the lighte of nature, have counted it shamefull for a Player to come on the stage without a slop (i.e. trousers) and therefore amongst Christians I hope suche beastly brutishnesse shal not let escape unpunished . . .' See also p. 135 above.

16 See Grace Frank, *The Medieval French Drama*, pp. 225–36. and Richard Axton and John Stevens, *Medieval French Plays*, pp. 257–301.

17 These were printed by J. M. Manly in *Specimens of the Pre-Shakespearean Drama*, I, pp. 279–88.

18 For illustrations see Brody, op. cit., Figures 5 and 6. The text of this play is also given.

19 Legislation in Parliament against May-games in the form of 'An Act to Restrain Abuses of Players' began in 1606. See *Statutes* (27 May 1606), IV, 1097.

20 See R. A. Wright, 'Mediaeval Theatre in East Anglia', M.Litt thesis University of Bristol, 1971.

21 See Malone Society *Collections VII*, ed. Giles E. Dawson (1965).

22 Ibid, pp. 199–200. See also Chambers, *The Mediaeval Stage*, II, 338 and R. A. Wright, op. cit.

23 On this subject see Sybil Rosenfeld, *Strolling Players and Drama in the*

Provinces, 1660–1795 (1939); Richard Southern, *The Georgian Playhouse* (1948), and Arnold Hare, *The Georgian Theatre in Wessex* (1958).

5: DRAMA AND NATURAL MAN

24 See Otto Demus, *Byzantine Art and the West.*
25 See G. Wickham, *Early English Stages,* I, pp. 13–50.
26 Ibid., Plate X and accompanying note, p. 393. The ceremonial attaching to the holding of tournaments and the prize-giving as practised in the fifteenth century is meticulously described and exquisitely illustrated in *Le Livre des Tournois du Roi René* (MS Français 2692: *Bibliothèque Nationale,* Paris). It was reproduced and printed by the magazine *Verve,* vol. IV, no. 16 (1946).
27 Ibid., pp. 17–18. See Ruth Clyne, 'The Influence of Romances on Tournaments of the Middle Ages', *Speculum* (1945), pp. 204–11, and N. Denholm-Young, 'The Tournament in the Thirteenth Century', *Studies in Mediaeval History presented to F. M. Powicke* (1948), pp. 240–68. The *Pas d'Armes* with its dual concepts of assault and siege proved to be a fertile source for the structuring of dramatic debates conducted within the Morality Play and Moral Interludes: see pp. 116–19 above.
28 Ibid., II, pp. 229–36.
29 Ibid., I, pp. 31–7 and Plates II–IX.
30 G. M. Trevelyan, *English Social History* (1942), pp. 64–70.
31 *Robert of Brunne's 'Handlyng of Synne',* ed. for EETS by F. J. Furnivall (1901).
32 See G. Wickham, *Early English Stages,* I, pp. 179–90.
33 Ibid., p. 197.
34 Ibid., p. 203.
35 Ibid., p. 218. See also Enid Welsford, *The Court Masque* (1927), and Hall's *Chronicle* (ed. 1809) pp. 516–19.
36 Ibid., pp. 191–207. See also *The Minor Poems of John Lydgate,* ed. for EETS by H. N. MacCracken, 2 vols (1934).
37 Ibid., pp. 212–16. See also L. H. Loomis, 'Secular Dramatics in the Royal Palace, Paris, 1378, 1389, and Chaucer's "Tregetoures" ', *Speculum,* XXXIII (1958), pp. 242–55. This has recently been reprinted by J. Taylor and A. H. Nelson in *Medieval English Drama: Essays Critical and Contextual* (1972), pp. 98–115.
38 See S. Anglo, *Spectacle, Pageantry and Early Tudor Policy* (1969), pp. 207–43.
39 See G. Wickham, *Early English Stages,* I, pp. 63–70, for Latin text, English translation and commentary.
40 See Robert Withington, *English Pageantry: An Historical Outline* (Harvard 1918–20), vol. I, and D. M. Bergeron, *English Civic Pageantry 1558–1642* (1971).
41 See Chambers, *The Mediaeval Stage,* II, pp. 181–5, and n.34 above.
42 Ibid., 324–6: Malone Society *Collections VII,* 120.
43 See Wickham, *Early English Stages,* II, (Pt 2), pp. 122–38.
44 Henry Medwall, *Fulgens and Lucres,* ed. for Tudor and Stuart Library by F. S. Boas and A. W. Reed (1926).

45 John Redford's *Wit and Science* is available in the Malone Society Reprints (1951), and John Bale's *Three Laws* in Tudor Facsimile Texts issued by J. S. Farmer (1907–14), On dress and its relationship to action in Interludes, see T. W. Craik, *The Tudor Interlude* (1958).

PART III: THEATRES AND COMMERCE

6: AMATEURS AND PROFESSIONALS

1 See pp. 125–8 above.
2 See *Durham Account Rolls* ed. Canon Fowler for Surtees Soc., and Chambers, *The Mediaeval Stage*, II, pp. 240–4.
3 See Chambers, *The Mediaeval Stage*, II, pp. 338–41 and p. 374.
4 Ibid., pp. 377–9
5 See *Coventry Leet Book*, ed. M. D. Harris for EETS, 2 vols (1907–9), II, pp. 707–8.
6 Henry VII's Privy Purse Accounts are to be found in the British Museum Add. MS. 7099, fols 22 et seq. They were printed by S. Bentley in *Excerpta Historica*, 1831, pp. 100 et seq. See also G. Wickham, *Early English Stages*, I, 217–25 and S. Anglo, *Spectacle, Pageantry and Early Tudor Policy*, Chapters 1–3 inclusive.
7 See pp. 107–9 above.
8 See M. B. Evans, *The Passion Play of Lucerne*, pp. 97–108.
9 See G. Cohen, *Histoire de la Mise en Scène*, p. 175. For an example of a complete balance sheet of income and expenditure see G. Wickham, *Early English Stages*, I, pp. 164–7.
10 Letter to an unknown correspondent dated 15 January 1591 printed by Chambers, *The Elizabethan Stage*, IV, p. 237.
11 On the whole question of the right to act in the sixteenth century see G. Wickham, *Early English Stages*, II (Pt 1), pp. 106–21; also M. C. Bradbrook, *The Rise of the Common Player* (1962).
12 See T. W. Craik, *The Tudor Interlude*, pp. 73–118.
13 Ibid., pp. 93–118; see also G. Wickham, *Shakespeare's Dramatic Heritage*, pp. 24–41.
14 An important link between the two was the traffic in plays between the Tudor choir-schools and the Court. The prayer for the sovereign thus provided a natural epilogue for the play.
15 See G. Wickham, *Early English Stages*, II (Pt 1), pp. 183–96.
16 See note 10 above.
17 *The Medieval Records of a London City Church (St Mary at Hill)*, ed. Henry Littlehales for EETS (1905), pp. 321 et seq.
18 See R. A. Wright, 'Mediaeval Theatre in East Anglia', M.Litt. thesis, University of Bristol, 1971, *sub* Heybridge, Bishop's Stortford, and Maldon.
19 For Bassingbourne see Chambers *The Mediaeval Stage*, II, p. 338: for the others see Wright, op. cit., *sub* Blighborough and Dunmow.
20 See Chambers, *The Mediaeval Stage*, II, p. 343 and Wright, op. cit., *sub* Bungay.

21 Chambers, *The Mediaeval Stage*, II, p. 342, and Wright, op. cit., *sub* Braintree.
22 See pp. 171-7 above: also A. M. Nagler, *Theatre Festivals of the Medici, 1539–1637* (Yale University Press 1964) and Jean Jacquot, *Les Fêtes de la Renaissance* I and II, ed. for CNRS, (Paris 1956 and 1956–60).
23 On the Dutch festivals see G. R. Kernodle, *From Art to Theatre* (Chicago 1944), pp. 111–29: on the German ones see H. Kindermann, *Meister der Komödie von Aristophanes bis Shaw* (Vienna 1952), 'Hans Sachs und Fastnachtspiel-Welt', pp. 111–20.

7: CHURCH AND STATE

24 See G. Wickham, *Early English Stages*, II (Pt 1), pp. 54–97.
25 For a detailed examination of the impact of the Reformation and Counter-Reformation on European religious drama, see H. C. Gardiner, S.J., *Mysteries' End* (Yale Studies in English, vol. 103) (Yale University Press, 1946; reprint 1967 – Anchor Books).
26 See G. Wickham, *Shakespeare's Dramatic Heritage*, pp. 67–83.
27 On the Italian Academies see L. B. Campbell, *Scenes and Machines on the English Stage during the Renaissance* (1923), pp. 9–70. This book was reprinted in 1961.
28 See F. S. Boas, *University Drama in the Tudor Age* (1914), and T. H. Vail Motter, *The School Drama in England* (1929).
29 This point is made forcefully in the anonymous Interlude *Respublica*, ed. W. W. Greg, for EETS (1952).
30 See G. Wickham, *Early English Stages*, II (Pt 1), pp. 60–75.
31 Ibid., pp. 329–31.
32 Printed by Chambers, *The Elizabethan Stage*, IV, pp. 266–7.
33 *Lincoln Diocese Documents*, ed. Andrew Clark for EETS (1914), pp. 216–19.
34 See pp. 145-50 above.
35 *Great Black Book of Hereford*, 10 December 1548 (fol. 27):
   'Forasmuch as there was before this time divers corporations of Artificers, crafts and occupations in the said City, who were bound by the grant of their corporations yearly to bring forth and set forwards divers pageants of ancient histories in the procession in the said City upon the Day and Feast of Corpus Christi, which now is and are omitted and surceased . . .' (spelling modernized).
   The money formerly raised and devoted to this purpose is to be switched to the general upkeep of the city.
36 For London and Ipswich see Chambers, *The Mediaeval Stage*, II, pp. 371–3 and 379–83; for New Romney see Malone Society *Collections VII*, ed. Giles E. Dawson, pp. 118–43 and 202–11.
37 See H. C. Gardiner, *Mysteries' End*, pp. 65–93.
38 See pp. 50, 113-14 and 164 above.
39 See G. Wickham, *Early English Stages*, I, pp. 237 et seq., and S. Anglo, *Spectacle, Pageantry and Early Tudor Policy*, pp. 238–43.
40 See *Early English Stages*, II (Pt 1), pp. 56–58.

41 As a painter, Manuel's style was deeply in debt to Holbein and Dürer. His self-portrait in stained-glass in Berne Cathedral, accompanied by the kneeling figure of Death, provides an allusion to the famous *Totentanz* which he painted for the Dominican Monastery in Berne.

   In a later work, *Barbali* (1526), he satirized the habit of forcing young girls to become nuns.

42 See Gardiner, *Mysteries' End*, pp. 51–7 and Thora Blatt, *The Plays of John Bale* (Copenhagen 1968).

43 See Blatt, op. cit., pp. 164–81.

APPENDIX

CALENDAR OF TWENTIETH-CENTURY REVIVALS OF ENGLISH MYSTERY CYCLES AND OTHER MAJOR RELIGIOUS PLAYS OF THE MIDDLE AGES

(This calendar is based, with revisions and additions, on the check list compiled by John R. E. Elliott, Jr in 1968.)

I 1900–14

1901   William Poel's production of 'The Sacrifice of Isaac' (Chester Cycle) and *Everyman* for the Elizabethan Stage Society at the Charterhouse, London.

1906   Nugent Monk's production of 'The Shepherds' and 'The Magi' (Chester Cycle) sponsored by the Chester and North Wales Archaeological Society for the English Drama Society at Bloomsbury Hall, London and at the Old Music Hall, Chester.

1909   Nugent Monk's production of 'Passion Play' (*Ludus Coventriae*; sometimes called the N-Towne, or Hegge Cycle, and recently attributed to Lincoln) for the English Drama Society in London.

    The appearance of Christ on the stage in this production resulted in the closure of the production by the police and the arrest of Nugent Monk on a charge of violating the Blasphemy Law.

1910   Nugent Monk's production of 'The Annunciation' and 'The Flight into Egypt' (Towneley Cycle, attributed to Wakefield) for the Norwich Players in Nugent Monk's own home.

1914   Nugent Monk's production of the Nativity plays from the *Chester Cycle* for the Norwich Players at the Old Music Room, Norwich.

1914–18   THE FIRST WORLD WAR

II 1918–39

1932   E. Martin Browne's production of plays on the life of Mary from *Ludus Coventriae* for the Chichester Diocesan Players at Chichester.

1934–5   Nevill Coghill's production of *Everyman* for the Dramatic Society of Exeter College, Oxford (1934) in the Fellows' Garden; repeated (1935) before the West front of Tewkesbury Abbey for the Tewkesbury Arts Festival.

1938   Cecil Quentin's production of *The Castle of Perseverance* for the Oxford University Experimental Theatre Club in St Mary's Church, Oxford, in a text translated and abridged by Cecil Quentin.

1938   Nugent Monk's production of the Passion Play from *Ludus Coventriae* performed privately by the Norwich Players at the Maddermarket Theatre Norwich before an invited audience.

            Monk's test for this production was published in 1939 by the Wherry Press, Norwich.

1939–45   THE SECOND WORLD WAR

III 1946–73

1951   '*The Festival of Britain*'

       1. E. Martin Browne's production of *The York Cycle of Mystery Plays* for the York Festival Society in association with the Arts Council of Great Britain and the Corporation of the City of York in the ruins of St Mary's Abbey, Museum Gardens, York.

          The text used was translated and abridged by Canon J. S. Purvis and consisted of plays 1, 3–6, 12–15, 17, 18, 21, 22, 24–26, 28, 30, 32–39, 42, 43 and 48. It was published by the SPCK in 1951.

       2. Christopher Ede's production of *The Chester Cycle* for the County Drama Committee of the Cheshire Rural Community Council in association with the Arts Council of Great Britain in the Refectory of Chester Cathedral.

The text used was translated and abridged by Betty and Joseph McCulloch. It was divided into three parts – (1) Old Testament plays; (2) New Testament plays from the Annunciation to the Flight into Egypt; (3) New Testament plays from the Last Supper to the Resurrection – and presented on successive days.

3. Carina Robbin's production of the two surviving plays from the *Coventry Cycle* (Sherman Tailors' and Weavers') for the Religious Drama Society in association with the Cappers' Company of Coventry in the ruins of Coventry Cathedral.

1952   1. Nugent Monk's production of the 'Norwich' Passion Play *(Ludus Coventriae)* at the Maddermarket Theatre Norwich. Unlike his 1938 production (q.v.) this was a public one licensed by the Lord Chamberlain.

2. Repeat performance of Christopher Ede's production of the *Chester Cycle* at Chester.

1954   1. Repeat performance of E. Martin Browne's production of the York Cycle at York.

2. Martial Rose's production of three plays from the *Towneley* (Wakefield) *Cycle* – 'Salutation', 'Second Shepherd's Play' and 'Flight into Egypt' – in Middle English dialect performed by students of Bretton Hall College at Wolley Hall, Wakefield.

1956   Glynne Wickham's production of *Ludus Coventriae* in Tewkesbury Abbey for the Friends of the Abbey presented by staff and students of the Drama Department of Bristol University in a text translated and edited by Jane Plunkett and Glynne Wickham.

1957   1. E. Martin Browne's production of the *York Cycle* at York. In this year Canon J. S. Purvis published his translation of the Complete Cycle (SPCK).

2. Christopher Ede's production of the *Chester Cycle* at Chester. This time the play was given in two successive days instead of three, the break coming after 'The Flight into Egypt.'

1958   Martial Rose's production of an abridged version of the *Wakefield Cycle* at Bretton Hall, Yorkshire, in his own translation.

1960   David Giles's production of the *York Cycle* at York.

1961   Colin Ellis's and Sally Miles's production of eighteen plays from the *Wakefield Cycle* translated by Martial Rose at the Mermaid Theatre, London.

H*

1962   1. E. Martin Browne's production of *Ludus Coventriae* in the ruins of Coventry Cathedral to mark the consecration of the new Cathedral. This production was later presented in the nave of Winchester Cathedral. The translation by E. Martin Browne was published under the title of *The Mysteries* by Samuel French in 1966.

2. Christopher Ede's production of *The Chester Cycle* in a new translation by John Lawlor and Rosemary Anne Sisson on the Cathedral Green in two successive days.

3. Jean Claudius's production of fourteen plays from the *Wakefield Cycle* for the Lambeth Drama Club, presented in Westminster Abbey for the City of London Festival and at the Edinburgh Festival, in a text adapted by the producer.

1963   William Gaskill's production of the *York Cycle* at York.

1965   Sally Miles's production of fifteen plays from the *Wakefield Cycle* at the Mermaid Theatre, London.

1966   1. Margaret Birkett's production of *Ludus Coventriae* in a text translated and edited by Martial Rose in St Wulfram's Church, Grantham, Lincolnshire.

2. E. Martin Browne's production of the *York Cycle* at York.

1967   1. Peter Dornford-May's production of the *Chester Cycle* in a revised text by Betty and Joseph McCulloch and Donald Hughes at Chester.

2. Robert Prior-Pitt's production of *Ludus Coventriae* in the ruins of Coventry Cathedral in the 1962 text by E. Martin Browne.

3. John Hodgson's production of the *Wakefield Cycle* at Bretton Hall College of Education, Yorkshire, in Martial Rose's translation.

4. Lynette Muir's production of the Anglo-Norman *Ordo Representacionis Adae* for St Adrian's Church, Leeds, in a translation by Lynette Muir published by the Leeds Philosophical and Literary Society, (Literary and Historical Section) vol. XIII, Part V, pp. 149–204, 1970.

1968   1. John Williams's production of the *Wakefield Cycle* for the Derby Playhouse, Derby (with one performance on Good Friday in Derby Cathedral): fifteen plays presented in two parts in Martial Rose's translation adapted by Peter Jackson.

2. Noah Greenberg's production of *Ludus Danielis* for the New York Pro Musica in Westminster Abbey, Winchester Cathedral and Wells Cathedral.

1969   1. Glynne Wickham's production of the Christmas and Epiphany plays from the *Chester Cycle* for the Bristol Old Vic Company in St George's, Brandon Hill, Bristol, using the original text.

      2. Glynne Wickham's production of The Life of St Meriasek (*Beunans Meriasek*) for the Drama Department of Bristol University in a text freely adapted and abridged from the translation from the Cornish by Whitley Stokes in the Vandyck Theatre, University of Bristol: this play was presented in a double bill with John Bale's *God's Promises* in the original text.

      3. Neville Denny's production of the *Visitatio Sepulchro* for the Drama Department of Bristol University in St George's Church Brandon Hill, Bristol, in the text and score by W. L. Smolden published by OUP.

      4. Neville Denny's production of the entire *Cornish Cycle* for the Drama Department of the Bristol University in association with the Cornwall County Council at St Piran's Round, Perranporth, Cornwall, in a text edited and adapted from the translation by Edwin Norriss by Neville Denny.

        The three parts of the play were presented on successive days, all three being presented in sequence on Sundays.

      5. Clare Venables and Rhys McConnochie's production of *Ludus Coventriae* for the Lincoln Theatre Royal Company, Lincoln Cathedral, in the 1966 text by Martial Rose.

      6. Edward Taylor's production of the *York Cycle* at York.

1971   No productions.

1972   1. William Tydeman's production of The Play Called Corpus Christi (*Ludus Coventriae*) in a text edited and abridged from the original by William Tydeman for the University College of North Wales Arts Festival in Bangor Cathedral.

      2. Kevin Robinson's production of the Passion plays from the *Cornish Cycle* for the Northcott Theatre Company, Exeter, in Neville Denny's adaptation. This production was subsequently presented in London at the Bankside Globe Theatre in Southwark.

1973   1. Repeat performance of Kevin Robinson's production of plays from the *Cornish Cycle* for the Northcott Theatre Company, Exeter.

      2. Edward Taylor's production of the *York Cycle* at York.

3. James Roose Evans's production of the *Chester Cycle* at Chester.

1. Many productions of single plays from all the Cycles have been given since 1945 in Churches and on pageant-waggons in the streets. These are not included in this Calendar.
2. The following productions are advertised for 1974,
   (a) A Medieval Cycle of Mystery Plays, Bishop's Palace, Winchester
   (b) The *Castle of Perseverance* at Manchester University.

LIST OF BOOKS REFERRED TO
IN THE TEXT AND NOTES

ANDERSON, M. D., *Drama and Imagery in English Medieval Churches*, Cambridge University Press, 1963.

ANGLO, S., *Spectacle, Pageantry and Early Tudor Policy*, Oxford University Press, 1969.

ART BULLETIN *see* LAVIN

ATCHLEY, E. G. CUTHBERT, *English Liturgical Colours*, SPCK, 1918.

AUDIAN, J., *Les Troubadours et l'Angleterre*, Paris, 1927.

AXTON, RICHARD and STEVENS, J., *Medieval French Plays*, Blackwell, Oxford, 1971.

BALE, JOHN, *Three Laws*, Tudor Facsimile Texts, ed. J. S. Framer, Early English Drama Society, 1907–14; reprinted by Charles W. Traylor, Guildford, 1966.

BARBER, RICHARD, *The Knight and Chivalry*, Longman, 1970.

BENTLEY, S., *Excerpta Historica*, London, 1831.

BERGERON, D. M., *English Civic Pageantry, 1558–1642*, Arnold, 1971.

BERNHEIMER, R., *Wild Men in the Middle Ages*, Harvard University Press, 1952.

BLACK, K. S., *Ludus Coventriae: The Play Called Corpus Christi*, ed. for EETS, 1922.

BLATT, THORA, *The Plays of John Bale*, Copenhagen, 1968.

BOAS, F. S., *University Drama in the Tudor Age*, Oxford University Press, 1914.

BRADBROOK, M. C., *The Rise of the Common Player*, Chatto & Windus, 1962.

BRODY, ALAN, *The English Mummers and Their Plays*, Routledge & Kegan Paul, 1970.

CAMPBELL, L. B., *Scenes and Machines on the English Stage during the Renaissance*, Cambridge University Press, 1923; reprinted 1961.

CHAMBERS, SIR EDMUND K., *The Mediaeval Stage*, 2 vols, Oxford University Press, 1903. *The English Folk Play*, Oxford University Press, 1933;

reprinted 1969. *The Elizabethan Stage*, 4 vols, Oxford University Press, 1923.

CLARK, ANDREW, *Lincoln Diocese Documents*, ed. for EETS, 1914.

CLODE, C. M., *Early History of the Merchant Taylors' Company*, London 1888.

COHEN, G., *Histoire de la Mise en Scène dans le Théâtre Religieux Français du Moyen Age*, Paris 1926. *Le Livre de Conduite du Régisseur et le Compte des Dépenses pour le Mystère de la Passion joué à Mons en 1501*, Paris 1925.

CRAIK, T. W., *The Tudor Interlude*, Leicester University Press, 1958.

CRAWFORD, J. P. W., *The Spanish Drama before Lope de Vega*, Philadelphia, University Press, 1922.

CREIZENACH, W., *Geschichte des neueren Dramas*, vols I–III, 1893–1903.

D'ANCONA, ALESSANDRO, *Origini del Teatro Italiano*, 2 vols, Turin, 1891.

D'ARCY, M. C., *Thomas Aquinas*, Oxford University Press, 1930.

DAVIS, NORMAN, *Non-Cycle Plays and Fragments*, with a note on the Shrewsbury Music by F.LL. Harrison, ed. for EETS, 1970.

DAWSON, G. E., Collections VII, 'Records of Plays and Players in Kent', 1450–1642, ed. for the Malone Society, 1965.

DEMUS, OTTO, *Byzantine Art and the West*, Weidenfeld & Nicolson, 1970.

DENHOLM-YOUNG, N., 'The Tournament of the Thirteenth Century', *Studies in Mediaeval History presented to F. M. Powicke*, 1948.

DENNY, N., *Medieval Interludes*, Ginn, 1972.

DIX, DOM. GREGORY, *The Shape of the Liturgy*, Daire Press, 1946.

DONOHUE, WALTER A., 'An Investigation, from a broadly Philological Standpoint, of the Rebirth of Organized Dramatic Entertainment in Europe in the Early Middle Ages', M. Litt. thesis, University of Bristol, 1970.

EARLY ENGLISH TEXT SOCIETY *see* Black, K. S.; Clark, Andrew; Davis, Norman; Evans, J. and Sergeantson, M. S.; Furnival, F. J.; Greg, W. W.; Harris, M. D.; Littlehales, Henry; Lydgate, John; Peacock, Edward.

EHRENBERG, R., *Capital and Finance in the Age of the Renaissance*, Bedford Economic Handbooks 2, London, 1928.

EVANS, M. BLAKEMORE, *The Passion Play of Lucerne*, MLAA, 1943.

EVANS, J. and SERGEANTSON, M. S., *English Mediaeval Lapidaries*, ed. for EETS, 1933.

FARNHAM, WILLARD, *The Mediaeval Heritage of Elizabethan Tragedy*, University of California Press, Berkeley, 1936.

FERGUSON, G., *Signs and Symbols in Christian Art*, Oxford University Press, New York, 1954.

FOWLER, CANNON J., *Durham Account Rolls*, ed. for Surtees Society, 1898, vol. 99.

FRANK, GRACE, *The Mediaeval French Drama*, Oxford University Press, 1954.

FRINGS, THEODOR, *Minnesinger and Troubadours*, Berlin 1949.

FURNIVAL, F. J., *The Digby Plays*, ed. for EETS, 1896. *Robert Brunne's 'Handlyng of Synne'*, ed. for EETS, 1901.

GARDINER, H. C., *Mysteries' End*, (Yale Studies in English, vol. 103) Yale University Press, 1946; reprinted 1967 (Anchor Books).

GIRADOT, A-T. de, *Mystère des Actes des Apôtres, représenté à Bourges en avril, 1536*, 1854.

GIRAUD, M., *Composition, mise en scène et représentation du Mystère des Trois Doms joué à Romans, les 27, 28 et 29 mai, aux fêtes de Pentecôte de l'an 1509*, Lyons 1848.

GREEN, ALICE STOPFORD, *Town Life in the Fifteenth Century*, 2 vols, Macmillan, 1894.

GREG, W. W., *Respublica* (Anon.), ed. for EETS, 1952.

HARDISON, O. B., JNR, *Christian Rite and Christian Drama in the Middle Ages*, Johns Hopkins, Baltimore, 1965.

HARE, ARNOLD, *The Georgian Theatre in Wessex*, Phoenix House, London, 1958.

HARMAN, ALEC, 'Mediaeval and early renaissance music (up to 1525)', *Man and His Music I*, Rocliff, 1958.

HARRIS, M. D., *The Coventry Leet Book*, 2 vols, ed. for EETS, 1907–9.

HATFIELD, RAB, 'The Compagnia dei Magi', *Journal of the Warburg and Courtauld Institutes*, (1970), pp. 107–61.

HILDBURGH, W. L., *English Alabaster Carvings as Records of the Medieval Religious Drama*, Oxford, 1949.

HUGHES, ROBERT, *Heaven and Hell in Western Art*, Weidenfeld & Nicolson, 1968.

HUIZINGA, J., *The Waning of the Middle Ages*, Edward Arnold, 1924; Penguin 1955.

HUYGHE, RENÉ, *The Larousse Encyclopedia of Byzantine and Medieval Art*, Paris 1958.

JACQUOT, JEAN, *Fêtes de la Renaissance I and II*, ed. for CRNS, Paris 1956 and 1956–60.

JODOGNE, O., *Mystère de la Passion d'Angers de Jean Michel*, Gembloux 1959.

KERNODLE, G. R., *From Art to Theatre*, Chicago University Press, 1944.

KINDERMANN, H., *Meister der Komödie von Aristophanes bis Shaw*, Vienna 1952. *Theatergeschichte Europas*, 9 vols, Salzburg 1957–70.

KLEIN, J., *The Mesta: A Study of Spanish Economic History, 1273–1836*, Harvard University Press, 1920.

KOLVE, V. A., *The Play Called Corpus Christi*, Stanford University Press, 1966.

KONIGSON, ELIE, *La Représentation d'un Mystère de la Passion à Valenciennes en 1547*, CNRS, Paris 1969.

LAVIN, MARILYN ARONBERG, 'The Altar of Corpus Domini in Urbino: Paolo Uccello, Joos Van Ghent, Piero Della Francesca', *Art Bulletin*, XLIX (no. 1), 1967, pp. 1–24.

LINCOLN *see* CLARK, ANDREW.

LITTLEHALES, HENRY, *The Medieval Records of a London City Church (St Mary at Hill)*, ed. for EETS, 1905.

LOI, RAIMON DE, *Trails of the Troubadours*, New York, 1926.

LOOMIS, L. H., 'Secular Dramatics in the Royal Palace, Paris, 1378, 1389, and Chaucer's "Tregetoures"', *Speculum*, XXXIII (1958), pp. 242–55; reprinted by J. Taylor and A. H. Nelson in *Medieval English Drama: Essays Critical and Contextual*, Chicago University Press, 1972.

LUCHAIRE, A., *Social France at the Time of Philip Augustus* (trans. E. Krebhiel), 1912.

LYDGATE, JOHN, *The Fall of Princes*, ed. for EETS by Henry Bergan, 4 vols, 1924–7. *Minor Poems*, ed. for EETS by H. N. MacCracken, 2 vols, 1934.

MÂLE, EMILE, *L'Art Religieux de la Fin du Moyen Age en France*, Paris (5th ed.) 1949.

MANDET, F., *Histoire de la Langue Romane (Roman Provençal)*, Paris 1840.

MANLY, J. M., *Specimens of the Pre-Shakespearean Drama*, 2 vols, Boston, 1897.

MARRIOT, W. B., *Vestiarium Christianum: The Origin and Gradual Development of the Dress of Holy Ministry in the Church*, Rivingtons, London, 1868.

MEDWALL, HENRY, *Fulgens and Lucres*, ed. for Tudor and Stuart Library by F. S. Boas and A. W. Reed, 1926.

MORRIS, COLIN, *The Discovery of the Individual, 1050–1200*, SPCK 1972.

MOTTER, T. H. VAIL, *The School Drama in England*, Longman, 1929.

MACCRACKEN, H. N. *see* LYDGATE, JOHN.

NAGLER, A. M., *Sources of Theatrical History*, New York 1952. *Theatre Festivals of the Medici, 1539–1637*, Yale University Press, 1964.

NELSON, A. H. *see* TAYLOR, J. and NELSON, A. H.

NICOLL, ALLARDYCE, *Masks, Mimes and Miracles*, Harrap, 1931.

NYKL, A. R., *Hispano-Arabic Poetry and its Relations with the Old Provençal Troubadours*, Baltimore, 1946.

OWST, G. R., *Literature and Pulpit in Medieval England*, Cambridge University Press, 1933.

PEACOCK, EDWARD, *Instructions for Parish Priests*, ed. for EETS, 1868.

PIRENNE, H., *Mediaeval Cities, their Origin and the Revival of Trade* (trans. F. D. Halsey), Princeton University Press, 1925. Reprinted in paperback 1969.

PROSSER, ELEANOR, *Drama and Religion in the English Miracle Plays*, Stanford University Press, 1961.

REDFORD, JOHN, *Wit and Science*, Malone Society Reprints, 1951.

RENNERT, H. A., *The Spanish Stage in the Time of Lope de Vega*, 1909; reprinted by Dover Publications, New York, 1963.

ROSENFELD, SYBIL, *Strolling Players and Drama in the Provinces, 1660–1795*, Cambridge University Press, 1939; reprinted by Octagon Books, New York, 1970.

SALTER, F. M., *Mediaeval Drama in Chester*, Toronto University Press, 1955.

SCHMIDT, N. C., 'Was there a Medieval Theater in the Round? A re-examination of the Evidence', *Medieval English Drama*, ed. J. Taylor and A. H. Nelson, Chicago University Press, 1972.

SEPTET, MARIUS, *Les Prophètes du Christ*, Paris 1878. *Origines Catholiques du Théâtre Moderne*, Paris 1904.

SCOTT, A. C., *The Theatre in Asia*, Weidenfeld & Nicolson, 1972.

SHOEMAKER, W. H., *The Multiple Stage in Spain during the Fifteenth and Sixteenth Centuries*, Princeton University Press, 1935.

SHERGOLD, N. D., *A History of the Spanish Stage from Mediaeval Times until the End of the Seventeenth Century*, Oxford University Press, 1967.

SOUTHERN, R., *The Georgian Playhouse*, Pleider Books, London, 1948. *The Mediaeval Theatre in the Round*, Faber & Faber, 1957.

STEMMLER, THEO, *Liturgische Feiern und Geistliche Spiele*, Tübingen 1970.

STEVENS, J., *see* AXTON, RICHARD.

STICCA, SANDRO, *The Latin Passion Play: its Origins and Development*, New York 1970. 'The Literary Genesis of the Latin Passion Play', in *The Medieval Drama*, SUNY Press. Binghamton, 1972, pp. 39–68. *The Medieval Drama*, SUNY Press, Binghamton, 1972.

STOKES, WHITLEY (ed.), *Beunans Meriasek: The Life of St. Meriasek*, (together with a translation from the Cornish), 1872.

STUBBS, PHILIP, *The Anatomy of Abuses*, 1583.

TALBOT RICE, DAVID, *Art of the Byzantine Era*, Thames & Hudson 1963.

TAYLOR, J. and NELSON, A. H., *Medieval English Drama: Essays Critical and Contextual*, University of Chicago Press, 1972.

TIDDY, R. J. E., *The Mummers' Play*, Oxford University Press, 1923.

TOULMIN-SMITH, LUCY, *English Guilds*, ed. for EETS, 1870.

TREVELYAN, G. M., *English Social History*, Longmans, Green & Co., 1944.

UNWIN, G., *The Guilds and Companies of London*, 2nd ed. Methuen, 1925; 3rd ed. Allen & Unwin, 1938.

WICKHAM, G., *Early English Stages, 1377–1660*, vol. I, 1958 (revised ed., 1963); vol. II (Part 1) 1962; vol. II (Part 2) Routledge & Kegan Paul, Columbia University Press, 1972. 'The Staging of Saint

Plays in England' in *The Medieval Drama*, ed. S. Sticca, SUNY, 1972, pp. 99–119. *Shakespeare's Dramatic Heritage*, 1969.

WITHINGTON, ROBERT, *English Pageantry, An Historical Outline*, 2 vols, Harvard University Press, 1918–20.

WRIGHT, R. A., 'Mediaeval Theatre in East Anglia', M.Litt. Thesis, University of Bristol, 1971.

YOUNG, KARL, *The Drama of the Mediaeval Church*, 2 vols, Oxford University Press, 1933.

Index

St Lawrence, 88, 89, 97
St Leonard, 96
St Louis (Gringore), 97
St Luke's Day, 132
St Martial, Limoges, 33
St Martin's Mass (Martelmass), 131
St Mary Magdalene, 94, 100; Plate 17
St Matthew's Day, 131–2
St Meriasek, 94, 97, 100–1, 116
St Michael, 27
St Michael and All Angels, Feast of, 132, 133, 206
St Nicholas, 44, 45, 47–8, 51, 70, 95, 97, 104, 113, 133, 183
St Nicholas Day, 131
St Olave, 102
St Oswald, 39
St Paul, 52, 109
St Peter, 20, 47, 73, 96, 109, 115
St Peter's Day, 133
St Piran's Round, Cornwall, 117; Plate 20
St Remy, 97
St Sernin, Toulouse, 19
St Simon and St Jude, Feast of, 132n
St Stephen, Feast of, 44
St Stephen's Cathedral, Vienna, 59
St Swithin, 196
St Thomas à Becket, 96, 102
St Thomas Aquinas, 108
St Ursula, 102
St Werburgh's Abbey, Chester, 70
sainte, 120
Saint plays, 43–55, 94–104, 115, 121, 168, 172, 181, 184, 199, 206–7; *see also specific plays*, e.g. *St Louis*
Salisbury, Wiltshire, 46n
Santa Sophia, Constantinople, 16, 17
San Vitale, Ravenna, 17
Satan, 109
Saturnalia, 45, 130
'Satyr' plays, 144
scarf-dances, 128
scenery, 87–90, 93, 99–100, 156, 165, 176, 182, 186, 187, 193, 195, 197
scenic devices, 75, 76, 81, 82, 86–7, 90, 93, 169–70, 182, 186, 193
Scope, Lord, 111
scribes, 65, 72
scripts, 70–4, 93, 186, 187; *see also* texts
Selby Abbey, Yorkshire, 111, 119, 173
Seneca, 23, 205

Septet, Marius, 33
sermons, 12, 59, 109–11, 112, 114
Seven Deadly Sins *see* Vices
Sévèrin the Martyr, 97
Seville, Spain, 79, 92
Shakespeare, William, 60, 97, 121, 144, 149–50, 157, 167, 191, 194
Shape of the Liturgy, The (Dix), 12, 25
shepherds, 33, 34, 63, 71, 73, 91, 144, 167
ships, 101, 164, 176; Plates 20 and 40
Shrewsbury, Shropshire, 68, 73
Shropshire, 68, 73, 140
Shrovetide, 134, 135, 136, 161
Sir Gawain and the Green Knight, 139
Slasher, 146
Sloth, 106, 114
Sol Invictus, 130
Somerset, 132, 140, 141, 143, 144
Sophocles, 205
Southern, Richard, 116
South Petherton, Somerset, 144
Spanish Tragedy, The (Kyd), 97
spatial concepts, 63–4, 88–90, 101
spectacula, 21, 22
Sponsus, 50
Stabat Mater, 33
Staffordshire, 144
stage directions, 46–8, 85, 101; *see also* rubrics
stage machinery *see* scenic devices
staging, 75–6
Stanzaic Life of Christ, 58
Staunch Goodfellow, 120
Steadfast Faith, 120
'Stowe' play, Essex, 195
street pageants, 168–71; *see also* pageants, civic
strolling players, 128, 145, 190, 200, 205, 209, 210
Stubbs, Philip, 126, 140, 141, 194, 205
Suffolk, 147, 173, 195, 207
superintendents *see* pageant-masters
Surrey, 140
Survey of Cornwall (Carew), 85
sword-dances, 128, 129, 135, 137–40, 150
symbolism, 5, 39, 43, 90, 109–10, 170, 177

tableaux, 95, 169
Tacitus, 137
Teatrum Mundi, 64, 89
Te Deum, 39, 40, 41, 43, 50, 73, 94